ADVENTURE TRAVEL NORTH AMERICA

Also by Pat Dickerman

FARM, RANCH & COUNTRY VACATIONS

Adventure Travel North America

by PAT DICKERMAN

Adventure Guides, Inc.

COVER PHOTO CREDITS:

Denali National Park—*Camp Denali, Alaska*

Whitewater Kayaking—*Madawaska Kanu Centre, Ontario*

Riding in the Sonoran Desert—*Don Donnelly Stables, Arizona*

Editor and Publisher: Pat Dickerman
Associate Editors: Julie Wheeler, Connie Smith
Contributing Editor: Steve Cohen
Cover and Book Design: Harrison Shaffer, Cristina Botta
Desktop Typography: Michael Szuromi—Avenue Business Centers
Printed by Arcata-Hawkins, New Canton, TN

Published by: Adventure Guides, Inc.
 7550 East McDonald Drive
Scottsdale, Arizona 85250
 (602) 596-0226. Fax (602) 596-1722.

Trade Distributor: Harbinger House
P. O. Box 42948
Tucson, Arizona 85733
(602) 326-9595. Fax (602) 326-8684.

Library of Congress Catalog Card Number: 93-071238

ISBN 0-913216-01-1

First Edition

Printed in the United States of America

10 9 8 7 6 5 4 3 2 1

CONTENTS

In 1971 we published an adventure travel newsletter as an insert in our book on farm and ranch vacations. It was the first manuscript ever printed about the outfitters in North America who set up trips down rivers, up mountains and across plains for neophytes as well as experienced outdoorsmen. It opened with the understatement: "There's a growing new vacation trend in this country."

In 1972 we published the predecessor of this current edition, and we have written and published the book every few years since. In these two decades the "growing new vacation trend" has entered the mainstream of the travel industry and has become its fastest growing segment.

INTRODUCTION

I'D LIKE TO TELL YOU . . .

WHAT ADVENTURE TRAVEL IS. . .

Years ago adventure travel was thought of as challenging, rugged expeditions mostly for very active adults. It has matured to include soft expeditions that today attract families and seniors as well—everyone who enjoys learning about the natural world and trekking into wild places without the necessity of excessive ruggedness.

Yet adventure travel is far from routine. It is unlike crowded tours which take people to crowded areas. Adventurers, noted for teamwork and close companionship, make their way in small groups—seldom over 20, more often close to ten, on some excursions only three or four. They penetrate some regions where few travelers have preceded them.

Adventures described in these pages differ widely, but all can be counted upon to enrich your vacations, and only a few require previous experience in outdoorsmanship. Many, however, require an inquisitive spirit and a desire for one-on-one participation with nature.

WHAT VACATIONERS LIKE ABOUT THESE TRIPS. . .

Adventure travelers enjoy activities in the outdoors—the beauty of a wilderness region, the joy of observing whales or eagles or bears or other wildlife in their natural habitat, the excitement of exploring.

Some like journeys with comfortable transport by van, by boat, by charter plane, by raft—or walking easy trails on their own two feet.

Others like the action involved in coastal sailing, rafting a wild river, kayaking among porpoises, riding in a pack string on mountain trails, climbing to a summit.

Adventurers enjoy exploring and learning about ecosystems and wildlife, mastering the techniques of reading a river, navigating the rapids, orienteering, paddling, horsemanship, trailing cattle, carrying a pack and making camp.

And they love the extra rewards—the beauty of an isolated canyon or alpine lake, watching a black bear eat berries, spotting deer at the water's edge, waking to the bugling of an elk or the honking of geese, sharing their experiences with family or friends.

On every page of this book are adventures that can introduce parents, grandparents and children to stimulating and refreshing vacations—some with challenges, others soft enough for a five-year-old.

WHO THE OUTFITTERS AND TRIP OPERATORS ARE. . .

It can hardly be claimed that adventure travel provides the amenities of a resort vacation, but unusual care and comforts not always associated with wilderness travel are part of the experience outfitters give.

These trip operators who guide, provision and plan all details for trips also teach you whatever skills are required, tell you what to bring and make it possible for the neophyte outdoorsperson to trek with safety and relative comfort into wild regions. They deeply desire to provide quality trips for each participant. Their journeys represent a unique blend of action, challenge and fulfillment.

They greatly enjoy what they're doing. We have known most of these adventure services for many years. Each edition of our book has reported on more than 200 of them—as many as can be contained within the limited number of pages. Most pay a nominal service fee which partially covers publishing costs and many provide photos to illustrate the book. Altogether they offer thousands of trips each year.

We sometimes are asked if we have been on all of their trips. It would take ten lifetimes to cover them all! But we do know a lot about each service through research and references and, of course, taking at least some of their trips each year.

We also are asked if we list all the good outfitters and adventure services. Heavens no! There are hundreds of excellent services not included here which we already know about, and hundreds more we likely would recommend if we researched their trips. But that would require a book many times this size, and it would challenge the vacationer even more than this one does to select a single trip from among so many possibilities.

HOW TO FIND THE FACTS YOU WANT. . .

Geographical headings appear in the margins for all the listings, either US WEST or US EAST or some such geographical umbrella, or states and provinces in alphabetical order. Indexes at the back of the book refer to the listings of travel companies operated by outfitters and adventure services, as well as to the geographic areas where trips are operated.

Marginal notations are added to indicate which wilderness regions or rivers or mountains are serviced by each trip operator. In the *Combos* chapter marginal notes indicate type of trips which have been combined. In other chapters they are intended to show at a glance the special areas in which trips are operated.

Family trips are reported in every chapter but are not isolated as such. For those services whose trips are especially good

---

HOW OLD ARE ADVENTURERS

"It was the most wonderful and unique experience our family has ever had," states the father of five children from seven to fifteen who rafted the Middle Fork of the Salmon for six days.

"The highlight of my childhood was a rafting trip through the Grand Canyon with my grandparents—exciting rapids and hikes each day and snuggled in my sleeping bag between them at night," recalls a father who now takes his own kids on river trips.

In Wyoming a participant who follows pioneer trails in a covered wagon every year didn't discover how much fun it was until her first trip four years ago when she was 82.

There seems to be few limits at either end of the age scale for participating in many of these adventures. When we recommend adventure travel for family vacations, we're thinking of grandparents, little kids and everyone in between.

for families, listings mention family rates and the suitability of trips for all ages.

Senior travel recommendations also are noted in various listings where trips are well adapted for seniors' requirements. These are noted in most chapters, especially in fly fishing, for example, and walking trips, one of which is offered *only* for people 50 and over.

For assistance in finding listings for services especially geared for **families** with young children or for **seniors**, please call our advisory service at (602) 596-0226.

Basic information such as details on what to bring, specific trip dates, itineraries and rates is available directly from the services. Telephone numbers and addresses for requesting this information are given in each listing. Questions also can be answered as to available space, correct matching of vacationer expectations to trip challenges, and the possibility of custom arrangements for small private groups.

Customized and/or scheduled trips are referred to in many listings. Most services schedule trips for various dates which are open for anyone to join. Others (such as for pack trips) customize trips for small groups (families or friends) who arrange their dates, itineraries and rates with the outfitter. A custom trip enables a family to make specific arrangements that not only meet their activity requirements but fit their vacation schedules.

Reservations are made directly with each trip service through telephone numbers and addresses noted in the listings.

If you have questions and want to talk over your selection of trips, please call our advisory service at (602) 596-0226, and we'll either supply the answers or suggest where you can get them. We also can help with some reservations and can plan special family or group trips. If a deposit or advisory fee is applicable, we will let you know about this in advance.

WHERE TO SEND YOUR COMMENTS. . .

One of the best things about writing a travel book is that when all the research is over and the information about unique and wonderful trips is in print, letters from vacationers tell about their experiences. This helps to guide us in selecting trips for the next edition. And it helps us to comprehend how vacation needs are best fulfilled.

Generally vacationers tell about the challenges and the fulfillment of adventure travel. But when disappointments are expressed, it helps us to re-evaluate and improve our information for future editions.

So please let us know where you have gone, what the trip meant to you and what you are planning for another year. It is my hope that these pages will open fresh and rewarding vacations for first-time adventurers and continued regeneration to those who have come to consider "adventure" as the essential ingredient of "vacation".

Sincerely

Pat Dickerman, *President*
Adventure Guides, Inc.
7550 East McDonald Drive
Scottsdale, Arizona 85250
(602) 596-0226

ON FOOT

Ken Schmitt for Hike Maui, Hawaii (page 21)

Backpacking / Hiking / Walking

Springtime hikes are accompanied by the gush and slurp of mud. In autumn the sounds are the crunch and crackle of leaves. Whatever the season, hiking is the way to experience the serenity of the wilderness—its nooks and crannies and vast majesty.

The outfitters who guide and provision trekkers contribute an extra measure of comfort, safety and knowledge of the region's history. They scout the trails, choose the most scenic or safest routes, plan the meals, do the cooking, know the best places to camp. They are naturalists and identify the flora and fauna, interpret the geology and spot and track wildlife.

There are hikes for all levels of ability. Novices may enjoy a leisurely five-miles-a-day amble down a carriage road or trail, with plenty of time to swim, fish and nibble on blueberries along the way. Seasoned trekkers opt for brisk and rugged forays which include rock climbing, rappelling and wilderness camping.

Once you've chosen the terrain you'd most like to hike—woods, rainforests, canyons, mountains, desert or beach—and the region and time of year you want to hike it, you'll need to decide just how far from civilization you'd like to go. Sleep under the stars? Hike hut-to-hut or inn-to-inn? Stay at a base lodge and take day hikes? Set up wilderness camps? There's a wide choice.

Your outfitter will provide a list of what to bring—and what not to bring. No matter how carefully you plan, once you hit the trail there's always that temptation to unload some gear. No one has figured out how to make a sleeping bag, pad, plastic ground cloth, dehydrated food, toilet articles clothing, cooking gear, raingear, first aid kit, flashlight, trail map and tent weigh less than forty-or-so pounds. So, how much is too much? Advises one trekker, "Before you leave home try on your pack and stand up. If you topple over, better pack it again."

U.S. WEST

Northern Rockies: Yellowstone, Tetons, Gros Ventre, Absaroka, Wind River and Bitterroot ranges.

Southwest: Sonoran Desert, Escalante Canyon, Gila Wilderness, Canyonlands.

WILD HORIZONS EXPEDITIONS

West Fork Road, Dept. AG, Darby, MT 59829. Attn.: Howie Wolke or Marilyn Olsen. (406) 821-3747.

If you backpack with a question mark—what's that? why? how?—a trip with Wild Horizons will satiate your outdoor curiosity. Howie Wolke is a well-known naturalist/conservationist and author of two books on the wilderness. He and his professional guides willingly pause to interpret the awesome flora, fauna and geology. Their emphasis is on safe, low-impact hiking and camping. The trips penetrate some of the wildest and most beautiful country in the northern Rockies—Yellowstone, the Tetons, Gros Ventre, Wind River, Absaroka and Bitterroot ranges—and the Escalante Canyon, Sonoran Desert, Gila Wilderness and Canyonlands National Park in the Southwest. Groups are limited to eight, and each one carries an average of 30–40 pounds six to seven miles a day. Howie is "most interesting and knowledgeable" according to a backpacker who plans a week on one of his trips every year. Trips Mar.–Sep., 6 days, $595; 7 days, $695; 8 days, $795. Minimum age 16 except for custom and family trips.

Floatplane transport for backpackers — *Arctic Treks, AK.*

ALASKA

Arctic National Wildlife Refuge

ARCTIC TREKS

Box 73452-G, Fairbanks, AK 99707. Carol Kasza and Jim Campbell. (907) 455-6502.

Trips for experienced hikers in the Arctic National Wildlife Refuge, the gem of the Brooks Range undiscovered for years, are the specialty of Arctic Treks. "Our trips are for those with a sense of adventure," they say, "—those wanting to shed their civilized trappings and recharge their spirits." They offer both day hiking and backpacking trips. You can take day hikes from a basecamp in a region of immense mountain lakes and glacier-covered peaks—either leisurely strolls or exhilarating ridge hikes, mixed with fishing for arctic char, lake trout and grayling. An Aug./Sep. base camp trip to observe the caribou migration is recommended for families (8 days/$2,250). Backpacking trips focus on putting you where the animals are—in spectacular wildlands of the higher mountain valleys or foothills and coastal plains. It's a chance to live in a great wilderness on its own terms. Hikers should be experienced and in good shape. Average rates $230/day include charter flights between Fairbanks and trailheads. Jun.–Aug. Also custom trips. (See also *River Running*.)

ALASKA

Gates of the
Arctic National
Park and Arctic
National
Wildlife Refuge

ABEC'S ALASKA ADVENTURES

1550-AG Alpine Vista Court, Fairbanks, AK 99712. Attn.: Ramona Finnoff. (907) 457-8907.

"Our trips are tailored to outdoor travelers who enjoy being active—who like to camp and hike, who prefer to paddle rather than sit as a passenger," explains Ramona. Her eight– to ten–day backpacking itineraries in the Brooks Range, some of them backpack/raft combos, start with a flight from Fairbanks to a remote location. In June, seasoned trekkers backpack 60 miles to view the migration of thousands of caribou—an exceptional wildlife trip! Or choose a leisurely 25-mile backpack into the Arctic National Wildlife Refuge. On a July trek in the Arctic Refuge, you see grizzly bears, caribou, moose, arctic fox, birdlife and muskoxen. In the Gates of the Arctic National Park, also a July trip, trails belong to the moose, bear and caribou. In August, join a 30-mile Arrigetch Peak backpack in the Gates of the Arctic. Another August backpack begins near the Noatak River with superb hiking and photo opportunities. Most treks average about 5 miles per day. Rates: about $141–$200/day. For six– seven participants. (See also *River Running*.)

ALASKA

Gates of the
Arctic, Wrangell
Mountains

HUGH GLASS BACKPACKING CO.

P.O. Box 110796, Anchorage, AK 99511. Attn.: Chuck Ash. (907) 344-1340. Fax (907) 344-4614.

"Wilderness living is much more 'here and now' than our normal social setting," says outfitter Chuck Ash. What better way to experience the Alaskan wilderness on a down-to-earth basis than by trekking? His high quality adventures through the finest roadless wilderness in Alaska are led by experienced Alaskan guides. Emphasis is on interpretation of natural systems, companionship and enjoyment. There are two treks in the Arctic National Wildlife Refuge to choose from—one through an entirely treeless tundra to follow the caribou herds ($1,850), and the other on the north side of the Brooks Range among diverse wildlife populations ($2,195). On the Wrangell Mountain Trek see volcanoes, blue ice and a "natural beauty so rugged, vistas so sweeping, that the mind cannot contain it all." This is the land of Dall sheep and grizzly bear, or wolf and moose. Only six backpackers per trip to reduce impact on the environment. (See also *Sea Kayaking, Wilderness/Nature Expeditions, Fly Fishing—Brightwater Alaska*.)

ALASKA

WILDERNESS ALASKA

Box 113063, Anchorage, AK 99511. Attn.: Macgill Adams. (907) 345-3567.

Brooks Range, Gates of the Arctic, Philip Smith Mountains

For backpackers who want to do something beyond the usual, Macgill Adams offers quality exploration and education trips across the Brooks Range. They are for no more than five hikers and himself, and they penetrate rarely visited regions, frequently using pioneering routes. For example, Mac describes his trip in the Jago Uplands as "exploring the interface of the hottest environmental debate of the decade. We will travel across the core of calving area of the Porcupine caribou herd. After the trip make up your own mind—wilderness or oil rigs?" In the Gates of the Arctic his group

Macgill Adams — *Wilderness Alaska®.*

walks on the North Slope and across a challenging pass near the Continental Divide—a region of breathtaking high mountains, glaciers, canyons, valleys and spectacular clear-water cascades. In the Philip Smith Mountains hikers this year pioneer a new route across the Continental Divide. A Philip Smith "Boots & Boats" trip in autumn combines trekking over the Continental Divide with floating a gentle river to an Athabascan village, a region filled with tundra colors by day and northern light displays at night. Trips are scheduled for one to two weeks, June–August. Rates: from $131–$257/day including group equipment, food, guiding fees and round trip transport from Fairbanks. (See also *River Running*.)

CALIFORNIA

Canadian Rockies, Olympic Peninsula (WA), Yosemite (CA)

KNAPSACK TOURS, INC.
5961 Zinn Drive, Oakland, CA 94611. Attn.: Cathy Harrison. (510) 339-0160. Fax (510) 339-0561.

"Our commitment is to provide carefully chosen, comfortable (not luxurious) lodging and tasty, nutritious meals at affordable prices," explains Cathy Harrison to potential hikers. Modeled after the European concept of "hutting", she personally leads all hikes, about five to six hours on the trail each day. Day tours in September in the Canadian Rockies include heli-hiking Mt. Robson. Hikers see spectacular waterfalls and walk on glaciers in the Lake Louise, Banff and Jasper regions with accommodations in cozy cabins, lodge and condos. Rate for 14-day trip is $1,475. Transportation is

In Yosemite —
Knapsack Tours, Inc.

by van. In Washington State's Olympic Peninsula they take alpine, beach and rainforest hikes in May and stay in a historic lodge. In California a popular "Yosemite on a Shoestring" trip (5 days, $315) headquarters hikers in a rustic bunkhouse at Yosemite Institute as a base camp. They group according to ability and head out to explore lightly traveled trails "beyond the valley," in full view of El Capitan, Half Dome and Cathedral Peak. For experienced, non-smoking hikers, small groups, no children. Does Cathy meet her goal? Claims a three-time Knapsacker, "If time permitted, I would go on every trip she directs."

A walking trip in Utah — *Walking the World, CO.*

COLORADO /
HAWAII /
MONTANA /
UTAH

San Juan Mountains, Kauai, Maui, Hawaii, Glacier National Park, Canyonlands

WALKING THE WORLD

P.O. Box 1186, Fort Collins, CO 80522. Attn.: Ward Luthi. (303) 225-0500.

People 50 and over are walking with Ward Luthi through scenic wilderness regions of the West and in Hawaii. "Our goal is to offer active, affordable experiences which enrich their lives," Ward says. His focus is outdoor adventures on which walkers discover the wonders of nature and gain a satisfying feeling of accomplishment at the same time. In Glacier National Park in Montana, for example, they have a close-up look at beautiful lakes, rushing streams and glaciers, with nine days of moderate to strenuous dayhikes and backpacking, one night in a lodge, and seven nights of basecamp camping, planned so that most days gear is left in camp and you carry only a light daypack. At a basecamp in southern Colorado a five-day program includes light hiking and instruction in bead work, basketmaking, fire starting and locating wild and edible plants. A two-week walk in three of the Hawaiian islands includes day hikes, moderate walking and indoor lodging—while experiencing a lush rainforest, snorkeling, stunning sunsets, a dinner cruise and daily walks to places like Haleakale Crater and a black sand beach. On Colorado trip llamas carry the gear. In Utah rafting is combined with walking. Daily rates average $90–$115 for most trips, $135 in Hawaii. Trips scheduled Apr.–Nov.

HAWAII

Maui

HIKE MAUI
P.O. Box 330969, Kahului, HI 96733. Attn.: Kenneth Schmitt. (808) 879-5270.

If you are visiting Maui, plan at least one day's hike with Ken Schmitt to explore the island's pristine and breathtaking natural beauty. Travel writers describe Ken as "a little-known treasure...a guide extraordinaire...a man who shares with quiet enthusiasm his encyclopedic knowledge of flora, fauna, history, geology and legends. Choose a coastal hike along cliffs with amazing caves and rock formations, and snorkel in a secluded marine preserve with colorful reef fish. Swim beneath cascading waterfalls. Climb high ridges to a tropical rain forest. Ken offers 50 different hikes which vary in ability level from easy to moderate to must-be-in-excellent-condition. Day hikes range from 5–11 hours, with average rates $75–$110 (under 15 years less), and include transportation from central Maui, waterproof day packs, rain ponchos and a gourmet picnic lunch. Group size is 2–6 except by arrangement. Private excursions with lodging, meals and extended itinerary can be planned. Advance reservations required. See photo on page 14.

NEW
HAMPSHIRE

White
Mountains

BALSAMS/WILDERNESS
Dixville Notch, NH 03576. Attn.: Jerry Owen. (603) 255-3400 or (800) 255-0600 in U.S. & Canada, (800) 255-0800 in NH. Fax (603) 255-4221.

Explore the North Country's geology, archeology, animal and plant life while relaxing at the Balsams Grand Resort Hotel. The Balsams estate is criss-crossed by numerous trails for walking, hiking or climbing. "Getting to the end of the trail is not necessarily the goal; the journey itself is intended to inspire," states the hotel's natural history handbook. Scheduled naturalist-guided walks every day range from an easy one-hour wildflower walk around Lake Gloriette to a more rugged four-hour climb of Sanguinary Ridge. Guests also go without guides, and special arrangements can be made for families or groups. Price is included in guest fee at the hotel. Other activities: professionally directed recreational program including golf, tennis, swimming. (See also *Ski Touring*.)

In Glacier National Park—*Glacier Wilderness Guides, MT.*

MONTANA

Glacier National Park

GLACIER WILDERNESS GUIDES
Box 535N, West Glacier, MT 59936. Attn.: Randy Gayner. (406) 888-5466 or (800) 521-7238.

GWG offers trips for all levels in Glacier National Park—a region John Muir called "the best scenery on the continent." One backpacker reports a trip that was rigorous because of the terrain but "done in a laid-back fashion that means vacation despite the physical endeavor." Trekkers agree that trips are efficiently run with quality guides. Groups are small, two to seven people. Custom trips also available. Average physical condition is required to carry packs of about 35 lbs, but sherpas may be hired to carry your gear. Trailside meadows are "carpeted in an unbelievable profusion and diversity of wildflowers," describes one hiker. "High, dramatic peaks surround you day after day, endless banks of glacial cirques curve their way downward with enormous waterfalls, small lakes dazzle in every direction." Weekly trips 3–6 days, $225–$450. Day hikes upon request, $50. (See also *Combos, River Running*—Montana Raft Co.)

VERMONT

Inn-to-inn

COUNTRY INNS ALONG THE TRAIL
R.R. #3, Box 3115, Brandon, VT 05733. Attn.: Roy and Lois Jackson. (802) 247-3300. Fax (802) 247-6851.

You can hike or walk Vermont's scenic trails and backroads, whatever your experience. Go at your own pace for several days on a self-guided trip, or stretch it into two weeks—with swimming, boating, shopping, antiquing or sightseeing added as desired. Off trail activities are varied, as well as the inns and cuisines along the way. Dating back to the 19th century, charming country inns are furnished with antiques and local handcrafts and offer hikers an evening's respite. The south to north hiking route includes sections of the Long Trail over the ridge line of the Green Mountains, popular with serious hikers who enjoy covering eight to ten miles of trail each day. Casual walkers opt for shorter scenic hikes. Rates for self-guided trips range from $57–$127/hiker depending on season, and include lodging, meals, car shuttle, tax and gratuities. One-day guided outings focus on wildflowers, birding or fly fishing. If you prefer hiking with a guide three-day weekend or five-day midweek trips for groups of ten are scheduled for May–Oct., 3 days/$429; 5 days/$629–$749, including meals and overnights at inns. In winter (Jan.–mid Mar.) this service puts you on skis following the Catamount Trail for four days, or a weekend, stopping at cozy inns; 4 days, $459/dbl/per person; weekend $359/dbl/per person. With inn-to-inn travel, you discover the "magic" of Vermont. (See also *Cycling*.)

HIKING HOLIDAYS
Box 750, Bristol, VT 05443. (802) 453-4816.

VERMONT

Vermont, Massachussets, North Carolina, Virginia, Quebec, New Brunswick

The hiking routes this company has selected for its weekend, three-day and five-day guided tours offer a wide variety of scenery and difficulty as well as short or long routes as you progress from one excellent country inn to another. "It's the natural beauty and getting to know the others in your group that makes these trips so rewarding," according to owner Bill Perry. Groups are small—usually 14–16 hikers who walk through historic villages, and panoramic valleys in the Green

Mountain scenes are a treat for hikers—*Hiking Holidays, VT.*

Mountains on tours in Vermont. On one day you ramble country backroads, on another wander through forest and field, or hike in the mountains and lake country, with summits and unforgettable mountain views highlighting trips. On one of the five day tours you hike from northern Vermont into Quebec. Other five-day tours follow trails through Quebec City and the Saguenay Fjord, and New Brunswick's Bay of Fundy, Virginia's Shenandoah Mountains with parts of the Appalachian Trail and the Blue Ridge Mountains of North Carolina. The hikes are graded easy and moderate. Experienced and enthusiastic guides lead each tour, and vans provide transport between inns and trails. Most Vermont hikes are scheduled June to October, and as early as April in Virginia. Rates for 5-day tours, $649–$799, and $299 for weekenders. (See also *Cycling*—Vermont Bicycle Touring.)

Sunrise on Pasayten Peak—*Shank Backpacking, WA.*

WASHINGTON

SHANK BACKPACKING

9835 N.E. 34th St., Bellevue, WA 98004. Attn.: William Becker. (206) 453-0502. Fax (206) 646-3671.

Pasayten & Glacier Peak wilderness areas

"Shank" is from the old Scottish verb meaning "to travel on foot." And on foot is the best way to reach the primitive wilderness areas where Bill Becker leads "free spirits of strong constitution." Bill, an aviation consultant, gets into the mountains on his own or with friends every summer and can guide a small group—one to four backpackers—on a customized trip for five days or longer. His trips are in the

Glacier Peak and Pasayten wilderness areas of the North Cascades. "Bill knows every lake and trail in this seemingly undiscovered wilderness," states one backpacker. "The trip exceeded all expectations—complete solitude in a mountain paradise." It's a rugged alpine land of glaciers, sky and water, where days include fishing, photography, bird watching. The excursions are for intermediate backpackers. Bill supplies transportation from Seattle to the trailhead and return. Rates average $125–$150 per day. Jul.–Sep.

CANADA / US

Grand Canyon (AZ), Canadian Rockies, Appalachian Trail (ME),White Mountains (NH), Great Smokies (NC), Ocala National Forest (FL), Alaska, Yukon

WILLARDS ADVENTURE CLUB

Box 10, Barrie, Ont., Canada L4M 4S9. Attn.: Willard Kinzie. (705) 737-1881 or 728-4787.

Willard Kinzie personally leads most of his eight- to ten-day basecamp and backpacking expeditions in widely separate regions. Trips in Florida's Ocala National Forest are scheduled in March, the Grand Canyon in April/May, and a hut-to-hut hike through New Hampshire's White Mountains in July. Other trips are in the rugged Canadian Rockies, Alaska and the Yukon's Chilkoot Trail July, the Appalachian Trail in Maine (Mt. Katahdin) and the Great Smokies of North Carolina in the fall. "All of these trips are for the adventuresome," says Willard. "They are coed with attention to details and safety instructions." He indicates that over 50% of the participants are repeaters—on their second to tenth trip! Rates average $650 Cdn. for 7–10 days.

ALBERTA

Kootenay & Assiniboine national parks, Kluane National Park in the Yukon

YAMNUSKA, INC.

Box 1920-A, Canmore, Alberta, Canada T0L 0M0. Attn.: David Begg. (403) 678-4164. Fax (403) 678-4450.

Yamnuska's classic backpack trips are in the Canadian Rockies and the Yukon. "In the Rockies the Mount Assiniboine Hike is ideal for beginners," says David Begg. "Meet in Canmore then helicopter to magnificent Mt. Assiniboine where, after some day trips, we do a three-day backpack to beautiful Sunshine Meadows near Banff." July and September, $575 US. The Rockwall Highline Hike, traversing Yoho and Kootenay national parks, is a six-day trip for strong beginners and intermediate backpackers. "For alpine meadows, lakes of turquoise and emerald and superb alpine scenery the Canadian Rockies are unsurpassed," claims Yamnuska. Further north in the Yukon is the Kaskawals Glacier Trek, a ten-day backpack to the snout of one of the mighty glaciers in Kluane National Park. Aug., $900 US. (See also *Mountaineering/Rock Climbing.*)

BRITISH
COLUMBIA

Vancouver
Island

WESTERN WILDCAT TOURS

P.O. Box 1162, Nanaimo, B.C., Canada V9R 6E7. Attn.: Roseanne Van Schie. Phone & Fax (604) 753-3234.

"Our tours bring people close to the land, and they leave feeling connected with nature," says Roseanne. "We consider ourselves educators in sensitive wilderness travel, focusing on our indigenous peoples and on traditional use and respect for the land." Vancouver Island is a hiker's delight, with mountain lakes pocketed in narrow alpine valleys. In its center, Strathcona Park offers half a million acres of wilderness brimming with history and picturesque terrain. Della Falls hikes are easy, with wild berries to munch along the way to this tallest cascade in Canada. Love Lake hikes ascent 3,100 feet from the falls to a remote alpine lakefront. The Grand Traverse is more rigorous; for experienced campers in good shape where in five days participants cover new territory each day. Rainforest tours celebrate firs, hemlocks and red cedars as you hike beneath their canopies. And a cultural feast at Cowichon Native Heritage Centre can be included in all trips. Rainforest and mountain tours on Vancouver Island are for two to eight hikers, at all levels of experience. Custom trips are also available. Trips include food, guides, group gear andtransportation from Nanaimo and average four to six hours hiking daily. Rates: $80–$102 per day. (See also *Sea Kayaking*.)

NORTHWEST
TERRITORIES

Baffin Island

BLACK FEATHER WILDERNESS ADVENTURES

40 Wellington St. E., Toronto, Ont., Canada M5E 1C7. (416) 861-1555. Fax (416) 862-2314.

For a two-week hiking expedition in Baffin Island, "Land of the Midnight Sun," Black Feather flies you from Ottawa to this island of amazing scenery, fascinating wildlife and remote, untouched wilderness. The trek is limited to ten fit and adventurous hikers accompanied by two guides. The chartered plane from Iqaluit lands just west of Tundra Lake. You spend the first week ascending a valley through Pangnirtung Pass, a scenic and rugged trek over talus, hummocks and moraines. You traverse ice bridges, negotiate the crevasses of glaciers and occasionally roll up your pants for a creek crossing. Each evening relax in tents at a panoramic campsite and enjoy a hearty dinner. You finally pass into the Owl River valley and Pangnirtung Pass, with an astonishing view of Mount Asgaard. From there, join the hiking trail of Auyuittuq Park and finish the trip exploring the inland fjord. Scheduled in Jul., $2,625 US, including air from Ottawa. BF offers other hiking expeditions which include the Canol Heritage Trail of the Mackenzie Mountains, Oldsquaw nature and photography camp and Ellesmere Island. (See also *Canoeing / Kayaking*.)

WHAT TO BRING

For guided backpacking trips, outfitters provide a list of the equipment you'll need. Most agree that well-made, properly fitted shoes are the hiker's most essential item. When trying on boots, allow a thumb's width between toes and boot tip. Try wiggling your toes, and check that your heels don't slip—slippage causes blisters. Finally, break in your boots well before the trip.

For day hikes over uncomplicated terrain, well-made sneakers will do. For more serious hiking, you'll need a pair of lightweight hiking boots; they're easier to break in and less expensive than medium or heavyweight boots. The latter, however, are essential for treks over rough terrain and in wet and cold weather. Most hikers wear two pairs of socks—a wool outer sock and either a cotton or silk liner. It helps eliminate friction.

As for clothing, one practical expert advises that most of what you need is probably already in your closet. Comfort is the key. Casual shirts, pants, a sweater and a windbreaker will get you started. Beyond that, check your outfitter's list.

Outfitters provide scheduled departures as well as custom trips designed to your specifications. Would you like to explore Baffin Island or the Alaska wilderness? The Appalachians or the Rockies? Canyons of the Southwest or Hawaii's Na Pali Coast? Do you prefer a rugged adventure on Vancouver Island, or walking Vermont's trails with overnights at comfortable inns? Go wherever your feet will take you. The longest journey, they say, begins with a single step.

Photo by Noah Llama Treks, North Carolina

Hiking with Packstock
(Llamas, Horses, Mules)

"Packstock" can mean a number of four-legged animals—horses, mules, burros or llamas. Friendly, amusing and sometimes ornery, whatever their temperament these trailmates tote the gear while you tote only yourself and perhaps a light daypack.

This has a direct bearing on the meals provided on these trips. Since the packstock carry the food, outfitters provide things too bulky and heavy to be carried in backpacks—fresh fruits, garden vegetables, whole grain breads and the makings for gourmet dishes of all kinds.

The use of packstock has extended hiking trips even for seasoned hikers. The animals can haul all the equipment and food, for example, for an eleven-day trip into Mexico's Copper Canyon—a rugged hike which could not be done without the gear-toting mules.

Packstock—especially llamas—have also opened dozens of new vacation possibilities for families. Even six-year-olds can manage a leisurely four- to eight-mile walk to a wilderness camp if they don't have to carry even a light daypack. Besides, leading a llama who follows wherever they go gives the kids a blast. These gentle, woolly animals are conditioned to work at any altitude and they don't mind waiting while trekkers take time out to fish, swim, explore or just relax. Today llamas are trekking with hikers through wildflower-blanketed regions all through the West and in the Appalachians of the East and regions in New England.

The outfitters listed here offer a variety of arrangements. On some treks you take trips each day from a basecamp. On others you move to new camps every day or so. Outfitters handle all the logistics and provide the camping equipment, care for the animals, meet guests at airports and offer shuttle service where needed.

COLORADO

Keystone Ski area

LLAMA TREKS AT KEYSTONE RESORT

P.O. Box 674, Clark, CO 80428. Attn.: Peter Nichols. (303) 468-4130 or (800) 451-5930.

From the last part of June to Labor Day it's possible that a gentle llama will be sharing your gondola at the Keystone ski lift. At the top you can hike with your llama for a few hours or stay overnight at a well-equipped basecamp, and catch the gondola for the ride down the next day. The llamas love the ride. They stick their heads out the windows taking in the awesome views of the Continental Divide. It looks like they are smiling. And they happily carry lunch, cameras, jackets, overnight camping gear or whatever for their hiking companions. For families staying at the resorts in and around Keystone, it's no big production to spend a night at the mountain basecamp even if they didn't bring camping gear along. Peter Nichols supplies the well-behaved animals along with cots, pads, raingear and everything else you might need for a spontaneous llama outing. A Llama Lunch Hike is offered daily from late June to early September at $45 per adult, $30 per child under 13. Llama Overnight Camps are

Riding the gondola with your llama for a high country trek—*Llama Treks at Keystone Resort, CO.*

offered three times a week, July to September at $110 per adult, $80 per child. Peter still offers regular llama hikes, a llama lease program and custom llama packtrips through his Elk River Valley Llama Company at the address above.

IDAHO /
WYOMING

TETON LLAMAS

673 North 4200 East, Rigby, ID 83442. Attn.: Mike & Kari Black. (208) 745-6706.

Teton Wilderness

Teton Llamas was the first to provide commercial llama pack trips in the Tetons. Their trips take in parts of the Teton Crest Trail within the Jedediah Smith Wilderness area. If you want to experience a backcountry adventure filled with spectacular scenery, high alpine lakes and breathtaking vistas, but without a heavy pack, Teton Llamas is for you. While the llamas carry the load, you're free to enjoy this mountain paradise with only a light pack. Then, after a day of hiking, savor hearty meals instead of freeze dried or powdered concoctions. "With llamas as your companions on the trail, you often see wildlife you would otherwise miss, due to their curious nature," Mike Black comments. "Our guides are trained and experienced in first aid, wilderness travel, minimal impact camping techniques and the natural and cultural history of the Tetons." Trips 4–5 days, 8 hikers maximum, Jul. and Aug. Rates $95/day, group discounts.

MAINE

TELEMARK INN

RFD #2, Box 800, Bethel, ME 04217. Attn.: Steve Crone. (207) 836-2703.

White Mountains

Steve Crone has developed three-day treks that are just right for families with children as young as six. Groups of eight to twelve take off from the Telemark Inn on Saturdays and Tuesdays, June through August. (Two-day adult trips are scheduled spring and fall.) It's a five-mile hike to their basecamp on a trail along the Wild River in the White Mountains—an easy trek since llamas, one for each hiker, carry all the gear. "The kids are having a blast with this big wooly animal out of Sesame Street walking behind them, and their parents are happy, too, with nothing they have to lug," says Steve Crone. "Along toward noon there's more excitement for everyone when they round a bend in the trail and behold tables set for a full buffet lunch on the riverbank—complete with tablecloths and fold-up chairs and an assortment of cheeses, meats, fruits, vegetable calzones and hummus (Indian chickpea dip with spices)." There's time to jump in a swimming hole before hiking on to the basecamp. Here trekkers have private dome tents with thick foam pads. They bring their own sleeping bags. Wake-up time in the morning starts with delivery of hot coffee and hot towels to each tent, followed by a sumptuous breakfast. On Day 3 an afternoon hike back to the Inn ends the trip, unless the more intrepid in the group elect to stay on for some canoeing, fishing or mountain biking, or for a four-day extension for canoe camping, making a seven-day combo when added to the llama trek. Rates for 3-day treks, $375/adult, $255/child. For the 7-day combo, $795/adult, $595/child. Also 1- to 7-day custom trips. (See also *Ski Touring / Snowmobiling*.)

Llama trekking in the White Mountains—*Steve Crone for Telemark Inn, ME.*

NORTH CAROLINA

Pisgah National Forest

WINDSONG LLAMA TREKS

310 Wilson Cove Rd., Swannanoa, NC 28778. Attn.: Sarah Gorder. (704) 299-9777. Fax (704) 298-6574.

WindSong views llamas as putting a "new wrinkle" in backpacking in the east, giving you a comfortable and relaxing camping adventure. Treks are topped by delicious food that is just icing on nature's cake according to Sarah. She encourages touching and becoming friends with the intelligent and tranquil llamas on her trips in the Pisgah National Forest of the beautiful Smoky Mountains. From May through October there are day trips with a gourmet picnic ($60), and two or more days with overnight camping ($90 per day). For groups of eight to ten people WindSong will design special treks. "Come and enjoy yourselves in these intimate Smoky Mountains," invites Windsong. "Our wooly llamas take you through forests dappled with wildflowers and past streams and waterfalls. Mid-June and July our trails are afire with native mountain laurel and rhododendron, and in September and October they're brilliant with fall colors."

OREGON

**Hells Canyon,
Eagle Cap
Wilderness**

HURRICANE CREEK LLAMA TREKS, INC.

*63366 Pine Tree Rd., Enterprise, OR 97828. Attn.: Stanlynn Daugherty.
(503) 432-4455 or (800) 528-9609.*

Stanlynn Daugherty's treks for up to ten hikers in northeast Oregon take you into stream-filled canyons, glacial-carved valleys and high-basin lakes with curious, intelligent, wooly companions transporting the gear. It's a land of wildflowers, mountain goats and bighorn sheep, and in the streams are rainbow, brook and rare golden trout. The itineraries for seven days (six nights), and a few for five days, are scheduled May to September in Hells Canyon and the Eagle Cap Wilderness at rates of $107 per day. They are leisurely to moderate, cover four to eight miles a day and include layover days to fish, explore, climb a mountain or just relax. Anyone can pitch in with camping and llama chores, or just sit back and enjoy. Meals highlight fresh fruits, garden vegetables, whole grain breads, with oriental, south-of-the-border and Italian dishes. Children six or so do well on the leisurely base-camp trips, and older youngsters go for the more strenuous

Trekking a glacial-
carved valley in
northeast Oregon—
Hurricane Creek, OR.

progressive ones. You are bound to learn a lot on Stanlynn's treks. She is the author of *Packing With Llamas*, the first comprehensive guide to llama packing. She also plans custom outings for groups. Trailheads near Enterprise or Joseph are the starting points.

UTAH

PACK CREEK RANCH

P.O. Box 1270, Moab, UT 84532. Attn.: Ken Sleight. (801) 259-5505.

Grand Gulch and Dark Canyon

Ken Sleight is a horseback, hiking and rafting outfitter, an expert on Indian cultures, a legendary storyteller and host at Pack Creek Ranch near Moab. His hikes into Utah's canyon country with packstock carrying the gear are scheduled April, May, September and October for 12 participants—four days, $500. They start and end at the ranch, and involve exploring, camping and five to eight miles of hiking each day. On a hike in the Lower Grand Gulch you camp near Indian ruins and explore cliff dwellings, rock art, side canyons and old trails, and meet a boat on the San Juan River for a final day of rafting. Anasazi pictographs and desert potholes highlight a trip in Dark Canyon. In the Upper Grand Gulch you walk into deep, winding canyons and explore ancient ruins and rock art panels. (See also *Trail Rides*.)

Horses pack gear into Grand Gulch Wilderness—*Frank Jensen for Pack Creek Ranch, UT.*

UTAH

Escalante River, Glen Canyon, Capitol Reef National Park

Trek along the red rock canyons of Utah—*Red Rock 'N Llamas, UT.*

RED ROCK 'N LLAMAS
P.O. Box 1304, Boulder, UT 84716. Attn.: Bevin McCabe or Steve Taylor. Phone or fax (801) 335-7325.

"Besides breathtaking scenery, our clients really enjoy interacting with llamas," says Bevin. Trips explore the splendid red rock canyons of the Escalante River, Glen Canyon and Capitol Reef National Park, some of the wildest and most remote terrain anywhere. Graceful slot canyons and archaeological sites abound. Lofty walls and grottos bespeak the ageless mysteries of this inaccessible landscape, and hanging gardens adorn gorgeous narrows. Throughout, spectacular canyon scenery is punctuated by rock art and ancient Anasazi ruin sites, and there's usually time for swimming. "Bevin and Steve are incredibly enthusiastic, bright, full of energy and knowledgeable about the geology and history of the area," says one recent guest. "It's really an incredible service in this very primitive, though very beautiful wilderness. It's an extraordinary trip and they're exceptionally good cooks." Each day you hike and climb from your basecamp. Trails range from very easy to moderately difficult. Scheduled trips 3–5 days, Mar. to Oct., for four to ten people to explore Hall's Creek Narrows, the Escalante River, Box Death Hollow, the Gulch or Choprock Narrows. Day trips and custom trips are available. Rates average $110 per day for fully outfitted trips.

VIRGINIA

Big Walker Mountain

VIRGINIA HIGHLAND LLAMAS

Rt. 1, Box 41, Bland, VA 24315. Attn.: Carolyn & Bob Bane. (703) 688-4464. Fax (703) 688-4659.

Spend a day on a guided hike to scenic High Rock on top of Big Walker Mountain in the beautiful southwest Virginia Mountains. Follow the historic three-mile pioneer trail, part of the old Appalachian Trail, used for generations as a north-south footpath on the Bane's 900-acre cattle and sheep farm. The majestic llamas will follow you anywhere you walk, carry your load and provide enjoyment as well. All you need are sturdy shoes, camera and raingear. Treks are offered in the springtime when wildflowers edge your path, and in the fall, when hills turn russet and yellow with the burnished glow of autumn colors. Take a break on top of the mountain for a delicious southern picnic lunch and to enjoy the expansive views. Located near I-77 and I-81. If you ask ahead, the Banes permit camping on their property, or you can stay overnight at the nearby Willow Bend Farm Bed and Breakfast. Rate: $60/person for day long hike.

Someone's looking over your shoulder—Scott Woodruff for Lander Llamas, WY.

WYOMING

Wind River, Absaroka Mountains

LANDER LLAMA COMPANY

2024 Mortimore Lane, Lander, WY 82520-9771. Attn.: Scott or Therese Woodruff, Dept. ATNA. (307) 332-5624 or (800) 582-5262. Fax (307) 332-5624.

Customize your own llama pack trip in the pristine wilderness of the Wind River and Absaroka Mountains of western Wyoming, just two hours from Yellowstone and Grand Teton national parks. Fully catered guided trips to glacial cirques and valleys, subalpine lakes and spectacular panoramic views of the Wind River Range vary in difficulty. "We supply everything—tents, food, daypacks, first aid and guides," says Scott, a seasoned llama handler and trainer. His educational background is in forestry and wildlife, and he has had years of backcountry experience. These trips are not difficult—you just need to be in respectable shape. A typical day on the trail starts early, with several stops before lunch and a mid-afternoon arrival at the next campsite. On layover days you can rise early or sleep late; the day's activities are tailored to your desires. Trips are three to ten days for up to six people, mid-June to mid-September, with transportation provided from the Riverton airport. Suggested minimum age for participants is six unless you are planning to carry your child. Scott and Therese are dedicated to their llamas and to providing guests with a quality backcountry experience. Rate: $125 per day. Group rates available.

MEXICO

Copper Canyon

ADVENTURE SPECIALISTS, INC.

Bear Basin Ranch, Westcliffe, CO 81252. Att: Gary Ziegler or Amy Finger. (719) 783-2519. [Dec.–Apr.: 515 W. San Rafael, Colorado Springs, CO 80905. (719) 630- 7687.]

"La Barranca del Cobre, or Copper Canyon, is a totally remarkable natural wonder—more than twice the size of Arizona's Grand Canyon and nearly as deep," says Gary Ziegler, who has hiked into it for many years. It's inhabitants, the Tarahumara Indians, maintain a centuries-old lifestyle— their villages perched among the cliffs where they farm and tend goats. Rare birds, tropical mango, orange groves and hundreds of uncharted archaeological sites await the hiker. Your trip starts in El Paso, Texas with driving to Chihuahua for overnight at elegant Hotel Victoria, then on by train for a night at a canyon lodge before descending to the river below. Burros carry the gear. Your first camp is by a secluded warm spring, then on a tropical deserted beach where you swim, hike, explore, photograph, see incredible plant life and tropical birds. On the trek back up to the rim visit 1,000 year-old cliff dwellings. Despite moderate to strenuous hiking the trip is leisurely with a week in the canyon, returning to El Paso the 11th morning. Departures Oct., Dec., Feb., Mar., Apr., $1,170/person. (See also *Pack Trips, Combos.*)

Yosemite Mountaineering School, California (page 40)

Mountaineering / Rock Climbing

"It's not all serious—it's tremendous fun," maintains one of the leading mountaineering services. "It was more fun and more educational than I expected," states the student of a climbing school. Despite the formidable look of granite walls and high peaks that are scaled by the experts, mountaineering and rock climbing instruction is open to the total novice—even to those who plan that their feet will never be more than ten feet off the ground.

Mountaineering is more than scaling a mountain or a steep wall of rock. It's not only about climbing high; it's about climbing well. Campcraft, map reading, orienteering, wilderness medicine and survival techniques are just the beginning. Other aspects include rope handling, rappelling, glissading, belaying and the handling of chocks, slings and other protective equipment. Steep ascents up snow-laden, ice-covered mountains involve the additional skills of using an ice axe, rope and crampons.

Where do you start? Small. There are half-day, day-long and weekend introductions to climbing just about anywhere there's a mountain. As your level of expertise increases, so do the opportunities to learn.

For those whose goal is to achieve top skills, mountaineering is a strenuous sport and can demand all the strength you possess. The rewards are many. There's the joy of self-confidence, the thrill of achievement, the discovery of what you can do if you have to and the indescribable exhilaration at the summit.

Still, it's also a sport for learning just the basics that bring enjoyment and perceptions of a mountain wilderness. One expert who has made more than 20 ascents of the Mt. McKinley summit also encourages and guides a family mountaineering vacation, or an easy climb well within the abilities of a group of friends, or a father and son.

ALASKA

Alaska Range

ALASKA-DENALI GUIDING, INC.
P.O. Box 566-ATNA, Talkeetna, AK 99676. Attn.: Brian and Diane Okonek. (907) 733-2649. Fax (907) 733-1362.

"The McKinley summit climb is the cornerstone of our mountaineering expeditions," explains Brian Okonek. He has made more than 20 ascents of "The Great One". ADG schedules a classic summit and traverse climb limited to nine climbers with three guides, Jun. ($2,550). "For those with skills, fitness and determination, it is an experience of a lifetime," Brian says. ADG also offers 24-day expeditions to climb the West Buttress route. Other expeditions are scheduled in the Alaska Range—to peaks along the Kahiltna Glacier and on Ruth Glacier. Both give climbers additional mountaineering experience and practice in climbing techniques. For hikers or seasoned backpackers ADG schedules treks for all experience levels in the Alaska Range (5 days/$675, 7 days/$950, 8 days/$1,150, Jun.–Aug.). They also plan personalized trips, "be it a honeymoon, a father-son outing, a family adventure or a gathering of good friends. Our hope is to share the exhilaration of visiting these wild places, and to add your insights and perceptions to our own enjoyment of the wilderness around us," the Okoneks say.

CALIFORNIA

Yosemite National Park

YOSEMITE MOUNTAINEERING SCHOOL
Dept. ATNA, Yosemite National Park, CA 95389. Attn.: Bruce Brossman. (209) 372-1335. [Sep.–Jun.: (209) 372-1244.]

Known for its excellent granite walls and domes and fine weather, Yosemite National Park has become a mecca for rock climbers the world over. The guides are expert mountaineers and alpinists, and capable teachers. In summer the school is headquartered in the Tuolumne Meadows, and in Yosemite Valley spring and fall. Courses include basic to advanced rock climbing, snow climbing, guided climbs and cross-country skiing. There are seminars for advanced climbers—alpencraft (5 days), snow and ice (2 days) and alpine climbing (3 days). The school also offers guided backpacking trips, three and four days into Yosemite backcountry, ranging from basic walks to strenuous multi-day excursions. Low impact backpacking and camping are part of the backpacking instruction, as are use of equipment, map and compass reading, proper food storage, trail and animal safety, emergency shelters, fire making, adverse weather survival and natural history of Yosemite's high country. Rates for rock courses are $100 for 1, $70 for 2, $45 for 3. On guided backpacks rates are $140/3-day trips, $180/4 days. (See also *Ski Touring*.) See photo page 38.

Climbing in
Yosemite—*John
Poimiroo for Yosemite
Mountaineering
School, CA.*

NEW JERSEY

Climbing and
Mountain Biking

MOUNTAIN SPORTS ADVENTURESCHOOL

*1738 Highway 31 North, Clinton, NJ 08809. Attn.: Lyle Lange.
(908) 735-6244.*

The first accredited rock climbing school in New Jersey,
Mountain Sports *AdventureSchool* offers instruction in technical rock climbing for beginners and advanced students
alike. "Climbing gear, including shoes, harness, helmet, and
alpine settings supplied," says Lyle. "Food, clothing, raingear,
hiking shoes, an open mind and nice weather are the responsibility of the participant." With a student-to-instructor ratio
of four to one, safety, quality of instruction and professional-
ism are the hallmarks of eight one- to two-day courses that
progress through four fundamental levels of climbing skills.
Beginners or those who haven't climbed for a few years are
taught how to inspect and care for equipment, and learn
common climbing knots and commands, before attempting
challenging climbs that require instruction in technique.
More advanced climbers learn leading, including placing
protection, dealing with ledges, rope management, weather

assessment, creating solid belay anchors and rescue techniques. Group lessons for two or more, $90/day. Private lessons, $135/day. An overnight biking-and-climbing adventure, $250. Equipment rentals and custom trips available.

NEW YORK

Adirondack
High Peaks
Wilderness

ALPINE ADVENTURES, INC.

Dept. 609, Route 73, P.O. Box 179, Keene, NY 12942. Attn.: R.L. or Karen Stolz. (518) 576-9881.

"The key ingredients to each of our adventures are learning and fun," the Stolzes say. The *Alpine Mastery Methods,* their own unique approach to structured experiential instruction in the mountains, get you out on the rock, ice or snow as soon as possible. A maximum of two students per instructor for most activities assures plenty of individual attention. Courses in introductory through advanced rock climbing are scheduled April–October (2 days/$169, 5 days/$499); ice climbing

On Chapel Pond
Slab in the
Adirondacks—*R.L.*
Stolz for Alpine
Adventures, NY.

and back country skiing scheduled December–March (2 days/ $169, 5 days/$399). Entering its 9th year, Alpine Adventures also offers extensive guiding services; and specialized, privately-taught courses in such topics as high-angle rescue, mixed climbing and advanced telemark techniques ($100– $165/day). Their facility, complete with indoor climbing wall and classroom, is situated on the edge of Adirondack High Peaks, the East's largest wilderness area. With over two-thirds of their business from repeat customers, the Stolzes can claim a high level of customer satisfaction. As one participant put it, "An outstanding course! It was more fun and educational than I expected. I'll definitely return."

OREGON

TIMBERLINE MOUNTAIN GUIDES

Mt. Hood

P.O. Box 23214, Portland, OR 97281-3214. Attn.: Roy Holland. (503) 636-7704.

Climb Mt. Hood, Oregon's highest peak. Standing at 11,235 feet, the peak rises one vertical mile above Timberline Lodge, with 12 glaciers on its flanks. Climbing routes vary in difficulty from fairly easy to advanced and all require proficiency with an ice axe and crampons. "Teaching you to climb safely and efficiently is our goal," says Roy, "so the climber-to-guide ratio is extremely low, both for safety and personal attention." Train in mountaineering, basic and advanced snow and ice climbing techniques, glacier skills and alpine climbing (rope handling, snow anchors, belaying and crevasse rescue). Descend on skis from 10,500 or 8,500 feet after summiting Mt. Hood's South Side route. Guides equip, train and guide you in a safe and enjoyable manner. "Timberline Mountain Guides never made us feel like the novices we were," offers an Oregon climber." Reaching the summit was a high that far exceeded the mountain's 11,235 feet. " Most courses offered April–October. Rate for basic one-day snow climbing classes range from $95 for four climbers, to $180 for personal instruction. A combination snow class and climb of Mt. Hood starts at $155 per person (4 people per guide).

WASHINGTON

AMERICAN ALPINE INSTITUTE

North Cascades, Sierras, Rockies, Southwest desert, Canada, Mexico

1212 24th-D, Bellingham, WA 98225. (206) 671-1505. Fax (206) 734-8890.

Now in its 19th year, AAI has become North America's most comprehensive guide service and expedition center for mountain climbing and backcountry skiing. Its teaching and guiding cover a complete range of rock, alpine and expeditionary environments throughout the world. Among its basic courses are those in Alpine Mountaineering and Rock Climbing. Its

6- and 12-day Alpine Mountaineering courses are taught May to October in the high country of the North Cascades in Washington. Beginners learn to be fully competent rope team members on alpine routes, and in the longer course learn the skills needed to lead a rope team on moderate glacial terrain and to be skilled "seconds" on rock. In addition to thorough instruction on route finding, safety issues and climbing technique, the courses include ascents of a variety of rock and glaciated peaks. (Rates: 6 days. $650, 12 days/$1,090.) A new Alpine Leadership program offers 24 days of instruction, first in the North Cascades then 12 days in the Bugaboos in British Columbia ($2,460). On a 36-day program another 12 days are added for instruction on Mt. Waddington in British Columbia ($5,120). AAI schedules courses year round for basic, intermediate and masters' levels, and guided climbs in the North Cascades and Leavenworth, WA; Joshua Tree, CA; Red Rocks, NV; Bugaboos and Squamish, BC; Baja, Mexico; high altitude volcanos of Mexico.

Mt. Baker—*Keith Gunnar for American Alpine Institute, WA.*

WYOMING

**Grand Tetons,
Wind River
Mountains,
Beartooth
Wilderness**

JACKSON HOLE MOUNTAIN GUIDES & CLIMBING SCHOOL

Box 7477D, Jackson, WY 83001. Attn.: Andy Carson. (307) 733-4979.

JHMG offers endless opportunities in an exceptional selection of climbing locales. "The Grand Tetons, Wind Rivers and Beartooths are our home," explains director Andy Carson, "but throughout the year we are active in Alaska, Devil's Tower and the Needles, City of Rocks, Canyonlands, Joshua Tree and Sierra Nevadas, and the Nevada Red Rocks." Participants of all ages and levels can choose any style of climbing in these diverse areas. At the Jackson Hole School beginners learn technical skills and acclimatize for a guided ascent on the four-day Grand Teton Climbers' Course, with three nights

Climbers' course in
the Grand
Tetons—*Jackson
Hole Mountain
Guides, WY.*

at the 11,000-foot High Camp ($450). JHMC offers fun climbing classes on rock or snow (1-day, $40–$65); multi-day courses, climbing camps and expeditions for personal accomplishment ($75–$125/day); winter ascents and ice climbing, ski mountaineering and ski touring, beginner to advanced ($50/day–$995 for 8-day winter ascent of Grand Teton). Your group can rent a backcountry ski hut—with guided instruction $100–$330. Private guides for climbing or trekking, $125–$165/day.

WYOMING

**Wind River
Mountains**

SKINNER BROTHERS, INC.

Box 859, Dept. AG, Pinedale, WY 82941. (307) 367-2270 or (800) 237-9138. Fax (307) 367-4757.

"For the outdoor enthusiast, there's no better investment than 30 days shared with companions in the beautiful Wind River Mountains," notes Skinner Brothers. The first six days of this course trains you in logistics—menu planning, equipment listing, packing and organizing for the assault on several peaks. You backpack into the Bridger Wilderness area for ten days of rock and snow climbing, followed by 12 days climbing major peaks in the Wind River Mountains. There is ample time for fishing in alpine lakes and streams or just watching the clouds pass over the mountain peaks. As in all sessions, there are highly qualified instructors with supervision by one of the Skinners. They point out the advantage of undertaking a longer-type trip: "Living in a mountain environment for 30 days means that handling and use of equipment becomes second nature. We also concentrate on the development of the leader and individual responsibility to the group." For up to 25 participants, 16 or older, with some previous climbing experience. Jun.–Aug. (See also *Pack Trips, Youth.*)

ALBERTA

**Canadian
Rockies**

YAMNUSKA, INC.

Box 1920-A, Canmore, Alberta, Canada T0L 0M0. Attn.: David Begg. (403) 678-4164. Fax (403) 678-4450.

Mountaineering and climbing at every level are Yamnuska's specialties. "It isn't all serious—it's tremendous fun," they say. For beginners a six-day program takes to the glaciers and peaks of the Canadian Rockies to enjoy easy climbs and scrambles with expert guides. Aug.–Sep., $685 US. Or newcomers to the sport can learn the basics in Basic Rock or Basic Rock Plus (3–4 days, $117–$226 US). For seasoned mountaineers and climbers programs range from weekends on famous Rocky Mountain peaks to six days in the Bugaboos, Columbia Icefields, and the Lake O'Hara/Louise region (May–Aug., weekends $218 US up, 6 days $645 US up). As for expeditions, Yamnuska emphasizes quality and style, low-ratio personalized guiding, well-organized logistics. Their seven-day Robson expedition attracts climbers from around the world (Aug., $1,065 US); for the seven-day Selkirk Route with high peaks and remote glaciers, you helicopter into the Battle Range (Jul., $1,165 US); the Logan three-week expedition, though not technically difficult, takes all you can give as weather and cold conspire to keep you from its heights, May–Jun., $3,630 US. (See also *Backpacking / Hiking / Walking.*)

**"Pigeon Spire" in
the Bugaboos—**
*David Begg for
Yamnuska, Alberta.*

BY HORSE

Photo by Buddy Mays

Cattle Drives / Roundups / Horse Drives

A *roundup*, one rancher explains, is when you move the cattle not too far in the home range. When you trail them 20 miles or more from one range to another, it's a *cattle drive*. When you round up a herd from an area that is grazed to one with fresh grass, you really are not rounding them up. You're *gathering* them and *trailing* them to new pastures.

When you move horses and pack animals to pack stations in the highcountry, where they are used on mountain pack trips, it's a *horse drive*. Whereas cows move at a walk, with horses you're following at a trot or a canter much of the time—several days of fast riding and spectacular scenery.

Some ranchers let "city slickers" try their hand at being cowboys on a paying basis—paying the rancher, that is. The fee helps to persuade ranchers to put up with greenhorns, and for the would-be cowpokes it's a Hollywood dream come true.

Besides cattle drives, there are other events involved with cattle ranching—branding, dehorning, castrating, pregnancy testing, vaccinating, taking salt to grazing areas, checking the cattle and moving them to new pastures. These activities are not for everyone. Days can be hot and dusty or cold and wet. It's a rough and rugged life. But it has an irresistible pull for the cowboy romantic who is enamored of every aspect of cattle ranching [from the smell of the sagebrush to the slurp of the mud as it grabs your boots].

Whatever the activity you sign up to do, days are apt to begin at the crack of dawn and end with a campfire cookout or a delicious chuckwagon dinner. On some cattle drives you sleep in a tent or under the stars. On others you return to the ranch house for a comfortable night. You follow whatever pattern the rancher has always used. Either way, for all the mud and dust and hard work, it's an experience no greenhorn will ever forget.

ARIZONA

**Chiricahua
Mountains**

PRICE CANYON RANCH

*P.O. Box 1065, Douglas, AZ 85607. Attn.: Scotty Anderson.
(602) 558-2383.*

At Price Canyon Ranch, 160 miles east of Tucson, Longhorns
and Brangas graze in the Chiricahua Mountains at elevations
up to 9,000 feet. Rounding up and trailing the herd between
mountain pastures and grasslands at 4,400 feet is an eight-
day event in early May and October. Scotty Anderson takes
up to ten guests on the roundups. In spring start with gathering, sorting, branding, dehorning, castrating and vaccinating the cattle before getting on the trail. Each night you're
back in the comfortable ranch house, with hearty family-
style meals. The fall roundup ends with separating the cows
for shipping. Rate: 4 nights, $400; 8 nights, $800. Unlimited
riding, hiking, birdwatching or pack trips other months.

**Roundup in the
Chiricahua Mts.—**
*Price Canyon Ranch,
AZ.*

ARIZONA

**Hassayampa
River Canyon
Wilderness Area**

WILLIAMS FAMILY RANCH

*Hassayampa Canyon Trails, P.O. Box 2691, Wickenburg, AZ 85359.
Attn.: Carrol Williams. Darlene King takes phone messages at
(602) 778-2694.*

A cattle drive or roundup at the Williams Ranch is the real
thing. The cattle ranch is located in the high desert 16 miles
north of Wickenburg, surrounded by the Hassayampa River
Canyon Wilderness Area. For 20 years friends and relatives
have joined in on roundups and cattle drives. Only recently
has the Williams family decided to invite vacationers to come
for the hard work, good times, beauty of the land and the
family atmosphere. "It's not a dude ranch and it's not posh,"

explains Carrol Williams. "But it's clean and nice and has all the necessities." The ranch has no electricity and no phone. They use a generator for power and get water from a spring. They have remodelled a bunkhouse into guest accommodations. Telephone communications with prospective guests are handled by a cousin, Darlene King (see number above), who also arranges travel by four-wheel-drive vehicle from Wickenburg to the ranch. At the ranch you participate in day-to-day activities—moving cattle to new pastures, branding calves, other cattle maintenance chores and a chance to ride. Year-round activities. For accommodations in the bunkhouse and family style meals, rates are $521 for 6 1/2 days, or $85/day for 3 to 5 days. ($585 or $90 for singles.) Families and youth welcome.

CALIFORNIA

Deer Creek

SHANNON RANCH

Route 4, Box 107, Porterville, CA 93257. Attn.: Sandi or Jack Shannon. (209) 535-4543.

"We are celebrating our 75th year of driving cattle," announces Sandi Shannon. "Join three generations of the Shannon family for life in the old west the way it was meant to be." On the spring drive, late May/early June, you'll ride from the Shannon Ranch on Deer Creek at 700 feet to the summer range at 8,000 feet in the Gray Meadow country of the High Sierra. In mid-September the drive (called the "Fall Gathering") is reversed, descending through quaking aspen and glowing fall colors amid fresh pine forests. Trailing 400–600 head of cattle, just the way it was done in 1918 when the ranch was started, is open to 12 participants who want to hook up with a real cowboy adventure. The seven-day drive includes two days at cow camp in spring and two days for gathering in the fall, with five days on the trail. "Don't miss the trout fishing in Little Kern River during cow camp," says Sandi. Bring your sleeping bag and working duds—and fishing gear. Everything else is provided, including bawling cattle and story-telling cowboys around an evening campfire. Horses are provided, or you can bring your own with approval of the Trail Boss. Rates: $1,050/7 days or $650/4 days. Nearest airport: Bakersfield.

CALIFORNIA/ NEVADA

California/ Nevada border

SOLDIER MEADOWS RANCH

c/o Spanish Springs Ranch, P.O. Box 70, Ravendale, CA 96123. (916) 234-2050 or (800) 272-8282. Fax (916) 234-2041.

Families and singles are urged to spend a week each June at Buckaroo Camp, a special one-a-year opportunity to ride with the cowboys and learn their skills. Have you ever wanted to rope and brand a calf? Do you know how to gather and sort cattle, mother up cows and calves, drive a horse-drawn wagon? Does riding the range appeal to you—in fact, riding, riding, riding for a week? Horsemanship clinics give a boost to beginning and intermediate riders. You'll find ruts from wagon trains of the 1800s—the Lassen-Applegate Emigrant Trail runs through this historic ranch—where you live the rugged lifestyle of the cowboy except for large canvas tents, a portable shower and delicious food. Also there will be gymkhanas (games on horseback), campfire songs, cowboy poetry and dancing, astronomy and history lessons. The ranch, owned by Spanish Springs (see above), is at lower elevations in Nevada, excellent wintering ground for cattle. For summer vacations (June only) at the Buckaroo Camp, the rate is $595/week + 15% service fee and taxes. (See also *Spanish Springs Ranch*.)

Riding at Buckaroo Camp—*Soldier Meadows Ranch, WY.*

CALIFORNIA

Northern California

SPANISH SPRINGS RANCH

P.O. Box 70, Ravendale, CA 96123. (916) 234-2050 or (800) 272-8282. Fax (916) 234-2041.

The Spanish Springs Ranch on the California-Nevada border gives riders the chance to join in all kinds of cattle-related activities involved with their herd of 5,000 cattle. On May and November cattle drives, 20 dudes ride for up to ten hours a day with stubble-faced buckaroos to drive 400–500 head of cattle over the rugged and spectacular trail between summer and winter range. At the six campsites along the trail, amenities are minimal but camaraderie is maximal. Drives are seven days, two scheduled in May and two in October/November at rate of $950 per rider. Fast-paced horse drives,

On an 80-mile drive in rugged country—*Spanish Springs Ranch, CA.*

limited to expert riders, are scheduled April and September to move 75 head of horses between winter pasture and outlying ranches. For these five-day drives the rate is $695. Still another option, seven-day roundups open to intermediate or expert riders in March/April and October/November offer the experience of working with the cow boss to gather, sort, wean and brand the calves. The rate is $595. (Add 15% service charge and taxes to all rates.) The 70,000-acre cattle ranch is known for the many authentic activities which fulfill riders' dreams of being cowboys for a time. (See also *Soldier Meadows Ranch*.)

COLORADO

BROKEN SKULL CATTLE CO.

Continental Divide, Routt National Forest

P.O. Box 774054, Steamboat Springs, CO 80477. Attn.: Jerry Garcia. (303) 879-0090 or 6487. Fax (303) 819-6044.

"Enjoy the West 1800s' style," urges trail boss Jerry Garcia. In early July drovers drive his Longhorn cattle over Buffalo Pass on the Continental Divide to summer pasture, and back again in late September Clydesdale horses pull the chuckwagon on the nine-day, 65-mile drive through sagebrush, mountains, canyons and river bottoms at elevations from 7,000–10,000 feet. The "grub" right off the old chuckwagon is cooked over an open fire. "Excellent," an Indiana drover rates it. A local cowboy-poet entertains evenings with cow-

Grub off the old chuckwagon—
David Adams for Broken Skull Ranch, CO.

boy songs and poems. At the drive's end drovers get involved in roping, branding and calf wrestling and receive their wages—a dollar a day in silver coin tucked in a buckskin "poke" etched with the Broken Skull brand. The Steamboat professional rodeo finishes the evening for some. Rate, 9 days, $1,300; five-day rates also available, as are 5-day stays in May at the ranch for roundups, tagging baby calves, checking fence and trailing from winter pasture about ten miles to spring range.

MONTANA

Thompson River Valley

HARGRAVE CATTLE & GUEST RANCH
300 Thompson River Road, Marion, MT 59925. Attn.: Ellen or Leo Hargrave. (406) 858-2284 (phone & fax) or (800) 933-0696.

"Don't tell too many people—heaven should only be trespassed a little at a time," says a recent participant on a week-long ranch stay. This "heaven" is near Glacier National Park in the Thompson River Valley. Leo and Ellen Hargrave invite up to 15 guests to join the activities on their 86,000 deeded and leased acres. Calving lasts from March to June, a busy time with more than 400 mother cows. May is branding month, and on the spring drive in June they move 400 cattle

"Cowhands" learning the ropes—*Hargrave Cattle Ranch, MT.*

to the mountains for summer grazing. The herd is moved to new pastures in July and August for feed and for conservation purposes, and on the fall drive in early October they are trailed back to lower pastures. "Scattering the cattle keeps the range grazed more evenly," Leo explains. "City 'cowhands' experience true cattle herding here," Ellen says. "Riding with the cowboys is a challenge, a lot of fun and very satisfying. We call it 'riding with a purpose.'" They're usually back at the log cabin and ranch headquarters rooms each night. Rate: $980 for 7 nights includes all but personal gear. (See also *Pack Trips*.)

MONTANA

KREBS RANCH

59 New Century Road, Belt, MT 59412. Attn.: Kathy Krebs Herman. (406) 736-5266.

Little Belts Mountains

In spring and fall about 500 head of cattle are moved between the home ranch and high pasture in the Little Belt Mountains, and up to six guests pitch in and help. You do a lot of riding over scenic acreage, see how a cattle ranch operates and visit the C.M. Russell Museum, Giant Springs, a buffalo jump and other local sights. You'll meet the whole family and neighbors and learn a lot from people who love ranch life. The spring drive begins with sorting and gathering cattle. Then you're into the dirt and dust, pushing the animals cross country into Monarch Canyon and up the mountainside, with days starting around 4 a.m. Each night back at the ranch.

The fall drive follows the same route in reverse. Much of the riding is over gentle hills and green meadows, but in the mountains be ready for high speed, hard turns and quick stops. Drives usually scheduled third or fourth weeks of June and fourth week of September. Arrival: Great Falls. Rate: $85/day including airport pickup/return, meals, lodging, horses, saddle, gear. Come April–May for cattle chasing, branding, etc. or end of August–September for lots of riding.

MONTANA

Bull Mountains

METCALF'S JA RANCH

Box 765, Big Timber, MT 59011. Attn.: Remi & Susan Metcalf. (406) 932-4572.

If you would like to experience life at a cattle ranch, do some cattle work for a few days or longer and ride to your heart's content, consider visiting the Metcalf's ranch in the Bull Mountains of Montana, not far from Billings. All through the summer guests can join in whatever work is going on—moving cattle to new pastures, bringing them in to worm and work the chutes or to ship them, or going to a neighbor's ranch to help with their cattle drive—a friendly custom in ranch communities. Activities are informally scheduled according to guests' interests and abilities. In 1919 Susan's family homesteaded the 5,000 acres in pine-covered hills with sandstone outcroppings. "We provide cow horses, not dude horses," Susan explains, adding that she also "feeds you well." The ranch accepts only one party (or family) at a time. Accommodations are in a rustic cabin with modern comforts, and meals are served at the main ranch house. Rate: $100/adult per day, $50 for children. Open for guests Jun. to early Sep.

MONTANA

Custer National Forest

TONGUE RIVER WAGON TRAIN & CATTLE DRIVE

Box 432, Ashland, MT 59003. Attn.: Jack Goss. (406) 784-2492 or (800) 345-5660.

When the Texans trailed their cattle north to railheads in Montana they did it on horseback, hauling their gear in covered wagons pulled by horses or mules. This is the experience re-enacted from June to September by Tongue River Ranch in the pine hills and prairies of southeastern Montana, an area on the Texans' route. Start with arrival in Billings and going to the Night Rodeo, with meals and motel included in the six-day rate. In the morning drive to the ranch with stops at the Custer Battlefield and Indian Museum in Ashland. By evening you are camping—wagons circled, tents set up, horses tethered, cattle corralled and chuckwagon producing hearty fare. You continue on the trail the next four days,

Chow time on the prairie—*Tongue River Wagon Train & Cattle Drive, MT.*

sharing the chores. The teamsters and outriders are your "tour guides". *Singles Only* trip end of July. Small or large groups (up to 100) can be accommodated. Rates are $1,095 for 6 days; $695 for 3 days. Discounts for children. Also offers custom pack trips and cross country rides.

NEVADA

The trail to Reno

RENO RODEO-TONY LAMA CATTLE DRIVE
223 Marsh Avenue, Reno, NV 89509. Attn.: Shelli Thomas. (702) 329-4200 or (800) 842-7633. Fax (702) 329-4283.

The Reno Rodeo Association and the Tony Lama Boot Co. have discovered that the best way to get their roping cattle to the rodeo grounds for the Reno Rodeo is to bring them to town from their winter pasture on a 60-mile cattle drive. It's a five-day drive, five to seven hours a day in the saddle to cover 12–15 miles, eating the dust kicked up by 300 head of cattle. You end the drive by moving the cattle right through downtown Reno to the rodeo grounds. Some 50 riders participate, camping out under Nevada's starry skies from June 14–18 in '93 (similar dates in successive years). You will travel on open Nevada terrain at an elevation of approximately 5,000 feet. Meals are served from chuckwagons that feature western gourmet cooking. An open bar and live entertainment also featured. Riders can bring their own horses or rent one, and you'll need a bedroll and western saddle. No previous cattle or horse experience is necessary. "Professional" drovers will be on hand to assist. Minimum age to participate is 12, and those under 18 must be accompanied by an adult. Cost is $695 for those who bring their own horse, or $1,070 if you need to rent one. Shuttle service from Reno airport to rodeo grounds is available.

OREGON

High desert region

IRON MOUNTAIN CATTLE CO., INC.

P.O. Box 487, Redmond, OR 97756. Attn.: Art Proctor. (800) 438-1389.

"We ride 10–20 miles a day through high desert sage and grassland, to pine and aspen forests and meadows at 4,000–6,000' elevations," says Dixie Weberg, whose family has owned the 44,000-acre ranch for 100 years. Wildlife abounds. You'll see deer, antelope, coyotes, elk, eagles and hawks while trailing 250–400 mother cows, plus yearlings, steers and heifers. Cattle drives are scheduled June, July and late September with a lot of riding and other cattle work going on between April and October. A few friends who wouldn't miss it have formed a company to book up to ten riders at a time on these old-time cowboy experiences at the ranch. After each day's ride they return to buckaroo quarters for the night—remote cabins built around 1900, complete with outhouses. Nights are crystal starry, and meals are hearty ranch fare. "An added bonus," Dixie explains, "is simmering in delicious hot, natural mineral spring water piped into a horse trough in the rustic setting. Can't beat it after a day of dust and aching muscles." There are no frills or luxuries here, she points out, but everyone who comes falls in love with this ranch and the "big country" experience it affords. Apr.–Oct., rate $100+ per day, including pickup at Redmond airport, a 2-hour drive. Small group discounts. Bring sleeping bag, boots, slicker.

UTAH

Blue Mountains

DALTON GANG ADVENTURES

P.O. Box 8, Monticello, UT 84535. Attn.: Val Dalton. (801) 587-2416.

The Daltons describe their ranch as "a real cowboy outfit" in the majestic country of the Blue Mountains bordering Canyonlands National Park and the Colorado River. "We're the third and fourth generation cowboys and we run the ranch the way it was done 100 years ago. We'd like up to six guests at a time to ride with us and share in a working ranch experience. This means days from sunup to sundown, dutch oven meals (no drinking on ranch) and camping out under the stars or in cabins with no electricity, some with modern bathrooms and running water, others where *you* do the running to get it." The cattle work varies from branding, roundups and trailing cattle and horses off the winter range in spring; to hauling hay, putting out salt, rounding up yearlings for market and driving cattle off the mountain in fall; to changing pastures, cutting ice and trailing cattle to new range in winter. The Daltons run about 300 head of cows and 350 yearlings on their 200,000 acres of rough, beautiful country—brushy, rocky, desert, canyons, aspen meadows. "It's a lot of range to cover, with long hours in the saddle. That's the way we like it." Guests fly to Moab via Salt Lake or to Cortez via Denver for ranch pickup. Spend arrival night at ranch or Monticello motel (not included in rate). Boots and hat a must; bedroll and tent can be rented. Rate: 3–6 days, $100/day.

Cattle work with the Dalton Gang— *Dalton Gang Adventures, UT.*

UTAH

Capitol Reef National Park, canyon country

PACE RANCH

P.O. Box 98, Torrey, UT 84775. Attn.: Pat or Gary George. (801) 425-3519 or (800) 332-2696.

"Your stirrups are too long if your rear end hurts. They're too short if your knees hurt. But if both hurt, your stirrups are just the right length," explains Gary George, whose Hondoo Rivers & Trails service guides horseback and river trips through canyon country. In spring and fall the Pace Ranch moves 700 head of cattle from winter to summer pasture and back again, and Gary takes a group of riders along. It's a six-day, 25-mile journey through the sculptured canyons of Capitol Reef National Park, over remote high desert, past rock escarpments, water holes and spectacular red rock spires. Pace Ranch has grazed cattle here since the 1880s. Take this historic ride while you can. The cattle-grazing rights will be suspended within a generation. Grand Junction, CO, is the fly-in point for arrival, with arrangements for van pickup, air charter or rental car transport to Torrey. Overnight at Torrey motel for a pre-trip briefing included in rate. Spring roundup May 28–June 3, fall Oct. 12–17, $760/rider. (See also *River Running, Pack Trips, Wilderness/Nature Expeditions*—Hondoo Rivers & Trails.)

WYOMING

**Thunder Basin
National
Grasslands, Cow
Creek, Coal
Bank, Red Hills**

CHEYENNE RIVER RANCH

*1031 Steinle Road, Douglas, WY 82633. Attn.: Don or Betty Pellatz.
(307) 358-2380.*

Plan to ride about six hours a day on cattle drives at the
Cheyenne River Ranch. The ranch was homesteaded by the
Pellatz family in 1917, and today Don and Betty Pellatz invite
up to ten riders to join the cattle drives at their own ranch as
well as some they handle for neighboring ranchers. You
camp out on these drives, with hearty chuckwagon meals
and a hot-water shower transported to each night's camp.
Aside from these amenities it's cowboy business as usual,
rounding up and trailing cattle, crossing streams and riding
through such places as the Thunder Basin National Grasslands, rough land along Cow Creek, high prairie country,
Coal Bank, the Red Hills, Wildcat Draw and ranchlands
brimming with tales of the early days. Betty fills you in with
all the local history. Casper pickup and return as well as first
and last nights at the Cheyenne River Ranch are included in
rates of $850 per rider for the week-long drives scheduled
each month from May to end of October.

WYOMING

**Big Horn
Mountains**

THE HIDEOUT

*Dave Flitner's Ranch, Shell Route, Greybull, WY 82426. (307) 765-2961.
Fax (307) 765-2777.*

"The cowboy is more than just a romantic historical figure,"
maintains Dave Flitner. "He exists today, doing much the
same work as a century ago. But it's work involved with
professional techniques, ranch management and issues involved with livestock grazing, conservation, environmental
planning and government and private landowner interaction." Dave has set up a five-day *Working Cowboy Adventure*
for eight guests every week from May to September at his
ranch in the Big Horn Mountains. The program starts with
horsemanship orientation and proceeds with whatever activities are in process at the four-generation cattle ranch.
From week to week they include such jobs as rounding up
and gathering a herd and moving them to high mountain
pastures, taking horses to the mountains, gathering strag-
glers, working with livestock, checking fences and watering
holes. Whatever the action, you are performing a cowboy's
chores and experiencing what cowboy life is all about from
shoeing, roping and riding to sleeping in a tepee with kerosene lanterns, chuckwagon meals and wrangler's tales around
a campfire. A videotape to take home records the week's
action. Rate: 5 days, $1,170. Customized programs offered
for eight or more riders.

WYOMING

Washakie Wilderness

HIGH ISLAND RANCH

P.O. Box 71-G, Hamilton Dome, WY 82427. (307) 867-2374. [Mid-Sep. to mid-May: P.O. Box 7, Fryeburg, ME 04037. (207) 925-3285.]

"Live the life of a cowboy on a week-long (Sat. to Sat.) adventure in the spectacular Washakie Wilderness," urges High Island. Between May and end of September the ranch offers two 1800-period cattle drives (with dress, food and action patterned to pre-1890s), four "authentic" cattle drives (wear what you want) and 11 round-up weeks. Enjoy chuckwagon grub, campfires, sleeping under the stars and unlimited riding every week on the 41,000 acres of this working ranch. They advise participants to "bring your own sleeping bag, towels and good sense of humor and join us pushing cows out of the sage, gullies and creek beds and trailing them over the prairie and into the mountains." Lots of fishing at the upper lodge. A branding week begins the season in May. Rates: $950/roundup week; $1,050/cattle drive weeks; $1,495 for special 1800s drives end of Jun. and end of Aug. (See also *Trail Rides*.)

Moving the herd in the Washakie Wilderness—*High Island Ranch, WY.*

WYOMING

Laramie Plains

TWO CREEK RANCH

800 Esterbrook Road, Douglas, WY 82633. Attn.: Nancy Daly. (800) 252-7899 or (307) 358-3467.

Twice a year, the last weeks in May and October, Dennis and Nancy Daly drive 1,000 head of cattle over a 75-mile route between their ranch at 5,000' and the Laramie Plains at 7,500'.

On each 11-day drive, 12 riders put in eight grueling hours a day while Dennis remarks, "Well, tommorow's another easy day." In spring they follow a trail along a creek and little-used road,up a hill, through a spectacular gorge, and across open range to high meadows. In fall the route is reversed. Folks from neighboring ranches sometimes come by for a wiener roast. Rate: $1,100. Other ranch events which vacationers join take place through spring and summer—a drive to spring range, a five-day branding weekend, a six-day roundup, eight days of gathering, weighing, giving shots, trailing, and marketing. Rates are about $100 per day. One rider reports, "We like the work, the food, the Dalys, the open land, and the awesome force of the weather. Great stuff!"

A glorious day for driving cattle—
Roberta Wright for Two Creek Ranch, WY.

BRITISH
COLUMBIA

TEEPEE HEART RANCH
Box 6, Big Creek, British Columbia, Canada V0L 1K0. Attn.: Hans Burch. (604) 392-5015 or 398-1061.

Chilcotin-
Cariboo country

Only six experienced riders may qualify to take part in two wild and rugged events at the Teepee Heart Ranch, 85 miles west of Williams Lake in the Chilcotin-Cariboo country of the coast range. Usually in February and March two Wild Horse Roundups are scheduled, and Horse Drives in spring and fall. These are fast and exciting rides. Rates and dates are available on request. (See also *Pack Trips, Fly Fishing.*)

BEFORE YOU GO:

Whether you wear new cowboy duds or an old pair of jeans, you'll need a rain slicker, a hat, boots and layered clothing you can take on or off as conditions change. Bandannas are not just for Hollywood cowboys. You will be glad to have one to cover your mouth and nose when riding drag with the wind howling and the dust flying in your face. It will help you breathe. Real cowboys even use chapstick. Without it, your lips may crack.

On real cattle drives, no special accommodations are made for paying guests. You pay to be treated the same as the help. Tents are normally provided along the trail, but you must bring your own sleeping bag. After a day on horseback, you'll be grateful for anything that cushions the hard ground. Several pickup trucks usually make the trip, and no one thinks any the less of you if you choose to ride in a vehicle for a day.

For more comfort though perhaps a bit less adventure choose a cattle drive where cowpokes return to the ranch house at night, or one that offers a variety of cattle ranching events in addition to trailing the cows. A shower and other plumbing facilities may be near at hand, or clean-up possibilities may consist of water dipped from an icy brook.

All of that is incidental. You are there to accomplish a purposeful job with the cowboys, and you may as well decide in advance that however they do it is good enough for you.

Great Divide Guiding and Outfitters, Montana (page 72)

Pack Trips

The beauty of a wilderness defies description—the awesome stillness, vastness, wildness, rugged peaks, rushing streams and millions of tiny flowers that set a mountain meadow ablaze with color…

Pack trip outfitters are the open sesame for exploring these regions on horseback. Usually four to eight riders (sometimes more) plus crew and pack animals to carry the gear set forth on these trips. Some are easy rides to a *basecamp*. Each day you follow trails in different directions to explore, spot wildlife or do some fishing, but return to the same camp at night. Others are *moving or progressive* trips—spending two nights or so at one camp, then riding on with the pack string to set up another camp. On these moving trips you go deeper into wilderness areas.

The expertise of a pack trip outfitter opens to even the least experienced rider the joy of wilderness travel on horseback. The outfitter provides all that is needed—the horses, pack animals, tents, food and camping gear as well as wrangler-guides and a camp cook. Basic riding instruction is part of the outfitter's service for neophytes.

Some outfitters schedule specific dates which singles or several riders can join. Others set up custom trips to fit the requirements of families or groups of friends.

Their what-to-bring lists include such essentials as sleeping bag and pad (unless supplied), jeans, long-sleeved shirt and t-shirts, sweater, windproof jacket, wide-brimmed hat, raingear, riding boots (comfortable and broken in) or smooth-soled hiking boots (no lug soles) with heels to keep from sliding through stirrups. If weather is apt to turn cold, bring thermal underwear and a jacket. Flashlight, sun lotion, chapstick, dark glasses, gloves, toilet articles, wash cloth, towel, camera, film and fishing tackle complete your gear. Other hand items are tennis shoes for day hikes, and waterproof boots or galoshes to keep your riding boots dry in the wet grass around camp in the morning.

ALASKA

**Kachemak Bay,
Kenai Peninsula**

ALASKA HORSEBACK VACATIONS
*58335 East End Road, Homer, AK 99603. Attn.: Mairiis Kilcher.
(907) 235-7850 or (800) 252-7899.*

"A very unusual and memorable trip," relates a guest. "The scenery was superb, and the opportunity to visit the homestead where Mairiis grew up and talk with her father was worth the whole trip." Her pack trip up the eastern shore of the Kenai Peninsula adds real adventure to an Alaskan itinerary. Starting near Homer (277 miles south of Anchorage), riders follow easy trails along Kachemak Bay's beaches timed to coordinate with the tides. Spectacular scenes hold their attention—bald eagles, glaciers, snow-capped peaks. Overnights are at historic homesteads—you see birds and wildlife, gather berries and mushrooms, dig for clams, or catch a salmon for dinner. "These are pleasant and gentle trips," Mairiis explains, "suitable for intermediate to experienced riders." She provides either English or Western riding (optional sightseeing in area), 1–4 days, May–Sep., $125/day, family and group rates. Custom trips combine riding and hiking.

**Trailing the tides
of Kachemak Bay—**
*Mairiis Hollister for
Alaska Horseback
Vacations, AK.*

COLORADO

**Sangre de Cristo
Mountains**

ADVENTURE SPECIALISTS, INC.
Bear Basin Ranch, Westcliffe, CO 81252. Attn.: Gary Ziegler or Amy Finger. (719) 783-2519. [Dec.–Apr.: 515 W. San Rafael, Colorado Springs, CO 80905. (719) 630- 76787.]

For more than 20 years Gary Ziegler has been packing into the Sangre de Cristo Mountains—a region filled with shimmering lakes, pine forests and miles of trails perfectly suited to exploring on horseback. For experienced riders Gary offers a five-day "ultimate pack trip" ($550, Jul.–Sep.). You ride trails above timberline, traverse the spine of the mountains and dismount to lead your horse over rugged terrain. "Each peak and ridgeline frames the vastness of the valley below," describes Gary. On his easier "hot springs horseback experience" (5 days, $575, Jul.–Aug.) riders follow trails over 13,000-foot passes, then descend to the joys of a hot springs resort complete with hot showers, wood-fired sauna and a system of pools. They camp in a wood glade and soak in the magical spot for two days before the spectacular ride back over the pass. For inexperienced riders a "Surf and Turf" trip includes three days of riding and camping and two days of river rafting—or take the three days of riding only. This combo is offered May to Sep. starting every Monday ($650, or $325 for 3 days only). (See also *Hiking with Packstock, Combos.*)

COLORADO

West Elk
Wilderness

BAR DIAMOND RANCH
Box 688, Hotchkiss, CO 81419. Attn.: Dellis & Linda Ferrier.
(303) 527-3010 or (800) 252-7899.

Families with children six years or older head for Dellis Ferrier's pack trips in Colorado's West Elk Wilderness from July 1 through Labor Day. Dellis tells us why. "We have some of the gentlest, best-trained trail horses in all of Colorado. If you've never ridden a horse or it's been a few years, don't let that stop you." His family has packed into this area for four generations. Trips start with Saturday arrival (they'll meet you at the Montrose airport) and the first night at the Ferriers' trailhead lodge. Next morning it's a five-hour ride with mules carrying your gear to a wilderness tent camp at 10,000 feet, the scenic headquarters for three nights. Each day you ride a different trail with a chance to see deer, elk, bighorn sheep, bald or golden eagles, bears and beavers. On a ride to the top of West Elk Peak the view stretches 100 miles in every direction. On Wednesday riders follow the trail back down to the trailhead, or move to another camp for two more days in the wilderness. Up to eight riders on each trip. Rates for 5 days, $425/adult; for 7 days, $600/adult; 10% less for children.

COLORADO

Fryingpan River

FRYINGPAN RIVER RANCH
32042 Fryingpan River Road, Meredith, CO 81642. Attn.: Jim Rea.
(303) 927-3570 or (800) 352-0980.

On pack trips in the spectacular high country of the Rockies riders start at the ranch and ride to camps along the Continental Divide. "It's a day's ride up Chapman Creek and over the ridge to our South Fork camp on the Fryingpan River," Jim Rea explains. "We ride through Dead Man Gulch and from the top look back to view Independence Pass and the Continental Divide." On a half-day ride from the ranch to their other camp at Granite Lakes at 11,000 feet, you are treated to great views and superb fishing. This is the camp generally used early in the season, with trips to South Fork camp later in the summer. Pack trips are scheduled for three or four days at rates of $450 or $600, discounted about 20% if staying at the ranch. They are for a minimum of four riders, but the ranch can match you with a group to make up the minimum. They provide Aspen airport pickup and return for fly-in guests. (See also *Fly Fishing*.)

COLORADO

**San Juan
Mountains**

RAPP GUIDES & PACKERS

47 Electra Lake, Durango, CO 81301. Attn.: Jerry or Anne Rapp. (303) 247-8923. Fax (303) 259-2953.

The quality and training of their 14–20 professional guides, wranglers, packers and teamsters, and maintaining a strong and healthy string of saddle horses, are all important to this pack trip outfitter in the San Juan Mountains of southwest Colorado. For over 12 years they have offered flexible and complete custom itineraries for small groups and frequently move their basecamps and pack trip routes to prevent over-grazing and other impacts. Expert guides handle the live-stock—large-boned Quarter horses, Morgan, Walker and Thoroughbred crosses—and all well-informed on the local history, flora and fauna of each elevation. Mules carry the gear on these trips. You ride about 12 miles on travel days, alternating with layover days to rest, explore or fish. Trips from three to six days are scheduled April to November into regions such as the Ute Tribal Park at Ute Mountain (with its Anasazi ruins, cliff dwellings and pictographs), the upper Animas River Canyon (guests can arrive or depart on the Durango/Silverton Train), Silver Mesa and Needle Mountain Range, along the Continental Divide to Starvation Gulch, and half-day rides to basecamps for several days of great trout fishing. Basecamps provide comfortable, heated wall tents with cots. Families with children or first-time adventurers find the trips easy despite their inexperience. Custom trips for 4–15 riders. Rates: $110–$150 per day.

*COLORADO/
ARIZONA*

**Weminuche
Wilderness,
Superstition Mts.**

WEMINUCHE & SUPERSTITION WILDERNESS ADVENTURES

17754 CR 501-A, Bayfield, CO 81122. Attn.: Dobbin & Caroline Shupe. (303) 884-2555. [Dec.–Apr.: P. O. Box 1899-A, Wickenburg, AZ 85358. (602) 684-7259.]

"Reach deep into majestic mountain backcountry and return to the joys and exhilarations of a lost way of life," urge the Shupes. They take you by horseback into the Weminuche Wilderness of the San Juan Mountains in southwest Colorado in summer and Arizona's Superstition Mountains in winter. You begin the Weminuche trip near Durango, marking a leisurely pace along meandering streams, through vast alpine meadows and forests to the delicate high altitude tundra above timberline. Cool mountain waters yield an abundance of trout which are served for breakfast. (Rides scheduled for 5 or 6 days, Jul.–Aug. $555–$655.) A horsepack trip in the fabled Superstitions puts action into winter doldrums. From Apache Junction (near Phoenix), ride into a remote region of stark beauty—deep rock canyons, giant saguaro cacti, rugged trails, the glory of the Sonoran Desert in bloom, sightings of wild quail, javelina, eagle—and stories of the Lost Dutchman and Spanish explorers. (Feb.–Apr., 5–6 days, $585–$685).

IDAHO

Selway-Bitterroot Wilderness

RENSHAW OUTFITTING, INC.

P.O. Box 1165, Kamiah, ID 83536. Attn.: Lynda Renshaw. (208) 926-4520, 935-0726 or (800) 452-2567. Fax (208) 935-0726.

A true wilderness pack trip is offered in the Selway-Bitterroot Wilderness by Idaho's longest licensed and bonded outfitter. Jim Renshaw has guided people into this area for 40 years. Three generations of Renshaw men have spent their lives exploring these rugged and remote mountains. His expertise spills over into a guide school, training a few select people each year. Jim deeply loves this country. "It's got rocks, lakes and meadows," he says, "and you can see forever." On a seven-day pack trip six riders follow trails to a camp on a wilderness lake or stream—a great family trip. Each day you ride in a different direction discovering fabulous scenery in the high mountains, crystal clear lakes and wild animals such as deer, elk, beaver, moose and mountain goat. You move to a different camp once or twice during the week, with pack mules carrying the gear. A guide and camp cook accompany each group. Best time —late Jul. and Aug. Rate: $900/rider, 7 days; family discounts. (See also *Fly Fishing*.)

MONTANA

Bob Marshall Wilderness

BOB MARSHALL WILDERNESS RANCH

Seely Lake, MT 59868. Attn.: Virgil and Barb Burns. (406) 754-2285. [Winter: St. Ignatius, MT 59865. (406) 745-4466.]

Experiencing the Bob Marshall Wilderness—vast, awesome, humbling—by packing into it on horseback is the only way to comprehend this remarkable region, Virgil and Barb Burns believe. They offer horsepack trips to explore this spectacular area with the assurance that you will be guided by the "tops" in the field. They consider the scenery and solitude, and fishing for wild trout in pristine lakes, rivers and streams, to be unsurpassed. They take riders on both moving and basecamp expeditions in July and August for five to ten days. One of their guests, the editor of American Forests Magazine, comments that their wilderness program wouldn't work "without reliable, competent, well-equipped outfitters" like Virgil and Barb. Another guest, editor of Outdoor Life, speaks of the Burnses pampering you "with superb food, gear, skilled guides and well trained horses." Rates of $155 per day include lodging and meals at the Burns' lodge nights before and after trip, also transport to and from Missoula.

MONTANA

**Lewis & Clark
National Forest**

**Along the edge of
Glacier National
Park**—*John Borsman
for Great Divide
Guiding, MT.*

GREAT DIVIDE GUIDING & OUTFITTERS
P. O. Box 315A, East Glacier Park, MT 59434. Attn.: Richard Jackson. (406) 226-4487.

"Escape to the Big Sky Country of the Northern Rockies and turn back the hands of time," urges Richard Jackson. With 18 years of packtrip experience, he offers moving or base camp custom trips. From the plains of the Blackfeet Indian Reservation in East Glacier, you ride high into the Lewis & Clark National Forest towards the Continental Divide. Richard adds a touch of the real West in the high mountains—moving cattle from one pasture to another. He guides you through high mountain meadows, across crystal clear streams and

into beautiful groves of quaking aspen. Trails lead to magnificent country along the southern edge of Glacier National Park. "The food is excellent, scenery fantastic and the fishing out of this world," reports a couple from Los Angeles. Richard tailors trips to your riding ability and interests, with everything provided except sleeping bags and fishing gear. Arrival: Kalispell, MT. Rates: $695, 5-days, up to 8 riders. Jun.–Sep. See photo on page 66.

MONTANA

Cube Iron
Wilderness

HARGRAVE CATTLE & GUEST RANCH

300 Thompson River Road, Marion, MT 59925. Attn.: Ellen Hargrave. (406) 858-2284 (phone & fax) or (800) 933-0696.

"Ours is a real working cattle ranch, but people also come here for wilderness pack trips," says Ellen Hargrave. The ranch customizes pack trips for small groups (up to six riders) in the proposed Cube Iron Wilderness just 25 miles from the ranch. "These trips are for people who want to experience the wilderness," Ellen adds. They are planned for three to four days in the extremely beautiful mountainous terrain with narrow trails through tall timber and rocky peaks, alongside towering cliffs and canyons. The region is home to deer, elk, eagles, trout, mackinaw, and kokanee salmon. The pace of riding and distance between campsites is planned according to each group's wishes and if riders also want a day or so of moving cattle at the 86,000-acre ranch, this usually can be arranged. Trips Jul.–Sep. Rate: $578/rider for 3-day trip includes all but personal gear. (See also *Cattle Drives / Roundups / Horse Drives.*)

MONTANA

Bob Marshall
Wilderness, Sun
River Game
Preserve

KLICKS K BAR L RANCH

Box 287, Augusta, MT 59410. Attn.: Nancy Klick. (406) 467-2771. [Winter & spring: (406) 562-3589.]

Beyond all roads, you reach this ranch, adjoining the Bob Marshall Wilderness, by driving from Great Falls or Augusta up the Sun River Canyon to Gibson Lake. Here the Klicks meet you for a scenic jetboat ride to the ranch. In fall when the water is low you ride in on horseback. Mountains and rivers are at your door. Pack trips follow trails through the wilderness in every direction—some to the Chinese Wall and White River and along the Continental Divide. It's a land of wildflowers and birds, and your catch of wild rainbow trout will vary from 12" to 20". These are custom trips, five to seven days, for small groups (up to six riders with wrangler and camp cook). For just two riders, contact the Klicks and join another small group. Comfortable log cabins at ranch before and after trip. Rate: $140/day per rider. (See also *Fly Fishing.*)

MONTANA/
WYOMING

R.K. MILLER'S WILDERNESS PACK TRIPS

P.O. Box 467, Livingston, MT 59047. Attn.: Ralph and Candace Miller.
(406) 222-7809.

Yellowstone
National Park

The eastern area of Yellowstone National Park is the domain of the Millers on the seven- to ten-day pack trips in this scenic backcountry for small groups—four to eight riders. The pace on each ride is set by the group, with layovers for exploring, fishing and spotting wildlife and birds—a specialty of the Millers after several trips for Audubon Society members. Ralph is a veterinarian and Candy an architect. They guide each of their trips. Guests learn to unsaddle and care for their horses, but that's the extent of their chores. The Millers and their wrangler do the rest. Ralph has packed into this remote highcountry for 20 years and knows it well—so well that he shuns the marked routes and follows game trails through open country. Candy produces what one guest called "a miracle of meals". The arrival point is Bozeman, and the Millers drive you to Livingston for overnight before packing into the wilderness. Your final night is back in Livingstone before return to Bozeman. Jul. to mid-Sep. Rates: $1,550/rider for 7 days, $2,200 for 10 days.

MONTANA

63 RANCH

Box 979-AG, Livingston, MT 59047. Attn.: Sandra Cahill.
(406) 222-0570.

Absaroka/
Beartooth
Wilderness

"We take you into some of Montana's most spectacular country," says Sandra Cahill, "up wooded canyons to rush-

A proud angler
displays the day's
catch—*Cahill photo*
for 63 Ranch, MT.

ing waterfalls and trout-filled lakes in the nearly million acre Absaroka/Beartooth Wilderness." Moving and basecamp trips run from four to ten days and are custom-planned to fit family needs, with special emphasis on scenic beauty and good fishing. On a five-day trip into the West Boulder area, you catch trout in placid water breaking into thundering falls. One day ride the length of the river to spectacular Mill Creek Divide through flower-filled cirques and beside melting snowbanks. On other trips ride into the Rainbow Lake country, a high mountain plateau (5 days); or over the divide to Buffalo Forks and headwaters of the Yellowstone (7 days); or over the Mission Creek Divide to wild Davis Creek. These are quality trips with good horses and equipment, hearty food and guides who love their work. Rates: $225/day per rider (or $100/day if you are retaining cabin at ranch.) Jul.– Sep. Arrival: Bozeman airport.

MONTANA

**Bob Marshall &
Scapegoat
wilderness areas**

WHITE TAIL RANCH OUTFITTERS, INC.

82 White Tail Ranch Rd., Ovando, MT 59854. Attn.: Jack and Karen Hooker. (406) 793-5666.

Since 1940 pack trips have been heading out of the White Tail Ranch into two spectacular wilderness regions—the Bob Marshall Wilderness and its famous Chinese Wall, and the Scapegoat Wilderness Area. "Participants will experience in depth one of the country's least disturbed primeval ecosystems," says Jack. "It's a paradise of fir, spruce and lodgepole pine forests, wildlife, tremendous geological fault lines, glaciated valleys and fascinating history." Jack is known for his wilderness savvy, packing skills and legendary campfire tales. Scheduled trips Jun.–Aug. for 4 to 10 riders, 2–11 days, $155–$165 per day. Children's discounts. Also custom trips. Rate includes Missoula pickup and return, and first and last nights at ranch.

OREGON

**Eagle Cap
Wilderness**

HIGH COUNTRY OUTFITTERS, INC.

P.O. Box 26A, Joseph, OR 97846. Attn.: Cal Henry. (503) 432-9171.

Custom trips into the beautiful Eagle Cap Wilderness are the specialty of Cal and Betsy Henry. It's a region Cal has packed into for more than 30 years. Peaks rise to 9,845 feet in this area, with dozens of lakes and streams, a lot of good fishing and many wildflowers, birds and wildlife. He arranges trips for small groups, from four to ten days with one or more layover days, camping each night near a lake or stream. It is a splendid alpine wilderness, and riders soon become immersed in the pleasures of outdoor living. Cal also arranges other types of horseback excursions—drop pack trips, a pack/float combination which includes running the Snake River through Hells Canyon and an overnight pack trip at $150/rider, young children less. The meeting point for all trips is Joseph, with transport from there to one of several trailheads. Cal's wilderness ranch on the Minam River can be a stopping point before or after trips. Pack trip rate: $120/day per rider.

OREGON

**Wenaha
Wilderness**

OUTBACK RANCH OUTFITTERS
P.O. Box 384, Joseph, OR 97846. Attn.: Ken Wick. (503) 426-4037.

Ken Wick takes riders into the Wenaha Wilderness on the Oregon/Washington border. Trails are in canyon drainage with old growth pine and fir. Riverbottoms are covered with hardwood and brush-type growth that turns red in fall. Riding is easy on meandering trails deep in the canyon—more strenuous along the border. Ken provides two or three guides with six to eight riders on each trip—small groups which result in close friendships. "There are almost no other riders in the Wenaha Wilderness," Ken says. "It's a somewhat undiscovered area with fantastic fishing, mostly catch and release—Dolly Varden and rainbow, and steelhead in the fall." The rate for 3- to 10-day trips, Apr. to Sep. is $125/day per rider. Arrival point is Lewiston, Idaho, where ranch picks up guests.

UTAH

**San Rafael
Swell, Capitol
Reef, Escalante &
Circle Cliff
wilderness,
Wasatch Plateau,
Henry Mts.**

HONDOO RIVERS & TRAILS
P.O. Box 98, Torrey, UT 84775. Attn.: Pat or Gary George. (801) 425-3519 or (800) 332-2696.

Gary George runs trailrides into backcountry of the Colorado Plateau, a land of color and canyons known for its rugged wilderness and spectacular scenery. Good to rugged trails are suitable for all levels of riders, with options of challenging terrain for the experience. Explore the San Rafael Swell—a region comparable to Capitol Reef National Park. Take entire 8-day ride (May 1–8, $960) or first 5 days ($590) or last 4 days ($470). Fall foliage ride into the adjacent spectacular region of Capitol Reef, Escalante and Circle Cliff wilderness is scheduled Sep. 26–30, $610. At this same rate other five-day rides into Capitol Reef are scheduled each month, June–September. A June trailride in the Wasatch Plateau is timed to coincide with the peak blooming period for wildflowers, and on one in July you see free-roaming buffalo herds and ride through forests of pinyon, juniper, fir and spruce in the Henry Mountains. (Both rides 6 days, $660.) All of Gary's trips are for ten riders and begin and end in Torrey, with a pre-trip motel night included in rate. Arrival point is Grand

Junction, CO, with transport to Torrey by van, rental car, or air charters. (See also *River Running, Wilderness / Nature Expeditions, Cattle Drives*—Pace Ranch.)

Backcountry
packing in the
Colorado Plateau—
*Hondoo Rivers &
Trails, UT.*

WYOMING

HIDDEN BASIN OUTFITTERS

Gros Ventre
Wilderness

P.O. Box 7182, Jackson, WY 83001. Attn.: Noel Meeks. (307) 733-9767 or (800) 253-7130. Fax (307) 733-7980.

"Top quality everything!" is Noel Meeks standard. He has been guiding pack trips for 20 years and his father before him for 25. With two basecamps established in the Gros Ventre

Wilderness, he takes riders to each for two nights on five-day progressive trips, with pack animals carrying the gear. He also schedules three-day basecamp trips. All trips start with riding orientation at the trailhead and continue with exciting rides through this scenic wilderness, over ridges and across valleys. Riding is interspersed with hikes for those who want them, fishing in streams or beaver ponds, or just relaxing around camp. "This adventure is truly a western experience. You'll learn a lot about mountain travel and horses," Noel promises. Trips are for a maximum of ten riders. Departures every Sunday on 5-day trips, late June–Sep.; every other Sat. for 3-day trips, Jul./Aug. Rates: $695/5 days, $375/3 days. (see also *Ski Touring / Snowmobiling*— Old Faithful Snowmobile Tours.)

"...truly a western experience."—
Hidden Basin Outfitters, WY.

WYOMING

Bridger-Teton National Forest, Teton Wilderness

PETERSON-MADSEN-TAYLOR OUTFITTERS

Box 1156, Afton, WY 83110. Attn.: Everett and Pat Peterson. (307) 886-9693 or (800) 447-4711.

This family-owned outfitter business combines years of experience in guiding scheduled and custom pack trips and fishing trips into the Yellowstone and Thorofare rivers country, a remote area in the Teton Wilderness. Guides, packers and a cook accompany each trip of eight to ten riders into this vast and beautiful wilderness where they camp four or five nights to enjoy some of the best cutthroat trout fishing in the west. On scenic rides they follow high mountain trails and view thundering waterfalls, wildlife and many beautiful species of wildflowers growing on the green slopes. Trail crosses the Continental Divide where you see the parting of the waters, with Two Ocean Creek dividing—half going to the Pacific and half to the Atlantic. Trips begin at Turpin Meadows trailhead 45 miles north of Jackson Hole, departing every Sunday or Monday. Pickup in Jackson is included in rates of $150/day per rider for 5-and 6-day trips; group discounts. (See also *Covered Wagons*—Wagons West.)

Cutthroat trout for this packtripper—
Peterson-Madsen-Taylor Outfitters, WY.

WYOMING

Shoshone & Teton national forests, Yellowstone National Park

RIMROCK DUDE RANCH
2728 North Fork Route, Cody, WY 82414. Attn.: Glenn Fales. (307) 587-3970.

"Our one-week progressive pack trips with a choice of two itineraries is best for most families," advises Glenn Fales, one of the most experienced outfitters in the region. "Both routes offer good fishing and unforgettable mountain scenery in the backcountry of Yellowstone Park and the Teton and Shoshone national forests—country tourists never see." Ride a trusty saddle-horse; mules carry the gear. Most trips run seven to ten days and are scheduled for three to eight riders, with a layover every other day to ensure plenty of time for trout

Packing up for the trail—*Jack Hollingsworth Productions for Rimrock Dude Ranch, WY.*

fishing, backcountry rides or spotting wildlife. These are custom trips for small groups which frequently are open for individuals or couples to join. Trails suit all riding abilities, but some riding experience is preferred. Rates: $125/day, family discounts. Jun.–Sep. Free pickup Cody airport, $25/person each way at Billings, MT airport.

WYOMING

Bridger Wilderness

SKINNER BROTHERS

P.O. Box 859, Dept. AG, Pinedale, WY 82941. (307) 367-2270 or (800) 237-9138. Fax (307) 367-4757.

Custom pack trips for adult and family groups are a Skinner Brothers specialty—on a limited basis in July, but easily available in August and early September. Horse-supported trek or trail ride along the Continental Divide is a special new feature. They take you into the Bridger Wilderness, "a fishing paradise with spectacular scenery." It's an area of the Continental Divide relatively unused, with great numbers of fish in every lake and different species of trout in each stream system. "Pack into this area for riding, camping, fishing and photography," the Skinners recommend. They cater to small groups (1–2 riders) or larger and provide guides, horses, food and all camping gear for moving or basecamp trips—also can pack you in on a spot pack trip or drop camp trip. The third week of August Skinner Brothers offers a Participation Pack Trip in which you can join other people and can bring your horse or use theirs. The Skinner Family started outfitting in the 1920s. (See also *Mountaineering / Rock Climbing, Youth.*)

In the Bridger Wilderness— *Skinner Brothers, WY* (photo next page.)

WYOMING

Yellowstone
National Park,
Absaroka, Teton,
Shoshone &
Washakie
wilderness areas

THOROFARE YELLOWSTONE OUTFITTING

Box 604, Cody, WY 82414. Attn.: Donald C. Schmalz. (307) 587-5929 or (800) 326-5928.

An Indian chief once said, "There is no country like the Crow Country. The Great Spirit has put it exactly in the right place." This is the region Don Schmalz has chosen for his pack trips—Yellowstone backcountry and the Absaroka, Teton, Washakie and Shoshone wilderness areas. For first timers he recommends a five-day camp deep in the wilderness, with rides from it each day, $680/rider. On a moving pack trip he guides riders to three different camps in eight days, $1,050. They pack up and move camp on this ride, and on a nine-day trip move to still another highcountry camp, $1,120/rider. Don describes this country as an area with broad meadows, rushing streams, lofty passes, ideal to ride, fish, photograph, walk and enjoy each night's campfire to your heart's content. Another trip is for 2–12 riders in America's only Wild Horse Preserve, 5 days, Jun.–Sep., $680. It includes nights at a motel and a boat tour in the Big Horn Canyon.

ALBERTA

Canadian
Rockies

ANCHOR D GUIDING & OUTFITTING

Box 656, Black Diamond, Alta., Canada T0L 0H0. Att: Dewy and Jan Matthews. (403) 933-2867.

In only 45 minutes from the Calgary International Airport, you can be at the Anchor D in the highcountry of the Canadian Rockies, the starting point for half- or all-day trail rides, basecamp rides, and three- to ten-day pack trips. Riders leave the ranch every Monday on pack trips, arranged according to how many days they have for riding and camping in the spectacular highcountry. They move camp every other day, with pack horses transporting the gear, in a region of mountain ranges, rivers, valleys and meadows. Two guides and a camp cook accompany up to 12 riders on these moving trips. On a seven-day "Great Divide" trip riders follow high mountain trails unencumbered with pack animals as the camping gear is hauled from camp to camp by teams of horses and wagons. By the time riders reach a new camp, it is set up and supper is cooking! Three-day basecamp trips which depart Fridays and Mondays focus on comfortable camps (wall tents and cots), riding in different directions or hooking cutthroat trout in mountain lakes. Rates: 1/2 day $40, full day $75, weekender $290, 3-10 days $125 per day, 7-day "Great Divide" $1,050. All rates in $ Cdn., plus tax.

The wagon hauls the gear not the guests—Anchor D, Alberta.

ALBERTA

Banff National Park, Canadian Rockies

HOLIDAY ON HORSEBACK

The Trail Rider Store, 132 Banff Ave., P. O. Box 2280, Banff, Alta., Canada T0L 0C0. Attn.: Warner Guiding & Outfitting Ltd. (800) 661-8352 or (403) 762-4551. Fax (403) 762-8130.

"The best things on our trips are free, and everything else is a bargain," claims Ron Warner. We tend to agree. Riders pay approx. $110/day Cdn. for HOH pack trips into the majestic beauty of Banff National Park in the Canadian Rockies. On trips scheduled from May to October, you view picturesque lakes and valleys against a backdrop of high peaks, snow-capped even in summer. HOH can arrange whatever you want from an overnight to a nine-day trip. From July until September, the Cascade Valley Range is a great place for riding, fishing, or hiking. Trips into the Cascade Valley are from three to six days. On overnight to six-day rides into Sundance and Halfway Lodge, you ride through glaciated valleys, down the Sundance Range, and over Allenby Pass at 8,000'—unmatched in ruggedness and beauty. Spend the night in Banff prior to trips, and meet at The Trail Rider Store for start of trip.

Packing into the Canadian Rockies—Ron Warner for Holiday on Horseback, Alta.

ALBERTA

Canadian Rockies

MCKENZIES' TRAILS WEST

Box 971, Rocky Mountain House, Alberta, Canada T0M 1T0. (403) 845-6708.

"Pack up your duffle bag, get into your old blue jeans and ride into the sunset with us," urge the McKenzies. Their "sunset trail" takes you into the heart of the Canadian Rockies, some of the most magnificent country in the world. With over 30 years experience in this rugged terrain they look after your safety and provide a vacation you will long treasure. Their six-day trip begins at a basecamp at the foot of Mr. Stelfax. Ride up Coral Creek, over Job Pass and into the scenic Job Valley for fishing, hiking, riding and wildlife viewing. Trips depart every Monday, Jul./Aug. Rate: $875 Cdn. + tax. Their

12-day trip begins near the Bighorn River just north of the basecamp. It's a circle tour including Wapiabi Creek, George Creek, Blackstone River, Brazeau River, Job Creek and Coral Creek, ending at basecamp. There's unlimited fishing, abundant wildlife, spectacular scenery and over 100 miles of wilderness trails. '93 departures Jun. 27, Jul. 18, Aug. 15. Rate: $1,600 Cdn. + tax. No charge for Calgary airport pickup. (See also *Fly Fishing*.)

ALBERTA

Eastern slope of Canadian Rockies

SADDLE PEAK TRAIL RIDES

Box 1463, Cochrane, Alta., Canada T0L 0W0. Attn.: Dave Richards. (403) 932-3299.

Riders from around the world come from May through September for these pack trips into the spectacular country along the eastern slopes of the Rockies. "We're not offering just a holiday," emphasizes David Richards, guide and outfitter at Saddle Peak Ranch. "It's a real experience by horseback, an outdoor retreat, far from the pressures of everyday life." His foothills ranch is located between Calgary (where guests can be met) and Banff. On three-day wilderness rides you follow trails to the mountain country of Devil's Head and Johnson Creek, a region known for its beauty, wild horse herds, bighorn sheep and good fishing. A five-day trip extends the riding, the scenery and the chance to kick back and relax. Even the two-day overnight trip gives those with limited time a feeling of the vastness of the wilderness. Rates

Packing into Devil's Head— *Saddle Peak Trail Rides, Alberta.*

range from \$107–\$145 Cdn. per day. Some rides can be combined with whitewater rafting.

ALBERTA

Jasper National Park

SARACEN HEAD OUTFITTERS

Box 7622, Edson, Alta., Canada T7E 1V7. Attn.: Ed & Maggie Regnier. (403) 723-3380.

For groups of ten riders in the Canadian Rockies, Ed Regnier takes a crew of six—guide, three wranglers, cook and helper. That's 16 on horseback accompanied by 20 packhorses carrying the gear! "Good food, comradeship, good horses and stunning scenery draw us back from year to year," comments a ten-time pack tripper. "The food is absolutely wonderful— no cans, all fresh, scones every morning and cake at night, all produced on a 3' x 3' metal stove." For 30 years Ed has been guiding rides over the adventuresome but not difficult trails through the unsurpassed scenery of Jasper National Park. These are custom trips, 3 to 14 days, Jun. to Sep., planned for 6 to 10 riders. The meeting point is in Hinton or Edson (motels in both places) or at the trailhead. Most trips planned for 3, 4, 6 or 10 days, with layovers for fishing, climbing, riding or relaxing. Rate: \$137/day Cdn. including tax. Also basecamp trips arranged.

Riding through open-range land— *Big Bar Guest Ranch, BC* (photo below).

BRITISH COLUMBIA

BIG BAR GUEST RANCH

P.O. Box 27, Jesmond, Clinton, B.C., Canada V0K 1K0. Phone or fax (604) 459-2333.

For a five-day pack trip in the Marble Range Mountains of the

Marble Range of the Cariboo Plateau

Cariboo Plateau, come to the Big Bar Ranch. An experienced guide and camp cook take you over breathtaking trails. You'll see Indian carvings and spot deer, black bear, coyotes, California bighorn sheep, eagles and ducks, and at each night's camp sit around a bonfire, sleep in two-person tents or under the stars except for one night in a cowboy cabin. These are progressive trips, May through September, for six to ten riders, with pack horses carrying the gear. From the ranch you ride through alpine forested country, open rangeland and meadows, then down a 4wd road and along the Fraser River, up a narrow ridge, over the top of the mountain and back to the ranch—about 60 miles in all. First and last nights at the ranch are included in rate of $625 Cdn., or $455 Cdn. for 8–14 year olds. Bring sleeping bag and personal items. The ranch is a six-hour drive from Vancouver, or take the train ("most scenic ride in the world") to Clinton where the ranch staff meets you. Discounts for groups and longer stays. (See also *Ski Touring / Snowmobiling*.)

BRITISH COLUMBIA

MCLEAN'S RIVER RIDGE RESORT

Chilko Lake, P.O. Box 2560, Williams Lake, BC, Canada V2G 4P2. Attn.: Ryan Schmidt. (604) 398-7755. Fax (604) 398-7487.

Chilcotin Plateau, Chilko Lake

"Join us for a riding experience of a lifetime," urges Ryan Schmidt. You ride with small groups into the spectacular high-alpine wilderness in the Coast Mountains of Chilko Lake and the rolling hills of the Chilcotin Plateau. It's an hour's flight from Vancouver to the airstrip and transfer to the basecamp. Spend the afternoon learning to saddle, bridle and care for your horse, take a short ride, and you're ready next morning to head into the mountains for a moving trip. The trip is for intermediate riders who follow steep trails to magnificent vistas as well as those across flower-filled meadows and along alpine lakes. Groups are small and develop a family atmosphere. Everyone helps with the chores. A barbecue and "Chilcotin Sendoff" celebrates the last night. *Mountain Rides*: Jun.–Sep., $1,275 US including Vancouver flights. On another specialty, the *Canadian Experience*, you become part of the family participating in chores at the resort, exploratory trips, trail clearing, horse care, camp cleaning and some long hours in the saddle. May–Oct., 2 weeks min., $595 US per week plus Vancouver flights. McClean's also offers riding vacations for the intermediate and experienced rider. For these vacations the rate is $975 US per week plus $300 US for the flights to and from Vancouver. Lake and river fishing packages also are featured at this rach. (For details please see the chapter on *Fly Fishing*.)

BRITISH
COLUMBIA

Chilcotin-
Cariboo country

TEEPEE HEART RANCH
Box 6, Big Creek, British Columbia, Canada V0L 1K0. Attn.: Hans Burch. (604) 392-5015 or 398-1061.

"Join our guests from Canada and around the world on fully equipped pack trips into the magnificent Taseko Mountains of the coast range," Hans Burch advises. "Explore by horseback the most beautiful country the historic Chilcotin-Cariboo has to offer." From July to mid-September he offers 10-, 14- and 20-day Wilderness Explorer trips, with everything provided except your sleeping bag and personal items. He considers these the ultimate trips for riding through the mountains. Trails are rated easy, and there are some river crossings and high passes. The rate is $150 Cdn. per day. These pack trips are for six to ten riders, and Tennessee Walking horses are provided and a cook, guide and wrangler. The ranch is 85 miles west of Williams Lake, accessible by good gravel road. The ranch will meet guests at Williams Lake, or at Big Creek, both serviced by air. (See also *Cattle Drives / Roundups / Horse Drives, Fly Fishing.*)

Karen Cummings for High Island Ranch, Wyoming (page 100)

Trail Rides

Many outfitters offer trail rides in scenic regions where access roads enable them to supply their basecamps by 4wd vehicle. With all the gear transported separately, riders do not travel with a pack string and are free to canter and lope where the terrain allows. They do not ride as deeply into wilderness regions as they do on pack trips, but unencumbered with a pack string they can go faster unless the trails are rugged.

Some outfitters use 4wd accessibility to create somewhat "cushy" camps as compared with wilderness camping where all gear must be carried in by horse or mule or burro.

At some of these camps participants are treated to spacious tents, hot showers and gourmet meals. In Utah's Monument Valley, for example, the comforts of camping are enhanced each evening by native people who provide entertainment.

In the Green Mountains of Vermont trail riders spend nights at charming country inns. In the Blue Ridge Mountains of Virginia, they reach rustic line camps with bunk beds after daily rides in a spectacular region. On California's Mendocino Coast they stop at B&B inns along the trail, and in the Canadian Rockies a mountain lodge provides dining and accommodations.

Whereas many trail rides are for small groups, others are equipped to handle 20 or more riders. For itineraries scheduled each year in the East as well as the West by the Appaloosa Horse Club, 150 or more seasoned riders bring their own horses and gather for a week of scenic trail riding, with live entertainment and dancing at camp each night. They have been doing this for nearly 30 years in regions such as the Southwest, the Rockies, The Appalachian and (an annual event) the Chief Joseph Trail in Montana.

Riding with other good riders and getting into a trot or canter are among the joys of trail riding. On some rides overnight accommodations are somewhat luxurious, comparatively speaking. On others, basic. Camaraderie and splendid scenery typify all, and you can count on some really great riding.

US WEST/EAST

Northwest,
Rockies,
Appalachians

APPALOOSA HORSE CLUB

5070 Hwy. 8 West, Moscow, ID 83843. Attn.: Susan Voile. (208) 882-5578. Fax (208) 882-8150.

Bring your own horse and join 150 or more seasoned riders for a week of trail riding in the Southwest, the Rockies or the Appalachians. Four rides are scheduled each year, April to September. On some itineraries you ride from a single basecamp; on others you move camp once. The Chief Joseph Trail Ride, the only one requiring registered Appaloosas, is planned for a different 100-mile segment of the famous trail each year, moving camp every day. "It epitomizes the best of any trail ride," says Susan Voile, Trail Coordinator, "in a gorgeous outdoor setting with some of the best riders and horses in the country." ApHC has organized trail rides for nearly 30 years. A physician, veterinarian and farrier ride the trails with you. All meals are supplied, as well as fresh water (for drinking and showers) and pellet feed for your horse. The Club helps to locate rental horses for riders who do not bring their own. Fun and friendship characterize these events, with live entertainment and dancing at camp each night. Rates: $225–$275 per rider + fee for non-members—$25/ adult, $10/youth 12–18, $40/couple, $50/family; also non-rider rates.

Scenic beauty on a trail ride—
Appaloose Horse Club, ID.

ALASKA

Minook Valley

LOST CREEK RANCH

Box 84334, Fairbanks, AK 99708. Attn.: Norma or Less Cobb. (907) 672-3999.

At this ranch 140 miles northwest of Fairbanks you'll experience real Alaska life. On daily rides in the Minook Valley of

An easy river crossing—*Lost Creek Ranch, AK.*

the Ray Mountains, stop to pick berries, pan for gold, observe lynx, moose, ermine and wolves, and fish for salmon, northern pike and Arctic char. Family-style meals include bread from a 50-year-old sourdough starter, local berries, mushrooms, and a large variety of dishes with fresh fish, moose, caribou and bear known only in Alaska. "The food is absolutely fantastic and the Cobbs make you feel completely at home, like one of the family," says a Virginia couple who have visited the ranch several times. "They're friendly, entertaining and Less tells great stories," comments a guest from South Carolina. "We hated to go to bed while he was still up. We didn't want to miss any of his tales." Daily rides for up to four riders up to six days, start with easy trails and progress to harder mountain rides. The ranch offers an overnight trip, camping at a natural hot springs, and moving pack trips and customizes outings for larger groups. Trails cross meadows covered with flowers, follow mighty rivers and lead to mountain tops, with terrain for both walking and loping. A log cabin and bunkhouse provide lodging, with inside plumbing and hot water showers recently added. Rate for trails rides: 6 days (Jun. through Aug., Sun. to Fri.), with lodging, meals and Fairbanks airport pickup/return, $1,000. Also daily rates.

*ARIZONA/
UTAH*

**Monument
Valley,
Superstition,
Bradshaw and
White
Mountains,
Mogollon Rim**

DON DONNELLY STABLES

*6010 Kings Ranch Road, Gold Canyon, AZ 85219. Attn.: Tammy Armour.
(602) 982-7822 or (800) 346-4403.*

Exploring the desert, canyons and mountains of Arizona and
Utah has been the specialty of the Don Donnelly Stables for
many years. "Everyone should see the magnificent beauty of
this region from the comfort of a well-made western saddle,"
Don maintains. Most of his rides start with airport pickup in
Phoenix, Tucson or Gallup, and feature "cushy" camps set up
with good-sized tents, cots, toilets, hot showers, a dinner
tent, gourmet chef and evening entertainment. Native peoples
and neighboring ranchers sometimes share stories around
the campfires. With gear transported by 4wd, there's no need
for pack animals, and rides are unencumbered. Donnelly's trips
focus on spectacular regions of the Southwest—Monument
Valley where so many John Wayne movies were filmed; the
Superstition Wilderness, one of Geronimo's last hideouts; the
Mogollon Rim with its fishing streams and lakes overlooking
the desert basin; the White and Bradshaw mountains with
camps in lush alpine meadows over 9,000 feet. These well
organized rides, open to adults, custom groups and families,
are scheduled April through October. Rates average $150 per
day. Overnight campouts $85.00. See cover photo.

Riders at Sunset—
*Gary Johnson for Don
Donnelly Stables,
AZ.*

ARIZONA/
COLORADO

**Walnut Canyon,
Weminuche
Wilderness**

HARTMAN OUTFITTERS
448 Lake Mary Road, Flagstaff, AZ 86001. (602) 774-7131.

In southwest Colorado, the heart of the Rockies, lies the Weminuche Wilderness. Its majestic beauty abounds with history, lost gold mines and wildlife. Stars by the millions light the sky and the moonlight is so bright that it lights the mountains. At dusk you often see herds of elk grazing high above timber. Coyotes yap at the moon, and the running waters of springs and brooks serenade you to sleep. This is the setting for Hartman Outfitters' six-day pack trips in the Weminuche Wilderness starting in Creede. You ride to a permanent camp, then take daily rides in different directions. (Scheduled in Sep., 6-day trips are $950/person.) From the Hartman's ranch—the Hitchin' Post Stables—in Flagstaff, rides or wagon trips into Walnut Canyon are scheduled every day—"five miles and 100 years from town". There are cowboy breakfast rides, steak rides, one- or two-hour rides, half-day and all-day or multi-day rides, and also rides on a horsedrawn wagon. Walnut Canyon was the home of cliff- and cave-dwelling Indians. You can observe pictographs, explore natural caves and follow hiking trails while staying at the ranch campsite where meals and overnight camping is provided. (May–Sep., 1/2 day $45, all day $65, overnight $90–100/day.

CALIFORNIA

**Horse trek along
Mendocino
Coast**—*Ricochet
Ridge Ranch, CA.*

RICOCHET RIDGE RANCH
24201 North Highway 1, Fort Bragg, CA 95437. Attn.: Lari Shea. (707) 964-7669.

Canter along broad beaches or ride the bluffs while the Pacific pounds below. Follow mossy trails through magnifi-

cent redwood forests amidst graceful ferns and a profusion of wildflowers. A horse trek adventure touring Mendocino's redwood coast starts from Lari Shea's Ricochet Ridge Ranch where you mount a well-trained Arabian, Russian Orlov, thoroughbred or quarter horse for a memorable week-long excursion. Lari, an experienced breeder, trainer and instructor and winner of the prestigious Tevis Cup 100 mile endurance race, is widely recognized for her adventurous trail rides. At each day's end, stay at one of the unique bed and breakfast inns or the elegant Mendocino Hotel. Entertainment by internationally acclaimed musicians three nights. Lunch is on a river, a picnic on the beach or high in an apple orchard. 5–8 days, $940–$1,580, Jun.–Oct. Also private and shorter rides arranged, English or Western.

COLORADO

Four Corners

FOUR CORNERS CENTER FOR EXPERIENTIAL LEARNING

1760 Broadway, Grand Junction, CO 81503. Attn.: Maria O'Malley. (303) 858-3607. Fax (303) 858-7861.

Ride along a high desert rampart, looking down to the Colorado River below. Or pick your way up a narrow canyon, cliffs towering above, with the feeling of excitement tingling as you strain to see what lies around the next bend. This is the adventure of the custom-designed Conquistador Rides in spectacular country offered by Four Corners Center. "Our groups are kept small, from two to eight riders, to enhance the feeling of adventure," explains Maria O'Malley. "We start with riding lessons in our arena and progress to half- or full-day or overnight trail rides or longer (up to 8 days). Your mount is a spirited Peruvian Paso horse, the horse of the Conquistadors and the world's smoothest riding horse." Top quality equipment, expert instruction and low impact horse camping are emphasized on these custom excursions, with day trips available Mar.–Oct., $125; and overnight trips Jul.–Oct., at $295/day including all but personal gear. "Conquistador Rides can provide the perfect opportunity to work on issues like self-confidence, self-esteem or improved communications for families or groups," Maria adds. (See also *Cycling / Mountain Biking, Combos.*)

NEW YORK

Adirondacks

COLD RIVER TRAIL RIDES, INC.

Coreys, Tupper Lake, NY 12986. Attn.: John and Marie Fontant. (518) 359-7559.

"Pack trips into the Adirondack Wilderness were our hobby— now they're our specialty," notes John Fontana. For over 20 years he has guided riders through this scenic area of mountain vistas, pure water and trout which you catch for campfire dinners. Try their overnight wilderness ride preceded by a night at the ranch on arrival, $150. Or a full day's ride at $65, including a trail lunch. Spend several days at the ranch— $115 per day includes riding and meals. Gentle, sure-footed horses are assigned according to experience, and you are grouped so as to ride at your own pace. Singles and couples join groups up to six riders (none under 14 unless experienced). Excellent home-cooked meals at the ranch dining room. For non-riding guests the rate with room and meals is $60, or $30 for B & B. (See also *Ski Touring / Snowmobiling*.)

UTAH/
ARIZONA

Monument Valley

MONUMENT VALLEY TRAILRIDES
P.O. Box 155, Mexican Hat, UT 84531. Attn.: Edward and Maybelle Black. (801) 739-4285 or (800) 551-4039.

With Navajo guides, explore fabulous Monument Valley on the Utah/Arizona border for an hour or all day, or on camping trips from overnight to five days. You ride into an unbelievably beautiful region of picturesque buttes and gigantic monoliths that rise precipitously 5,000 feet from the valley floor, carved through eons by wind and rain. This is Navajo country and home of the ancient Anasazi. On the longer trips your guides take you to remote places not seen before by white people where you can find pieces of pottery and see pictographs made by earlier inhabitants, and hear coyotes at night. This Navajo-owned outfitter has guided riders through the region for a decade. These are custom trips for groups of 4 to 25 riders. Two or more Navajo guides accompany each group. Rates range from $25 for a one and a half-hour ride to

Fabulous Monument Valley—
Stephen Daboul for Monument Valley Trailrides, UT.

$325 for a five-day camping ride where you supply food, sleeping bags and tents. With these items provided the rate is $500 per rider for five days. A 4wd truck meets the group each night with fresh provisions. You'll return with a new comprehension of this land of Indian heritage.

UTAH

PACK CREEK RANCH

P.O. Box 1270, Moab, UT 84532. Attn.: Ken Sleight. (801) 259-5505.

La Sal Mountains

An overnight horseback excursion to a basecamp in the La Sal Mountains is only a three-hour horseback ride from Ken Sleight's Pack Creek Ranch, 20 minutes from Moab, but Ken calls it "the ultimate get-a-way" trip. You scout out old cowboy trails, drink cold, clear natural spring water, inhale the scent of pine forests and take in superb views of Utah's canyon country. Dutch oven cooking is the best, and tales of the Southwest around the campfire, true or not, create vivid scenes to dream about in snug tents. Ken supplies sleeping bag and pad, tents, food, horses and tack. Bring only personal gear. Rate: $150/ rider, family discounts. Nights before and after at Pack Creek Ranch optional. (See also *Hiking with Packstock*.)

A ranch ride—
Frank Jensen for Pack Creek Ranch, UT.

VERMONT

MOUNTAIN TOP INN

Mountain Top Road, Chittenden, VT 05737. Attn.: Bill Wolfe. (802) 483-2311 or (800) 445-2100. Fax (802) 483-6373.

Green Mountains

This inn in the Green Mountains of central Vermont has become a center for riding vacations. It is a place where you can bring your own horse if you wish. Instruction includes dressage, jumping, driving and polo clinics. In the latter you learn the basic strokes on "Splinter," the wooden horse, and practice "stick and ball" at a walk and slow canter. Riders get a feel for the action in practice chukkers and low goal games. Mountain Top offers both English and Western riding, instruction for beginners or experienced, and daily rides where you can walk, trot and canter through mountain pastures, over miles of forested trails and by scenic lakes and ponds. After a lesson or two from an instructor, even beginners qualify for rides of 3–6 hours daily with excellent on trail lunches, following trails through the countryside where wildlife abounds. May–November riding vacations include lodging and use of all the inn's facilities at rates of $94–$143/day with discounts for multiple-day stays. Breakfast and dinner $30 additional daily per person. (See also *Ski Touring/Snowmobiling*.)

In Green Mountain pastures—*Jerry LeBlond for Mountain Top Inn, VT.*

VERMONT

Mad River Valley, inn-to-inn

VERMONT ICELANDIC HORSE FARM, INC.
RR 376-1, Waitsfield, VT 05673. Attn.: Kristina Calabrese. (802) 496-7141.

Your four- or five-gaited purebred horse has been used for generations in Iceland for competitive and pleasure riding, and also for driving, carrying packs and farm work. In Vermont you'll use an Icelandic for riding through the beautiful Mad River Valley. The horses' small size, 13–14.2 hands, belies their stamina, speed and strength to comfortably carry a rider up to 250 lbs. over great distances. Four-day inn-to-inn rides scheduled every other week May–September for novice or experienced riders. For experienced riders only there are five- to six-day rides. On weekends you can have two riding days and overnight (or longer) at an inn. A winter program includes five days of riding and ski-joring through the crisp, snowy countryside. "The Icelandic horse with its comfortable 'tolt' gait gives you the feeling of floating across the scenic countryside," promises Kristina. Rates: 2 days, $325; 4 days, $745; 5 days, $885; 6 days, $1,040, including overnights and meals.

VIRGINIA

Blue Ridge Mountains

MOUNTAINTOP RANCH

Rt. 1, Box 402, Elkton, VA 22827. Attn.: Virgle and Bettie Cunningham. (703) 298-9542.

Wilderness trail rides in the Blue Ridge Mountains for groups up to 20 riders "come with all the fixings—a rustic line camp with bunkbeds, sleek quarter horses, and a trail boss and camp tender to provide the leadership and campfire culinary skills for the group," reports Virgle Cunningham. At his 1,000-acre working ranch with spectacular views overlooking the Shenandoah Valley, he customizes one- to four-day wilderness rides paced so that riders with no previous experience can come along. One day's lunch break is at an isolated waterfall complete with swimming hole, and at night folks gather around the campfire and swap tales. Each ride, spiced with renditions of folklore and history, geology, flora and fauna becomes a lesson on horseback. Virgle, a former Texas

Rides overlook Shenandoah Valley—
Mountaintop Ranch, VA.

cowboy, describes his outings as "rustic"—no TV, telephones, highways or electricity—but an abundance of beauty, wildflowers and pristine streams. Wilderness rides, Apr.–Oct., range from $225 for 2 days, to $395 for 4 days. Year-round day rides are $75, or with cabin overnights $185 for 2 days, $260 for 3 days.

Like Butch & Sundance— following the Outlaw Trail— *Equitour, WY.*

WYOMING / ARIZONA / UTAH

Absaroka & Wind River Mountains, Superstition Wilderness, Monument Valley

EQUITOUR

Box 807, Dubois, WY 82513. Attn.: Bayard Fox. (307) 455-2778 or (800) 545-0019. Fax (307) 455-2354.

Equitour's trips in Wyoming and Arizona/Utah are steeped in the history of the Old West. An *Outlaw Trail* ride in Wyoming takes riders to the famed hideout of Butch Cassidy; on the *Pony Express Ride* you follow trails of the famous "mailmen" of yesteryear; and a *Wild Horse Mountain Ride* in beautiful Rocky Mountain Country crosses passes at 11,000 feet. Meeting point for these trips is Riverton. For a taste of cowboy life, sign up for five days of trailing and working cattle (7- to 8-day trips) at the *Mountain Cow Camp* in the Wind Rivers (from Dubois), with departures every Sunday All rides scheduled June–September. In spring and fall Equitour's trips follow trails in Arizona's Superstition Mountains or Utah's fabulous Monument Valley, land of the Navajos and the mysterious Anasazis. Comfortable camps are equipped with spacious tents, hot showers and gourmet meals. Most trips scheduled for eight days, seven nights, with motel night and dinner at start of trip. Rates: $1,000–$1,200 per rider (some cow camp weeks $950). Equitour's expanded service includes worldwide riding holidays.

WYOMING

Washakie
Wilderness

HIGH ISLAND RANCH

*P.O. Box 71-G, Hamilton Dome, WY 82427. (307) 867-2374. [Mid–Sep.
to mid-May: Box 7, Fryeberg, ME 04037. (207) 925-3285.]*

Ride the range, round up strays, fix fence, check cattle, move
them to fresh pastures and cast a line into Rock Creek and
hook a cutthroat trout for supper. Riders come to High Island
Ranch for unlimited riding in May and early June, also late
July and early August, and the last half of September. Ride
horseback or in a wagon on a two-day wagon train with an
overnight campout on the 35-mile trail to the high country.
Stay at a rustic but comfortable lodge at 9,000' in the Washakie
Wilderness. Ride a trail overlooking the Continental Divide
and the Needles, a 12,000'-peak which dominates the landscape. Ride with the cowboys to pack salt and minerals to the
cattle. End each day spinning yarns around the blazing
campfire, then sleep to a coyote lullaby. "It's the life that
legends are made of." (See also *Cattle Drives / Roundups /
Horse Drives*.)

WYOMING

Big Horn
Mountains

In red-rock canyon
country—*Janice Ott
for S-N-S Riding
Tours, WY.*

S-N-S RIDING TOURS

*P.O. Box 4187, Casper, WY 82604. Attn.: Sy Gilliland or Steve Berdahl.
(307) 266-4229.*

Explore Butch Cassidy's Hole-in-the-Wall hideout and red-
rock canyons. Ride tough, rocky trails in the rugged foothills
of the Big Horn Mountains. Examine Indian tepee rings and
rock art. Follow trails through the Red Desert to observe the
wild horses who live there. And each night, return to the

comforts of the S-N-S basecamps equipped with spacious wall tents, cots, foam pads and chairs, luxurious in comparison with camping out. You split the week between two basecamps. Your personal gear is transported separately, leaving you free for lots of riding and loping. Sy Gilliland has outfitted trips in this area since 1977 with his partner, Steve Berdahl. You start and end these trail rides with overnights at a Casper motel (with two meals). This as well as transport to and from the S-N-S basecamps, 5 nights of comfortable camping, all meals and riding are included in the Sun.-to-Sun. rate of $1,050. Families and all levels of riding skills are welcome. Up to 12 riders per week, Jun. to mid-Sep.

ALBERTA

Banff National Park

TRAIL RIDERS OF THE CANADIAN ROCKIES
Box 6742, Station D, Calgary, Alta., Canada T2P 2E6. (403) 263-6963.

Encouraging trail riding through the backcountry of Banff National Park has been TRCR's goal since 1923. Riders come from around the world to explore the magnificent region. For both experienced and novice riders, six-day family trips provide for 21 participants, and adult-only trips take 35 riders. They follow scenic trails up Pipestone Creek to a Teepee Camp, their headquarters for five nights. Each day they ride different trails, and in evenings gather at the canvas Sundance Lodge for singing, dancing and hot chocolate. For adults the 6-day rate is $630, and for under 18 years it is $360 Cdn. TRCR offers seven experienced riders 6- to 9-day moving trips at $960–$1,404 Cdn. These rides penetrate further into the mountains, establishing new camps at night. With a guide, wrangler and cook they participate in camp chores and explore the spectacular Kootenay Plains, Ya Ha Tinda, Johnston Creek, Dolomite Pass and Palliser Pass. All trips are scheduled July–September include van transport from Banff to the trailhead and a roundup supper (optional) the final night. TRCR membership fee of $10–$15 and 7% tax is added.

ON WHEELS

Wagons West, Wyoming (page 108)

Covered Wagons

A long time has passed since the early pioneers first crossed the vast open plains, pushing westward and carving their way into the wilderness and into history. But the ruts are still visible in many parts of the West. You come across deep, grass-covered furrows etched by iron-trimmed, wooden wheels of the wagons that lumbered across the plains more than 100 years ago.

The idea of modern-day covered wagon trips started over 30 years ago when the State of Kansas held its Centennial. A rancher from Quinter, along with neighbors, decided to travel to the Capitol in covered wagons. To their surprise the locals along the way stopped them for pictures and handshakes and to beg for rides. The result was a covered wagon trip along the old Butterfield Trail the following year, and the idea caught on.

These are great trips for families. For children the anticipation is second only to the moment when the wagonmaster cries "Wagon Ho!" He whips his hat in the air, and your wagon lurches forward as the team of horses (or mules) tugs hard at the harness. Soon you are accustomed to the rhythmic rocking motion, the squeaking of the harness and the sound of the wheels on the hard, dry ground.

The pace of the wagon train is slow by today's standards— about 20 miles per day. "After three days of rolling across prairie, I got into my car and drove back to our starting point in less than an hour," laughs one New Yorker with no regrets. It's sometimes a rocky ride. A little gully is a very big deal in a wagon. When you ride inside and look out on the prairie framed by the pleasing shape or the wagon's cover, you wonder if this shape might have been the inspiration for the graceful Gateway Arch in St. Louis.

At day's end the wagons circle and dinner preparations begin. You dine at dusk on grilled steaks, potatoes and ranch-style beans, filling your plate not once but twice and washing it down with some steamin' joe. Later there's a square dance or you listen to tall tales around a crackling campfire. At a fairly early hour most "pioneers" are ready to climb into bedrolls and count the skyful of stars.

KANSAS

Flint Hills

FLINT HILLS OVERLAND WAGON TRIPS, INC.

Box 1076, El Dorado, KS 67042. Attn.: Ervin E. Grant. (316) 321-6300.

Spend Saturday night in a covered wagon in the Flint Hills! Today's pioneers leave I-35 at Cassidy and join the locals (a lawyer, doctor, teacher and others) at the Cassidy Cafe for driving to the embarkation point and a day and overnight of rolling over prairie land into the scenic Flint Hills. Trips start on Saturday mornings. You roll across the prairie in a wagon train with authentic mule-and horse-drawn wagons and a stagecoach. Sleep overnight beside a stream "out in the middle of God's creation." (Restrooms provided, but no showers.) A chuckwagon offers "a hefty trail lunch," and a hearty pioneer-style dinner is cooked over an open fire—followed by tall tales and strumming guitars. Bring a sleeping bag (and tent if you want one) and bunk down in or under the wagon or on open ground. After a stick-to-the-ribs breakfast, roll on to the end of the trail, back to Cassidy by early afternoon. Participants write lyrically of soft breezes, meadowlarks, earth smells, the wide horizon, an incomparable sunset and a star-studded sky. Jun.–Oct. Adult, $130; under 12, $75; family and group rates.

Life 100 years ago (almost)—*Flint Hills Overland Wagon Trips, KS.*

MONTANA

Custer National Forest

TONGUE RIVER WAGON TRAIN

Box 432, Ashland, MT 59003. Attn.: Jack Goss. (406) 784-2492 or (800) 345-5660.

Jack Goss combines a covered wagon trek with a cattle drive, as did the Texans a century ago when they moved their cattle north to railheads and new pastures in Montana. On a typical day on this wagon train, you're up at six saddling and harnessing the horses. Breakfast at seven. Leave camp when the wagons roll at nine, and get to that night's camp with chores completed and supper ready by seven. Cards, horseshoes, cowboy songs and walks wind up the evening. These trips are for everyone—families, adults, grandparents, singles. (For further details, please see page 58 in *Cattle Drives* chapter.)

WYOMING

Targhee National Forest

BAR-T-FIVE OUTFITTERS
P.O. Box 2140S, Jackson, WY 83001. Attn.: Bill Thomas. (307) 733-5386. Fax (307) 739-9183.

In 1889 "Uncle Nick" Wilson drove the first covered wagons over Teton Pass into Jackson Hole. Today his great-grandson Bill Thomas, with his wife Joyce and their three children, recapture the experience with covered wagon treks. "Roll the wagons," Bill calls, and the "Prairie Schooners" line out for the trek along the backroads of the Targhee National Forest, between Yellowstone and Grand Teton national parks. It's a trip for all ages. Wagons move to a new camp each day—two of them on the shores of high mountain lakes. Horseback rides, canoeing, chuckwagon style meals and campfire singing round out the day's fun. Group size: 20–40 people. 4 days/$545 (9–14 years/ $495, 4–8 years $445). All sleeping gear and airport pick-up/return included. Group discounts. June–September. (See also sleigh rides in *Ski Touring / Snowmobiling.*)

WYOMING

Oregon, Mormon and Pony Express Trails, Overland Stage Route

TRAILS WEST, INC.
#65 Main Street, South Pass City, WY 82520. Attn.: Nona Bates. (307) 332-7801 or (800) 327-4052.

"We'd like to show you an area where covered wagons lumbered along the Oregon, Mormon and Pony Express trails and the Overland Stage Route," says Nona Bates. "Hundreds of wagons heading to a new land came through here. We follow the same trails, and the pungent odor of sage and rattle of wheels are reminders of 150 years ago." On the three-day wagon trip you can ride a horse, ride or drive a wagon or walk. You sleep in a tepee and have meals cooked over an open fire as the pioneers did. You learn a lot about our forefathers and their struggles to settle a new land. "A real and authentic experience—not commercialized," say participants. "It's like stepping out of a Louis L'Amour book." Along the way you talk with cattlemen and sheepherders, and either before or after the trip you wander through the

On the Pony Express Trail—In Sync Productions for Trails West, WY.

South Pass ghost town, one of the best preserved in the West, 37 miles south of Lander off Rt. 28. Trips are for 2–20 participants, Jun.–Sep., 3 days starting Tues. and Thurs. Rate: $350, or $250 for kids 6–12. Wagons can carry wheelchairs. No charge for pickup and return at Riverton airport.

WYOMING

Teton National Forest

WAGONS WEST

Peterson-Madsen-Taylor Outfitters, Box 1156A, Afton, WY 83110. (307) 886-9693 or (800) 447-4711.

There's a lapse of either an hour or a century, depending on how you look at it, from your Jackson Hole motel to a Conestoga wagon at Sagebrush Flat or Skull Creek Meadows. Travel in covered wagons with the new owners of L.D. Frome's long-established Wagons West. They bring their love of this way of life and years of outfitting experience. Repeat guests can count on the same experienced guides and wranglers and Dutch oven meals (all you can eat). Modernized covered wagons with rubber tires and foam-padded seats that convert to deluxe bunks look like the real thing. Gentle horses and mules pull wagons over trails and remote backroads in the Grand Teton area. Fishing, riding, spotting wildlife and cowboy songs are all part of a day's trek. Jun.–Sep. Rates: 2 days, adults, $260; children under 16, $220; 4 days, adults, $490; children, $390; 6 days, adults, $675; children, $550. Jackson pickup. Bring sleeping bag. (See also *Pack Trips*—— Peterson, Madsen, Taylor Outfitters.) See photo page 104.

**Conestoga wagons
in Teton National
Forest**—*Wagons
West, WY.*

Otter Bar Lodge, California (page 116)

Cycling /
Mountain Biking

Astride a streamlined 10-speed or a clunky-looking hi-tech mountain bike with knobby, fat tires, you follow winding roads or backcountry trails through New England towns and Nova Scotia villages, over the Carolina and Tennessee Smokies, in southwest deserts, Baja beaches, Rocky Mountain vistas, California vineyards, a Bahamas' island, wind-swept bluffs of the Pacific Northwest, the Canadian Rockies and even in Alaska.

You move slowly or fast at your own pace. You have time to experience the environment with all your senses.

If you can ride a bike you can ride a mountain bike, only the places you can go on one of these durable machines expands your touring possibilities dramatically. While touring bikes are limited to routes accessed by roads, mountain bikes literally chew up rugged terrain. With sophisticated gearing, rugged frames and all-terrain tires, mountain trails and gorgeous backcountry (on approved biking trails, of course) are well within the capabilities of the equipment, if you're up to it.

Some trips are easier than others, perhaps covering only 10 miles or so a day, with time to shop, snack, chat with locals, sightsee and enjoy a picnic. Other itineraries are more strenuous, traveling up and down hills, across streams or over mountainous terrain. Although most organized tours do provide a sagwagon for transporting gear, bike repair equipment and tired cyclists, it is important to align your biking capabilities with a tour that suits your strengths and weaknesses.

Operators provide detailed maps and itineraries, with alternate routes to accommodate various riding abilities—including families with young children. They also provide 10-, 12-, 18- or 21-speed touring or mountain bikes depending on terrain, though you can probably bring your own bike if you prefer.

US EAST /
WEST /
CANADA /
MEXICO

**Inn-to-inn and
camping tours**

BACKROADS BICYCLE TOURING, INC.

*1516 5th St., Suite PR, Berkeley, CA 94710-1740. (510) 527-1555 or
(800) 245-3874. Fax (510) 527-1444.*

In just 14 years, Backroads has grown from selling a few trips to the world's #1 active travel company. Itineraries for road biking, staying at inns or camping, follow routes in 22 states and provinces, nationwide. Most are five-day trips with some California weekenders. Some are for singles, others for teenagers or families, for "fit folk over 55", for jogging enthusiasts or for art lovers. But most groups are mixed, their size averaging 19 pedallers, with spring, summer, fall and some year-round departures. Count on rates of $1,000 (more or less) for 5-day inn trips, and $600 for 5-day camping tours. For groups of ten or more, trips can be customized and rates discounted. On a five-day inn or camping trip in the Shenandoah Valley of Virginia, for example, you follow country roads past Civil War sites, tiny colonial villages and historic country inns. Starting in Lexington, stop at a museum, restored homes and the McCormick Farm of reaper fame. Shuttle or bike up the mountains and ride the scenic Blue Ridge Parkway, then cycle along Walker Creek past weathered farmhouses and grist mills back to Lexington. Delightful inns each night, or camping in wooded countryside. Cover about 35 miles per day, or 50 with optional extensions. Inn trip $995, camping $595. (See also listing for *Mountain Biking* in this chapter: US West / Mexico.)

**Two bikes and a
burley trailer on a
family trip—**
*Markham Johnson for
Backroads, CA.*

US WEST /
MEXICO

BACKROADS BICYCLE TOURING

1516 5th Street, Suite PR, Berkeley, CA 94710-1740. (510) 527-1555 or (800) 245-3874. Fax (510) 527-1444.

MOUNTAIN
BIKING

Arizona,
California,
Idaho, Oregon,
Utah, Mexico's
Baja

Backroads' first mountain bike tours were launched in 1987 in the low-slung hills of Marin County—a two-day tour they still offer with camping overnight. Now their itineraries for off-road bikers have expanded to five- and six-day tours with nights at inns or lodges over scenic routes in four western states, plus a six-day inn trip (or seven days camping) in Mexico's Baja, and a nine-day inn tour in Costa Rica. In southern California's Anza Borrego State Park you explore mysterious canyons and waterpockets on a two-day camping trip. The extensive system of dirt roads through Oregon's Mt. Hood area are ideal for five-day trips with nights at places such as Timberline Lodge and the Columbia Gorge Hotel. In Utah bikers use off-road biking and jeep trails and a few paved roads on six-day routes through the Arches and Canyonlands national parks with their intricate red-rock landscapes carved by wind, water and time over eons. Six days in Arizona focus on Sedona's red-rock country skirting the southern edge of the Colorado Plateau's mesas, buttes and towering cliffs. In Idaho's Sun Valley and the Sawtooth Mountains riders see more bears, mountain goats and moose than on other trails. For an ideal winter escape, they choose the southern tip of Mexico's Baja Peninsula with its seaside attractions for a six- or seven-day tour. Rates for the 5- or 6-day trips, staying at inns, range from $166 to $240 per day, with departures scheduled seasonally according to the areas you choose to travel. (See also listing in this chapter: US East / West.)

US SOUTH

CAROLINA CYCLE TOURS

13077 Hwy 19 West, Bryson City, NC 28713-9114. (704) 488-6737 or (800) 232-7238. Fax (704) 488-2498.

CYCLING /
MOUNTAIN
BIKING

Southern
Appalachians

Carolina Cycle Tours, a division of Nantahala Outdoor Center, specializes in small groups (10–15 cyclists) and van-support for all tours, with itineraries in the Southeast. Accommodations reflect the character of each region. Escape into the dramatic scenery of the Southern Appalachians on the Blue Ridge Parkway, or the Franklin or Joyce Kilmer ride. Plan to bring a swimsuit for the popular Carolina Lowcountry and Beaufort Bike & Beach tours. For mountain bikers, Carolina provides a truly "off-road" experience with two- or three-day tours in the Nantahala and Pisgah national forests, and half- and full-day guided trail rides and rentals. Rates average $150 per day for 2- and 3-day weekend tours, and

$158 per day for 5-day tours. Carolina enjoys sharing their love of travel, adventure and bicycling through quality vacations at reasonable prices. (See also *Canoeing / Kayaking, River Running, Combos*—Nantahala Outdoor Center.)

US EAST /
WEST /
CANADA

Coast to coast

BIKECENTENNIAL

P.O. Box 8308-QC, Missoula, MT 59807. (406) 721-1776. Fax (406) 721-8754.

Bikecentennial has been putting cyclists on the road for 25 years, offering both self-supported camping tours (depend on your own power, cook your own meals, carry your "home" with you), and light tours (the freedom of cycling self-supported combined with the luxury of spending nights at country inns). "Bicycle touring without a support vehicle brings a sense of independence and accomplishment that is unique to our style of tours," says tour coordinator Steve Robertson. Spend five days to three months with them on journeys that explore America's quiet backroads. Take a 10-22 day Glacier Park journey. If a coast-to-coast tour is your dream trip, spend three months on their history-making TransAm or Northern Tier routes. Light touring itineraries include five days cycling in Door County, WI for example, or mountain biking near Jackson Hole, WY which Bikecentennial calls "Fat Tire Heaven!" Bikecentennial is the largest non-profit recreational cycling organization in the U.S., having started in 1976 to celebrate the nation's 200th birthday. Mem-

Pausing in Glacier National Park—
Bikecentennial, MT.

ber benefits include the most comprehensive cycling information available.

Scenic road in nat'l park—*Timberline Bicycle Tours, CO.*

US/CANADA
EAST/WEST

Inn-to inn trips, national parks, & other scenic areas

TIMBERLINE BICYCLE TOURS

7975 E. Harvard, #J, Denver, CO 80231. Attn.: Dick and Carol Gottsegen. (303) 759-3804.

"In ten years of creating bicycle tours and other outdoor-related vacations, we have become a leading proponent of 'adventure cycling' with the industry's most athletic program," say TBT's directors Dick and Carol Gottsegen. They now offer 58 itineraries through the western U.S. and Canada, northern Great Lakes, Nova Scotia and Prince Edward Island. Their tours highlight more than a dozen national parks. With both on-road and off-road routes, all accompanied by support van, TBT specializes in inn-to-inn trips featuring overnights in the magnificent, historic lodges of the national parks. Groups range from 8–14 cyclists, two leaders with each group, and tours range from five to nine days. Rates from $695 to $995 include cost of all lodging and meals. "Accept our invitation to share with us the beauty of this land," Carol and Dick urge. "Experience its undulating terrain, its majestic grandeur, the awesome challenge of its mountains and incomparable peace and solitude of isolated valleys." It's not hard to say 'yes' to that invitation. (See also *Combos.*)

CALIFORNIA

OTTER BAR LODGE

Forks of Salmon, CA 96031. Attn.: Peter or Kristi Sturges. (916) 462-4772.

MOUNTAIN
BIKING

**Salmon River
canyon**

Biking & kayaking
at a wilderness
retreat—*Phil
DeRiemer for Otter
Bar Lodge, CA.*

"It's an undiscovered mountain bike mecca," writes one California biker. With three quarters of a mile of the California Salmon running through its property, the Otter Bar is located between Marble Mountain and Trinity Alps wilderness areas. From August through October bikers come for remote trails and hundreds of miles of dirt roads. Top-notch experts provide instruction if you want it as well as bike repair maintenance, the "how-tos" of riding in all types of terrain and the philosophy of trail etiquette. Shuttle service is provided to "gain altitude" (up to 5,000 feet above the lodge) for biking back via different routes. One day you may ride to a mountain lake with spectacular views. Another, ride down to the river's edge where a raft will take you downriver for an afternoon of Class III whitewater. It's for those who love biking with the comforts of a luxurious lodge and gourmet dining at day's end. See photo on page 110.

*COLORADO /
UTAH /
ARIZONA /
NEW MEXICO*

FOUR CORNERS CENTER FOR EXPERIENTIAL LEARNING

1760 Broadway, Grand Junction, CO 81503. Attn.: Maria O'Malley. (303) 858-3607. Fax (303) 858-7861.

Small-group custom trips are Four Corners' specialty for mountain bikers. They take from two to eight cyclists on trips

MOUNTAIN
BIKING

Colorado
National
Monument,
Moab, Unaweep
Divide, Grand
Mesa, Kokopelli
Trail, Pollock
Canyon

for 1-12 days on their various mountain bike cruisers. For a laid back, easy ride they recommend the Rim Rock Drive, most scenic route across the Colorado National Monument where every bend in the road brings a new breathtaking vista. The one-day trip is priced at $69 including pickup and return to Grand Junction hotel, high quality bike, helmet, wind/rain jacket and fanny pack, transport to the top of the Monument and lunch. The 20-mile cruise back is mostly downhill. Other day routes for mountain bike cruisers include the Grand Mesa Descent, the Dewey Bridge to Moab, the Unaweep Divide to the Colorado River and all-day or overnight trips on the Kokopelli Trail between Grand Junction and Moab, the Tabaguache Tour, Pollock Canyon, Horsethief Look, Rabbit Valley and others. No minimum age requirement—only the ability to ride a bike. Rates for long trips on request. (See also *Trail Rides, Combos*.)

COLORADO /
NEW MEXICO /
UTAH

ROADS LESS TRAVELED

P.O. Box 8187, Longmont, CO 80501. Attn.: David Clair. (303) 678-8750 or (800) 488-8483.

Escape the ordinary and discover the uncommon. Explore quiet backroads and trails visited by few. Stay in century-old inns, secluded guest ranches and mountain huts. Gain better insight and appreciation of lands less traveled. This is David Clair's view of what bike trips should offer. "Our success comes from the tour routes we use and variety in where we

Scenery with off-
road biking—*Roads
Less Traveled, CO.*

MOUNTAIN
BIKING

Crested Butte
(CO), Santa Fe,
Taos (NM),
Canyonlands
(UT)

stay," he says. We explore many backroads and trails to create a trip. Our routes are less traveled, very beautiful and immensely interesting. Our goal is to offer a personal, unique and rewarding experience." Trips along the White Rim in Utah's Canyonlands move at a relaxed pace with time for hiking to hidden canyons, Indian ruins and afternoon swims. Bike and camp along the Kokopelli Trail in dramatic canyon country—a premier off-road adventure ending with a 4,000 foot descent you'll never forget. On a Crested Butte Hot Springer tour you cycle the Rockies rooftop. In northern New Mexico ride on "some of the finest trails we have found anywhere," says David, "—an undiscovered paradise for off-the-beaten-path cycling." One biker comments, "It's exactly the right combination of exercise, relaxation, scenery, and fun." Trips for up to 13 riders, $125-$170 per day, Apr.–Oct. (See also *Combos.*)

FLORIDA /
CARIBBEAN

BOTTOM TIME ADVENTURES
P. O. Box 11919, Ft. Lauderdale, FL 33339-1919. Attn.: A.J. Bland. (305) 921-7798or (800) 234-8464. Fax (305) 920-5578.

The Bahamas

An Eleuthera
beach—*Bottom Time
Adventures, FL.*

Imagine a 100-mile-long island with picturesque beaches, rolling hills, quaint villages, friendly natives and a seldom-traveled paved road the length of the island. Imagine also a 90' private yacht as your floating sagwagon, meeting you from port to port. Eleuthera in the eastern Bahamas is the destination for these dreamy bike trips which start in Nassau aboard the luxury 90' catamaran, *Bottom Time II*. A.J. Bland describes Eleuthera as "reminiscent of a New England village with a tropical setting, well kept homes dating back to the 1700s and natives so friendly that you should not be surprised if, along the way, you are invited into someone's home for refreshments." Roads meander past pineapple plantations, along high bluffs and to pink-sand beaches where you plunge into turquoise waters whenever you want. If you prefer shorter rides, return to the *Bottom Time II* before lunch and cruise to the next rendezvous where you're free to explore, shop, visit craftsmen or do some sea kayaking or snorkeling. The 7-day tours scheduled Oct. to Apr. include a/c double cabin, chef-prepared meals, 12-speed cross-trainer bike, leader/guide. Rates start at $1,195. (See also *Boats / Cruises / Scuba*, *Wilderness / Nature Expeditions*.)

On Keweenan Peninsula along Lake Superior— *Michigan Bicycle Touring, MI.*

MICHIGAN

Upper and Lower Peninsulas

MICHIGAN BICYCLE TOURING, INC.
3512 Red School Road, Kingsley, MI 49649. Attn.: Michael Robold. (616) 263-5885.

"We're the touring expert in Michigan," says Michael Robold whose company has been leading bike trips for 16 years. From May through October. MBT offers trips every weekend and five-day Sunday–Friday trips on some 20 itineraries that include Mackinac Island, the Leelanau Peninsula and other picturesque regions with crystal-clear lakes and clean, un-crowded beaches. You spend nights at historic inns, deluxe resorts, at lighthouses and on a Great Lakes schooner and are treated with great regional cuisine. Seeing hidden waterfalls and abandoned mines and visiting with local artists and craftspeople are in the itineraries as well as seeing historic and well-known sites. Many tours combine biking with canoeing, kayaking, hiking and sailing. These are adventures for small groups (8–24 riders) with non-competitive riding suited to all levels of cycling ability. Specialty trips include bike mainte-nance clinics and relaxation retreats at an antiques-furnished country inn. Bring your own bike or rent a 12-speed touring bike, an 18-speed off-road bike or an 18-speed tandem. Rates include lodging, meals, tax, tips, tour leaders and support vehicle. Weekend trips $199–$299; 5-day trips $585–$829.

In canyon country—Kaibab Mountain Bike Tours, UT.

UTAH

MOUNTAIN BIKING

White Rim Trail in Grand Canyon, Maze

KAIBAB MOUNTAIN BIKE TOURS
P.O. Box 339, 391 South Main Street, Moab, UT 84532. (800) 451-1133. Fax (801) 259-6135.

"You're cruising along a smooth dirt road. Red-rock cliffs tower over your shoulder. Blooming cactus adorn the trail. Snow-covered mountains loom in the distance. Welcome to Kaibab's Mountain Bike Tours!" says Brett Taylor, founder of Kaibab. Formed over the eons as an ancient sea floor was thrust skyward, then sculpted by wind and water, the terrain

District in Canyonlands National Park

of southeastern Utah is unlike anywhere else in the world. "The best way to experience this country is from the seat of a mountain bike," Taylor insists. Tours with Kaibab follow hidden roads in deep red-rock canyons and across towering mesas, such as along the legendary White Rim Trail, routes in the mystical Maze District, and passages along the North Rim of the Grand Canyon. Tours are planned for all ability levels and range from one-day descents to five days of biking. Each tour is accompanied by a fully-equipped support vehicle. Professional, enthusiastic guides see to all the details of your tour, including gourmet trailside dining and unexpected luxuries along the way. (Trips for 4–12 cyclists with 2–3 guides. Min. age 15.) Bicycle and equipment rentals available; tours range from $50 for a day to $1,069 for a week of mountain biking and whitewater rafting. (See also *Combos.*)

VERMONT

Inn-to-inn

COUNTRY INNS ALONG THE TRAIL
R.R. #3, Box 3115, Brandon, VT 05733. Attn.: Roy and Lois Jackson. (802) 247-3300. Fax (802) 247-6851.

Create your own tour and experience the charm of Vermont—rolling farmlands, narrow valleys, low mountain passes and quaint villages. Try a leisurely route through the Champlain Valley or a more challenging ride through the Green Mountains. All trips begin at Churchill House Inn in Brandon, one of many historic inns to visit. These self-guided tours are custom designed according to preference of dates, mileage and what you want to see. They are for "fun loving folks from 7 to 70," Lois Jackson notes. Rent panniers for your gear as self-guided tours have no sagwagon or luggage shuttle. Or take luggage in your car and start your bike loop at each inn. Rates range from $65–$110/day per person plus trip planning fee, and includes lodging, meals, tax and gratuity. Trips May–Oct. Rental equipment available. (See also *Backpacking / Hiking / Walking.*)

VERMONT

Inn-to-inn tours in Hawaii, Maine, Massachusetts, Nova Scotia, Pennsylvania, Vermont, Virginia

VERMONT BICYCLE TOURING
Box 711, Bristol, VT 05443. Attn.: Bill Perry. (802) 453-4811.

VBT specializes in "Roundabouts, Rambles, Wanderers and Vagabonds"—trips that vary from a weekend to five days, each tour with routes graded easy, moderate or challenging. With a mix of singles, families and couples, trips average 16 per group. Distances vary from 10–20 miles/day to 60 miles/day. Choose the route that fits the distance you want to ride. Having pioneered van-supported, deluxe inn-to-inn cycling through Vermont in 1972, VBT has you pedaling your way along back roads that lead to crystal clear lakes and secluded waterfalls, romantic covered bridges, 18th century villages, fields of wildflowers and panoramic views. Weekend trips from $259, 5-day tours from $599. SuperSaver early season rates offer discounts. Fly & Cycle packages arranged through VBT's in-house travel agent offer reduced rates on air, hotel and rental cars when you book your tour. Special trips include sail-and-cycle combos on the coast of Maine, and five-day trips in Virginia, Pennsylvania, Cape Cod in Massachusetts and itineraries in Nova Scotia and Hawaii. Custom tours are arranged. (See also *Backpacking / Hiking / Walking—Hiking Holidays.*)

WEST VIRGINIA

ELK RIVER TOURING CENTER
Slatyfork, WV 26291. Attn.: Gil and Mary Willis. (304) 572-3771.

MOUNTAIN BIKING

Pocahontas County

"This has been a great exposure to the unseen and undiscovered beauty of West Virginia, a super mixture of climbing, awesome downhills and single track terrain," says one recent participant on Elk River's six-day mountain bike trip. "If any place could be said to have been created for mountain biking, that place would be Pocahontas County," says Gil Willis who launched these trips. Riders find immediate access to miles of diverse terrain in this birthplace of eight rivers and home to 302,000 acres of national forest. Some routes are old narrow-gauge railroad beds converted to scenic bike trails. Tours of one to three days include a *Single Track Weekend Clinic*, the *Canaan Valley Sampler* which covers high alpine terrain, and a self-guided *Inn-to-Inn* tour. *Cranberry to Canaan*, "the ultimate West Virginia mountain bike experience" according to Mary, is a six-day off-road trip and covers 150–175 miles. One August departure is reserved for tandem riders only. A *Tour of the Virginias* crisscrosses Virginia and West Virginia for 150–175 miles in six days, with stops at historic inns and cabins. All tours include guides, maps, meals and accommodations at B&B's, inns, historic lodges, modern lodges and cabins; or custom trips can be arranged. Rates: $75–$125 per day. Trips scheduled May–Oct.

ALBERTA

ROCKY MOUNTAIN CYCLE TOURS
Box 1978-A, Canmore, Alberta, Canada T0L 0M0. Attn.: Mary Jane and Larry Barnes. (403) 678-6770 or (800) 661-2453. Fax (403) 678-4451.

Canadian Rockies, Hawaii

"If you really want to experience the Canadian Rockies," say the Barneses, "why not do it on a bicycle?" Their luxurious, week-long "Hike 'N Bike" mountain resort tour combines days of cycling and hiking with nights at handsome, rustic inns and lodges. Other trips in this spectacular region involve crossing back and forth over the spine of the Rockies, cycling through Kootenay and Yoho national parks, and following challenging trails to the mountain lakes of British Columbia. All trips are six days, and begin and/or end in Banff. It's a region of mighty waterfalls and deep blue glacier-fed lakes, bear and moose, natural hot springs and Northern Lights! Camping tours, $775 US; inn tours, $1,090-$1,680 US. RMCT also schedules an 8-day/$1,610 Hawaii trip. All trips limited to 20 participants.

In the beautiful Rockies—*Rocky Mountain Cycle Tours, Alberta.*

CampAlaska Tours, Alaska (page 127)

Van / Jeep / Rail

Van, jeep, and rail tours are not a lazy person's vacation. They are energetic expeditions into backcountry where you explore remote canyons, Indian ruins, high mountain meadows and crystal clear lakes.

Van and jeep trips are designed for small groups who travel as a team. Together you shop for food, cook, set up camp, plan your menus and make destination decisions. Sometimes you camp in the wilderness under the stars; other times you stay in the best hotels.

Van camping trips are generally planned for a week or two, although some expeditions cover the length and breadth of the country in up to nine weeks. The long treks are a very economical way to go and are especially popular with young adults.

Jeep excursions, on the other hand, usually last for a day or up to a week. While vans are easier on the seat, a jeep can travel where a van cannot—up and down rocky ledges, small cliffs and sloping rock walls.

If you are particularly fond of fishing, fossil and rock hunting, geology or photography, jeep services are willing to accommodate with customized trips.

Among the sights to be leisurely seen from a train is Mexico's Copper Canyon. The Sierra Madre Express cores into a wilderness accessible only by train, covering a challenging route that took 60 years to build.

Colorado's Durango-Silverton narrow gauge steam train explores similarly difficult terrain in the San Juan Mountains, where it once hauled miners and ore and now carries tourists on an evocative, historic trip in impeccably restored rolling stock. The Grand Canyon Railway, transports passengers in a restored 1920s Harriman railcar from Williams, AZ.

For a guide to train travel in North America, *Rail Ventures* by Jack Swanson and Jeff Karsh is available from Rail Ventures Publishing, Box 1877, Ouray, CO 81427 for $16.95 including mailing.

US / CANADA /
MEXICO

Camping tours

TREKAMERICA

P.O. Box 470, Blairstown, NJ 07825. Attn.: Cynthia Rowlands.
(908) 362-9198 or (800) 221-0596. Fax (908) 362-9313.

"Our treks are for friendly, free-spirited young adults, 18–38, who love action-packed vacations and the rewards of traveling in a small group with like-minded people from around the world," Cynthia says. TrekAmerica has been running affordable camping tours throughout the U.S., Alaska, Canada and Mexico for 22 years. How about van camping through national parks or Indian tribal lands? Or exploring prairies, lakes, deserts, rivers—or the sparkle of New York or Hollywood? You'll do it in air-conditioned luxury. Vans are equipped with AM/FM cassette tape decks, CB radios, roof racks for luggage and camping equipment and large tinted windows. Well-trained professional tour leaders guide each trip, organize group activities and see to it that it's a vacation of a lifetime for each one—while getting an inside look at the "real America". Tours range from seven days to nine weeks starting at $440. Year-round departures. Pack a sleeping bag and bring a spirit of adventure. (See also *Youth*.)

Van travel into
scenic wilder-
ness—*TrekAmerica*,
NJ.

US WEST

Arizona,
Colorado, New
Mexico, Utah

SVEN-OLOF LINDBLAD'S
SPECIAL EXPEDITIONS, INC.
720 Fifth Avenue, New York, NY 10019. (212) 765-7740 or (800) 762-0003. Fax (212) 265-3770.

Small groups of no more than ten explore the mind-boggling Four corners area—Arizona, Colorado, New Mexico and Utah—on two different 13-day itineraries guided by knowledgeable expedition leaders. The mode of transportation varies to suit the terrain from comfortably designed four-wheel-drive vehicle, light plane, narrow gauge train or sturdy raft. *Canyons of Time* focuses on the Grand Canyon country, the Anasazi, Hopi and Navajo, and the geologic wonderland of Monument Valley in southern Utah. *Impressions of Native America* delves into the Pueblo Indian and Hispanic cultures of northern New Mexico and the high alpine country of southwest Colorado. "Journey with us to the rim of a canyon whose depths are deep in shadow," urges Sven-Olof Lindblad. "Watch the last rays of sun ignite a distant sandstone pinnacle. Let the mystique of this high desert country, the land of Georgia O'Keefe, Zane Grey, John Wayne and Tony Hellerman, touch your soul and imagination." It is indeed a remarkable region, from the mysterious prehistoric ruins of the Anasazi to the arts, crafts and traditions of contemporary Pueblo and Navajo people. Trips scheduled May, Sep., Oct. Rate: $3,600–$3,700, including stays at lodges or inns. (See also *Boats / Cruises / Scuba*.)

ALASKA

Camping tours

CAMPALASKA TOURS
P.O. Box 872247, Wasilla, AK 99687. Attn.: Tim Adams. (907) 376-9438. Fax (907) 376-2353.

Travel by van with a small group (12 adults), and tent-camp in state and national parks. "The flexible pace gives you a chance to experience Alaska as you travel," Tim Adams explains. "Our itineraries include national parks and wild and historic destinations, and enroute we hike, canoe, kayak, raft whitewater rivers, take scenic flights, or simply relax and enjoy." Twelve itineraries scheduled from June to September for 6–22 days fit varied calendars and budgets. Rates average $60–$80 per day, and a food kitty covers provisions for the nights you cook over a campfire and sleep under the stars. Other meals at restaurants and aboard ferries are paid as you go. On a seven-day trip out of Anchorage, for example, visit Portage Glacier, cross Prince William Sound by ferry, continue by van to Fairbanks and Denali with time for a scenic flight around Mt. McKinley and for rafting a river ($600). A 15-day adventure starts with a flight from Seattle to Prince Rupert, then a ferry through the Inside Passage to Ketchikan, cruise to Juneau, ferry to Skagway, then van travel to the Yukon, Fairbanks, Denali and Anchorage ($1,075). CampAlaska's goal for each trip is the right blend of travel and sightseeing, free time for independent activities, and a chance to really experience the rugged beauty of this vast land. See photo page 124.

Van camping in Utah's spectacular Canyonlands—*Tag-A-Long Tours, UT.*

UTAH

Canyonlands National Park

TAG-A-LONG EXPEDITIONS
452 North Main St., Moab, Ut 84532. Attn.: Bob Jones. (801) 259-8946 or (800) 453-3292. Fax (801) 259-8990.

Hear the song of the lone coyote, lose yourself in a galaxy of stars sprinkled across the endless night sky or curl up in front of a campfire and hear stories of a lost Indian civilization. "Tag-A-Long's three-day overland Canyonlands National Park wilderness adventure is shared with only few others," says Bob Jones. During the day, botanists and Canyonlands specialists will take you through the remote areas of the Needles District where you'll discover by foot gulches and grottos unspoiled by the touch of modern civilization. Trek to towering Indian ruins nestled in an arched rock overhang, or be greeted by a Collard lizard sunning on a warm rock. "Every experience is one of a kind, and every one your own," assures Bob (3 days/$425). Tag-A-Long also schedules 4wd charter trips for groups of three or more. A full menu of half- and one-day 4wd Canyonlands National Park explorations include the Island in the Sky—a high mesa with panoramic views. Or drive south to the incredible Angel Arch. Blend a 4wd exploration with a scenic calm-water jetboat into the backcountry of Canyonlands National Park—a Tag-A-Long exclusive (Day trips $45–$89). (See also *River Running, Ski Touring / Snowmobiling*.)

BRITISH COLUMBIA

Land Rover wilderness tours

GREEN ROAD WILDERNESS EXPEDITIONS LIMITED

3396 Marine Drive, West Vancouver, B.C., Canada V7V 1M9. (604) 925-1514. Fax (604) 922-8340.

In a fleet of Land Rovers, explore some of the most spectacular country in North America. This safari in western Canada

Discovering ghost towns by Land Rover—*Green Road Wilderness Expeditions, B.C.*

is for conservation-minded travelers who want to experience outstanding wilderness beauty first hand, along with comfortable camping (roomy tents, thick mattresses, hot showers, staff-prepared meals). You may opt to drive or sit back and enjoy the ride. From Vancouver you travel north to a wilderness, largely bypassed by "progress." Turn-of-the-century miners passed through here during the Yukon gold rush. Today only ghost towns, isolated villages and Indian reservations remain. You cross ranges of mountains with peaks up to 10,000 feet, from dense coastal forest to semi-desert inland. Crystal clear lakes and wildflowers abound. Groups average 15 people; 6 days/$995 Cdn., children 8–16 half price. Custom group expeditions. Jun.–Sep.

RAIL

MEXICO

Copper Canyon

SIERRA MADRE EXPRESS
P.O. Box 26381, Tucson, AZ 85726. Attn.: Patricia Rondelli. (602) 747-0346 or (800) 666-0346. Fax (602) 747-0378.

"Top-rated service" aboard the Sierra Madre Express is the appraisal of recent passengers who have taken this eight-day tour through Mexico's Copper Canyon. The restored train which accommodates up to 47 guests is deluxe by Mexican standards and serves good though not gourmet meals. The trip is a comfortable and adventurous journey into a remote and spectacular region. Copper Canyon is accessible only by train, and it took 60 years to construct this railroad with its 87 bridges and 35 tunnels at elevations from sea level to 8,500 feet. The mountains and canyons through which you travel are magnificent, and meeting and learning about the Tarahumara Indians who live here and seeing their villages is a fascinating highlight. The trip begins and ends in Tucson with first class hotel accommodations, and you travel by motorcoach to Nogales to board the train. Guests sleep on the train two nights and spend other nights at country-style Mexican inns—the Posada Barrancas near Divisadero and Hotel el Mission in the picturesque pueblo of Cerocahui. Travel from one point to the next is by train, with school buses providing local transport in the primitive areas at each stop. You view vast canyons (deeper than our Grand Canyon) and roll through landscapes from giant saguaro and organ pipe cacti, tropical fruits, pine and cedar to mountains with great chasms, granite peaks and sculpted rocks. It is a journey for outdoor-loving people seeking soft adventure and for rail buffs. Sep.–May, 8 days, at $2,190 dbl. occupancy.

By rail to Copper Canyon—*Sierra Madre Express, Mexico.*

ON WATER

Alaska Frontier Adventures, Alaska (page 137)

Boats / Cruises / Scuba

If puttering around on a little day sailer has spurred grand visions of exploring faraway islands or shores, then perhaps you should consider chartering a boat. This chapter describes everything from do-it-yourself bareboat charters to houseboats, skippered yachts, canalboating on the Erie Canal and cruising in waters from the Caribbean to Alaska.

Although it's still a very romantic way to go, there have been some changes in *who* cruises in recent years. Whereas boat chartering used to be predominantly a retiree's adventure, it's now popular with families and groups of couples, singles or college students who get together to share the adventure—and the cost.

For children, Erie Canal boating is not only exciting but teaches history and how to work the locks. Boat chartering with or without crew is equally instructive in seamanship, navigation and sailing skills, and ample provision for water sports makes boating a favorite with children of any age.

Among the most appealing aspects of chartering a private boat is the independence. You set the agenda, stop at any port you wish, stay for as long as you please, roam a deserted island or discover a private reef for snorkeling.

On crewed charters—roomy catamarans or luxury yachts in the 65' or longer class—everything is supplied. A bareboat charter comes with varying degrees of bareness—with or without food, beverages and specific equipment. There are sailing schools (please see pages 212-213) which specialize in transforming landlubbers into qualified bareboat skippers. These training sessions are great vactions as well as instructive.

Boat charters frequently include scuba equipment. For scuba enthusiasts who would like three to five incredible dives a day we've included details on a special 90', 3-decked catamaran that provides a divers' paradise in the Bahamas (page 147). Trips scheduled year round take you to reefs that have never been visited.

US EAST/
CARIBBEAN

New England,
Atlantic Coast

NICHOLSON YACHT CHARTERS

432 Columbia Street, Cambridge, MA 02141. Attn.: Julie Nicholson. (617) 225-0555 or (800) 662-6066. Fax (617) 225-0190.

"Yacht cruising with us is bustling markets, long sandy beaches, pearly pink dawns and exhilarating sailing," enthuses Julie. The oldest established service for yacht charters in the world, Nicholson brokers upwards of 500 beautiful yachts—sail and motor, bareboat and crewed. Head for the Caribbean in winter for cruising the Windward, Leeward Islands or Virgin Islands—or choose New England in summer. For crewed charters, the captain and his crew become guests' personal guides, tailoring a vacation to individual requirements. Accommodations are for 2-18 guests in private staterooms. Snorkel and fishing equipment is always carried on board, and usually wind surfers and scuba gear. All inclusive rates average $150/person/day. Mediterranean charters also a specialty.

ALASKA

Southeast Alaska

THE ADVENTURESS

Marine Adventure Sailing Tours, 945 Fritz Cove Rd., Juneau, AK 99801. Attn.: Andy Spear. (907) 789-0919 or (800) 252-7899.

For a group of four (or a family of six) wanting to explore Glacier

Exploring
spectacular Glacier
Bay—*Pat Dickerman
for The Adventuress,
AK.*

Bay, Tracy Arm, Ford's Terror, or the inlets and inside passages of Admiralty, Baranof and Chichagof islands, consider *The Adventuress*—a luxurious 50-foot motor sailer with a wilderness-oriented skipper and gourmet-skilled cook. These are custom cruises which Andy Spear arranges to fit your time frame, general itinerary, and the ship's availability. He has operated vessels in Alaska since 1969, is a professional oceanographer and holds a degree in geography and biology. Glaciers, whales, unbelievable scenery and a feeling of vastness are all part of the trip. You anchor in protected inlets in view of calving glaciers at night. Put out a crab pot and gather a harvest of Dungeness crab in the morning. Ride the Zodiac to shore to find bear tracks along a salmon stream, or to explore an old miner's cabin or glacial moraine. Hoist the sails to skim silently across the water, or paddle a kayak. Andy's inexhaustible knowledge and tales of Alaska are a welcome and informative bonus. May–Oct. Rate: $3,400/3 days and up.

ALASKA

Inside Passage, Southeast Alaska

ALASKA FRONTIER ADVENTURE YACHT EXCURSIONS

P.O. Box 32731, Juneau, AK 99803. Attn.: Capt. Charles Kelly. (907) 789-0539. Fax (907) 789-0539.

Captain Kelly is a seasoned expert at hosting four to six guests aboard his 50' *Frontier Queen* on cruises in the fabled Inside Passage and the intricate waterways of Southeast Alaska. He also can charter other privately-owned yachts, matching your group and expectations to the right vessel, whether for two guests on a 34' boat, crewed or bareboat, or up to 12 guests on a luxury yacht in the 65' to 105' range. Whatever the arrangement, these cruising waters offer extraordinary beauty—glacial fjords, ice-packed peaks, dramatic waterfalls. Also incredible marine and wildlife viewing, fantastic salt-water fishing and tremendous river and stream fishing. Yachts are equipped with Zodiacs for shore explorations and kayaks for extra fun. Rate for crewed charters range from $200 to $500/person/day, depending on size and luxury of vessel. See photo on page 134.

ALASKA

Prince William Sound

ALASKA WILDLAND ADVENTURES

P.O. Box 389, Girdwood, AK 99587. Attn.: Kirk Hoessle. (907) 783-2928 or (800) 334-8730.

"Think of the *Discovery* as a floating lodge," advises Kirk Hoessle. "She provides comfort, custom equipment and classic ambience for exploring the raw beauty and wildness of Prince William Sound." With staterooms for twelve guests, she is the smallest cruise ship in Alaska offering scheduled

Cruising fjords and
inlets—*Alaska
Wildland Adventures,
AK.*

cruise departure dates. There are six staterooms, dining/sitting
room and covered and open outside viewing areas for guests.
The boat's size and design allow it to venture into seldom-
visited bays, fjords and inlets. Follow a pod of killer whales.
Scope the high slopes for mountain goats. Wander through a
lush rainforest or remote beach on a shore excursion. Explore
spectacular glaciers and view sea otters, harbor seals, sea lions
and thousands of puffins, kittiwakes and oystercatchers. This is
an intimate cruise in complete comfort into one of the earth's
richest and most scenic seacoast environments. Your voyage
begins and ends in Whittier, including van service to and from
Anchorage. Your interesting hosts, Rose and Dean Rand and
their three children, a long-time Alaskan family and owners of
the *Discovery*, live aboard year round and participate in research, resource development and educational projects. Rate
for 5-day cruises, May-Sep., $1,795-$2,095/person with weekly
departures. (See also *Wilderness / Nature Expeditions, Fly Fishing*.)

ALASKA

GLACIER BAY TOURS AND CRUISES
*520 Pike Street, Suite 1610, Seattle, WA 98101. (800) 451-5952.
Fax (206) 623-7809.*

Glacier Bay,
Inside Passage

For Alaska travelers who wish their itineraries included
close-up glacier viewing, wildlife or whale watching, coastal
exploring and sea kayaking, Glacier Bay Tours and Cruises

Breaching
Humpback
whale—*Glacier Bay
Tours & Cruises, AK.*

offers three to eight day trips starting in Juneau, Glacier Bay
or Inside Passage ports, as well as shorter half-day or one-day
excursions. Aboard the deluxe small cruise ship *Executive
Explorer*, with 25 staterooms and deluxe baths, or the lower
cost "cruising basecamp" *Wilderness Explorer*, with 18 cabins
and pullman-style baths, you can do all these things in
comfort, even sea kayaking from the cruise ship. Combine an
overnight stay at Glacier Bay Lodge with a day cruise of the
Bay's West Arm, or cruise overnight and explore both East
and West Arms. Cruise the Inside Passage, Glacier Bay,
national parks, monuments and scenic wilderness areas of
southeastern Alaska, including spectacular fjords and picturesque towns on a seven-day tour. Or choose a package
that provides whale watching and natural history walks.
Guided sportfishing packages in cabin cruisers can be arranged. Rates start at $89 for a 1/2 day of whale watching,
and average $130–$300 per day for multi-day cruises, depending on itinerary, dates and cabin selection; airfare extra.

ALASKA

HYAK CHARTERS
*Box 2071, Wrangell, AK 99929. (907) 874-3291. [Oct.–Apr.: Box 382,
Indianola, WA 98342. (206) 297-2490.]*

**Southeast Alaska
and Inside
Passage**

"We design our trips around the specific interests of our
charterers—relaxed to just enjoy the magnificent scenery, or
do you also want to canoe a river or climb a mountain? Let's
go!" urges skipper Gary McWilliams. He likes to explore the
nooks and crannies, to get off the beaten track. He finds
special places to show you—whales' feeding grounds and
bears' favorite salmon holes, sea lion rookeries and eagles'

**At the end of
Nature's rainbow—**
Hyak Charters, AK.

aeries, petroglyphs and pictographs, caves and hot springs, ghost towns, wild berry patches, crystals and fossils. The *Hyak* does seven-day tours from Ketchikan, Juneau, Wrangell, Sitka and other ports, all serviced by Alaska Airlines. The *Hyak* is a 52-foot wooden boat of classic and picturesque design. She comfortably accommodates four guests (five in special arrangements) and has a canopy-covered aft deck for all-weather nature observation and photography. A motorized skiff, canoe, binoculars and fishing gear are provided. Guests enjoy catching their dinner and the cook knows how to prepare it. "It was one of the great adventures in our family life," comments a passenger from Wisconsin. "Ten times better than I expected," reports a Tennessee passenger. The *Hyak* also offers art and photography workshops. All-inclusive rate: $1,850/person/week. May–Sep.

ALASKA

**Misty Fjords,
National
Monument**

OUTDOOR ALASKA

P.O. Box 7814, Ketchikan, AK 99901. Attn.: Dale Pihlman. (907) 225-6044.

Cliffs tower thousands of feet high above the deck of your comfortable 32-passenger excursion yacht as you cruise the dramatic Misty Fjords National Monument from Ketchikan. Cascading waterfalls add to the beauty of the scene. Owner Dale Pihlman explains the geological drama as "a young and spectacular land, still being shaped by ice and water. "He and his guides—most lifetime residents—lead highly personalized excursions through this majestic, primeval wilderness. "Midway on each cruise we turn off our engines so you can 'hear' the overwhelming silence," Dale points out. "The greatest disturbance may be the splashing of a salmon or the cry of an eagle." Round trip cruise from Ketchikan takes 11 hours. Combine a cruise with a flight on a float-equipped bush plane for the "ultimate way" to experience this national treasure. Rates: 11-hour cruise, $140; 8-hour cruise/fly, $185. Kayak transport for campers and paddlers, $175. Guided kayak trips.

Towering cliffs in Misty Fjords dwarf a yacht—*Outdoor Alaska, AK.*

ALASKA

Inside Passage

SVEN-OLOF LINDBLAD'S
SPECIAL EXPEDITIONS, INC.
720 Fifth Avenue, New York, NY 10019. (212) 765-7740 or (800) 762-0003. Fax (212) 265-3770.

"Our goal is immerse a small number of people in the natural beauty of Southeast Alaska. We want to show you the bears, whales and eagles," states Special Expeditions. Each voyage is accompanied by a natural history staff who know Alaska well, have discovered where bears are likely to come to the shoreline, where humpback whales congregate, where the good trails penetrate deep into the forest. Cruise a maze of fjords, channels and rivers past glaciers gliding towards the sea on a comfortable, highly maneuverable, 70-passenger ship. A fleet of Zodiacs "launched at a moment's notice"

Photographing sea lions on a rocky shore from the deck of our ship— *Special Expeditions, Inc.*

allow you to explore and experience this spectacular display of nature up close. May–Aug. 10 days/$2,970–$4,200, plus air. Arrival: Seattle. (See also this chapter—Oregon, Mexico. See also *Van / Jeep / Rail.*)

ARIZONA / UTAH

ARA'S LAKE POWELL MARINAS
P.O. Box 56909, Phoenix, AZ 85079. (800) 528-6154. Fax (602) 331-5258.

Lake Powell stretches for 186 twisting, scenic miles between red-rock canyon walls where the Colorado River once flowed

HOUSEBOATING

Lake Powell

Red-rock canyon walls are houseboaters' scenic backdrop— *ARA's Lake Powell Marinas, AZ.*

freely. It overflows the old riverbed into hundreds of side canyons. Red buttes, spires and multi-colored cliffs rise precipitously, creating a colorful wonderland for cruising, climbing, exploring, fishing or just relaxing. Marinas provide houseboats, 36' to 50', from their docks at Wahweap, Bullfrog, Hall's Crossing and Hite. Instruction is included with rentals. Excellent striper, largemouth and smallmouth bass, walleye and crappie fishing. Rent and tow a powerboat for daytime cruising on the spectacular lake while living on your houseboat. Average rates, low to high season, 36' houseboat, 3 nights, $400–$675. 18' powerboat $111–$185/day. Year-round service with low season Nov.–Mar. (See also *River Running*—ARA's Wilderness River Adventures.)

NEW YORK /
FLORIDA

MID-LAKES NAVIGATION CO., LTD.

11 Jordan St., P.O. Box 61-AT, Skaneateles, NY 13152. (315) 685-8500 or (800) 545-4318. Fax (315) 685-7566.

The Erie Canal, Okeechobee Waterway

Cruising New York's 550-mile canal system—*Mid-Lakes Naviagtion Co., Ltd., NY / FL.*

Imagine the freedom of being captain of your own canalboat. Chart your own course on the western Erie Canal aboard a steel-hulled, European-styled *Lockmaster*. From the boat dock in the Finger Lakes you can cruise past wild woodlands, tidy farms and historic canalside villages. Take to the towpath on a bike (one is provided), or laze the day away on the comfortable vessel. The *Lockmaster* is self-sufficient; each is equipped with galley, two heads, a shower and three separate sleeping quarters. No need for a marina—you can tie up just about anywhere. The *Lockmaster 41* sleeps up to six, the *Lockmaster*

44, up to eight. Mid-March through October. For a winter adventure, choose a *Lockmaster* week on the Okeechobee Waterway in South Central Florida. Escape the cold and discover the quiet anchorages and friendly towns of this lovely canal system. December through May. Rates: $1,400-$1,900 per week. Mid-Lakes also offers three-day cruises on its 45-passenger vessel *Emita II*, plying New York's entire 550-mile canal system. Scheduled departures from Albany, Syracuse and Buffalo, about $435 per person double. The fare includes all meals as well as overnight lodging at hotels along the waterway. Discover the quiet joy and restful pace of canalling.

OREGON

Columbia & Snake rivers

SVEN-OLOF LINDBLAD'S
SPECIAL EXPEDITIONS, INC.
720 Fifth Avenue, New York, NY 10019.   (212) 765-7740 or (800) 762-0003. Fax (212) 265-3770.

"In the Wake of Lewis & Clark," a voyage along the Columbia and Snake rivers aboard the comfortable *M.V. Sea Bird* or *M.V. Sea Lion* takes you through forested mountains, arid plateaus and fertile farmland. Trips start at the mouth of the Columbia River in Astoria, the pathway for the epic explorations of Lewis & Clark, and end 450 miles upstream on the Snake. Along the way, you pass through numerous locks and dams, cruise through the spectacular Columbia River Gorge with majestic Mt. Hood as a backdrop and take a thrilling jet boat ride into Hells Canyon, the deepest gorge in the U.S. Naturalists and historians on all voyages. Vessels are one-class ships which accommodate 70 passengers in 37 outside cabins and provide maneuverability and access to otherwise unreachable waterways and anchorages. They carry a fleet of rubber landing craft (Zodiacs) which transport passengers for explorations ashore. May, Sep.–Oct., 7 days / $1,800–$2,700, plus air. Arrival: Portland. (See also this chapter: Alaska, Mexico. See also *Van / Jeep / Rail*.)

WASHINGTON

Pacific Northwest waters

NORTHWEST MARINE CHARTERS, INC.
2400 Westlake Ave. N., Suite 2, Seattle, WA 98109. Attn.: Robey Banks. (206) 283-3040.

"The Pacific Northwest has the finest protected cruising water anywhere," Robey Banks maintains. "There are fossils and driftwood on the island beaches; clams, crabs, wild oysters on shore; whales and porpoises offshore; Coho, silver and king salmon fishing for the 'pro' and flounder and cod for the 'meat' fisherman; tea and crumpets in Victoria—and unbelievable beauty everywhere!" NMC offers a choice of over 100 boats 28 to 125 feet, each completely equipped for extended cruising (6-day minimum). Sample rates: $1,300/ week for 34-foot U-Drive cruiser (sleeps 6); $1,800–$2,500/ week for 37- to 41-foot diesel trawlers (sleeps 6); $1,500/day for 60-foot skippered and crewed luxury yacht for four–six passengers. Also houseboats and U-sail sailboats. Charters available in southeast Alaska, May–September, and in Sea of Cortez, November–March. To avoid disappointment and have best selection, Robey suggests reserving 3 to 6 months in advance.

CARIBBEAN / MEXICO

THE MOORINGS

19345 U.S. 19 North, Suite 402, Clearwater, FL 34624. (813) 535-1446 or (800) 535-7289. Fax (813) 530-9747.

Tortola, St. Lucia, Grenada, St. Martin, Guadeloupe, Sea of Cortez

Bareboating has long been a specialty of The Moorings. Their flagship base in Tortola in the British Virgin Islands provides programs and an expanded fleet to encourage first-time charterers to break into the world of bareboating. Sailors do so not only in Tortola, where there are 16 anchorages within an hour's sail of the marina, but at other Moorings bases in St. Martin, Guadeloupe, St. Lucia, Grenada and Mexico. The Moorings have increased their crewed yacht fleet—offering charters complete with professional captains and cooks— perfect for vacationers who like the pleasures of the sailing lifestyle but would just as soon skip the responsibility for the yacht and meal preparation. A fleet of roomy 48' catamarans and 50'-60' yachts serving this growing interest has been increased with 65'-90' luxury yachts. The Moorings considers their crewed yachts to provide exciting vacations especially for families. "Children love boats and water sports," they point out, "and love the day-to-day change of scene. Sharing a cruising adventure gives families an opportunity for unique bonding." For those who want a resort vacation with just a look at what sailing is all about. The Moorings operates Club Mariner Resorts on Tortola, St. Lucia and Grenada. Visits there almost inevitably lead even confirmed landlubbers sooner or later to board a sailboat.

CARIBBEAN

WINDJAMMER BAREFOOT CRUISES, LTD.

1759 Bay Road, Miami Beach, FL 33139. Attn.: Glenn Dean. 305) 672-6453 or (800) 327-2601. Fax (305) 674-1219.

Bahamas, British Virgin Islands, West Indies, Grenadines

"Our two-week itinerary aboard the *Amazing Grace* covers virtually every island south of Florida and north of Venezuela," says Glenn Dean. The 80-passenger ship is the most recent addition to WBC's fleet and is the most spacious. She worked as a lighthouse tender in the North Sea for the British Royal Navy, and regularly lodged Queen Elizabeth. This cruise will take you through the Bahamas, British Virgin

Islands, West Indies and Grenadines, and offers activities to suit every traveler's needs: snorkeling, scuba diving, water-skiing, hiking expeditions, horesback riding, education tours and long stretches of white, black and pink sand beaches for swimming, sunning and beachcombing, or gathering exotic coral and shells. "With handsome luxury and comfort in impeccable style, she serves as supply ship for our Windjammer fleet," Dean says. All inclusive rates start at $950. Also, 6- and 13-day trips on historic Tall Ships, $600–$1,625. Year round cruises. (See also *Windjammers / Sailing*.)

MEXICO

Sea of Cortez

SVEN-OLOF LINDBLAD'S
SPECIAL EXPEDITIONS, INC.
720 Fifth Avenue, New York, NY 10019. (212) 765-7740 or (800) 762-0003. Fax (212) 265-3770.

"Among the Great Whales" is a spectacular voyage to Baja California and the Sea of Cortez. Each winter California gray whales migrate by the thousands to lagoons and bays along the Pacific coast. Spend three days exploring the vast Bahia Magdelena, one of the prime congregating grounds for these magnificent animals, before cruising the Sea of Cortez with its 50-odd, mostly uninhabited islands. See many species of seabirds, desert creatures, and a myriad of cacti. Don a mask and snorkel, and discover the remarkable array of life below the surface—a ballet of sea lions, brilliantly colored fish, curious moray eels and maybe a graceful manta ray. Natural-

A gentle encounter with a barnnacle-encrusted, friendly gray whale—*Tom O'Brien for Special Expeditions, NY.*

ists on all voyages. Vessels are comfortable one-class, 70-passenger ships with a fleet of Zodiacs for a gentle encounter, perhaps, with a gray whale. Mar.–Apr., 12 days, $3,100–$4,600; or 8 days, Sea of Cortez only, $2,070–$3,150, plus air. Arrival: Tucson, AZ. (See also this chapter: Oregon, Alaska. See also *Van / Jeep / Rail.*)

SCUBA

FLORIDA /
CARIBBEAN

BOTTOM TIME ADVENTURES
P.O. Box 11919, Ft. Lauderdale, FL 33339-1919. Attn.: A.J. Bland. (305) 921-7798 or (800) 234-8464. Fax (305) 920-5578.

The Bahamas

The Bahamas Islands, 50 miles off the Florida coast and 600 miles into the Caribbean, provide a divers' paradise with millions of reefs that have never been visited. From aboard BTA's 90' catamaran, *Bottom Time II*, built with three decks and double cabins for 28, you can explore in comfort and safety. Trips are scheduled year round. Experience high-speed drift diving over beautiful shallow reefs, or dive on incredible walls that descend to more than a mile. Explore the "Blue Hole of Cay Sal," the "Walls of the Exumas" and countless unnamed reefs far away from civilization. Each trip is different, each dive an adventure. "Count on three to five dives a day, all at a fair price," reports one enthusiast, "and a crew that goes out of its way to give you the best diving." Rates: $1,195 for seven days, including cabin, meals, beverages, air tanks and refills, dive weights, dive master, licensed crew and captain. (See also *Cycling / Mountain Biking, Sea Kayaking, Wilderness / Nature Expeditions.*)

An enchanting undersea world—
—Bottom Time Adventures, Caribbean / FL.

Wilderness Outfitters, Minnesota (page 154)

Canoeing / Kayaking

You are paddling down a slow, meandering river. A brimmed cap shades your eyes, a lifejacket hugs your body. Your waterproof duffels with all your camping gear are securely tied to the canoe—easier to retrieve in case you should tip over. As you glide along, the pleasant and sometimes dramatic scenery rolls by. You hear splashing water ahead—louder—then you see the rapids. You aim for the smooth-water tongue, bordered by froth, and slide into the turbulence, using your paddles to steer around rocks and maintain balance. You make it—and resume the gentle paddling rhythm and your quiet reverie.

Exciting moments make canoeing on whitewater rivers sportier but no more enjoyable than paddling on lakes. Experts say that on gentle Class I or II waters, canoes are the way to go. Beyond that they recommend kayaks—smaller and more maneuverable than open canoes.

New craft now popular on rivers and coastal waters are the Kiwi Kayak (small, stable and easy to paddle on Class III whitewater) and the two-person Klepper Kayak (standard equipment in coastal regions).

Information in these pages includes trips in the famous Minnesota Boundary Waters Canoe Area and Maine's Allagash Wilderness Waterway as well as on rivers and lakes east and west. Also details on faraway excursions in Alaska and the Arctic regions of the Yukon and Northwest Territories, and far to the south in Baja. Glacier viewing, whale watching and snorkeling are the prime focus of some trips. For other canoe and kayak trips please see chapters on *Combos* (page 217), *Wilderness / Nature Expeditions* (page 241) and *Sea Kayaking* (page 201).

One of the prime delights of canoeing and kayaking is the stillness—broken only by the rhythmic splash of your paddle, the occasional sound of whitewater rapids, the call of the loon, the wind in the trees or waves lapping on shore. It's a gentle, close-to-nature vacation.

US WEST

**Rivers in
Arizona,
Colorado, New
Mexico, Utah**

DVORAK EXPEDITIONS

*17921 U.S. Hwy. 285, Suite AG, Nathrop, CO 81236. Attn.: Bill Dvorak.
(719) 539-6851 or (800) 824-3795. Fax (719) 539-3378.*

"From flat water to whitewater, the river is the best teacher,"
asserts Bill Dvorak. On this whitewater skills seminar you
begin on flat water learning the basics, then move down the
river practicing—mastering the skills in moving water. Bill
offers instruction and raft-support trips in 29 canyons on ten
rivers across the West. Seminars vary from a half day introductory lake session to a 12-day paddling trip. Sample trips:
six days on Utah's Green River through Desolation and Gray
canyons with their progression of rapids is a place to hone
river running skills; or three days on New Mexico's Rio
Chama with its warm climate and easy pace is good for
paddling a kayak or canoe. Rates from $80/1 day to $2182/
12 days. Reduced rates for families and "special population"
groups—those with physical or emotional problems. A 22-
day whitewater skills camp is another specialty. (See also
River Running, Youth.)

**An experienced
kayaker on the
Selway River—**
*Dvorak Expeditions,
CO.*

MAINE

**Allagash, St.
John, Penobscot,
Moose,
Kennebec, Lower
Dead rivers**

ALLAGASH CANOE TRIPS

*P.O.Box 713, Greenville, ME 04441. Attn.: Warren Cochrane or Linda
Koski. (207) 695-3668.*

"We take pride in our methods of cooperative, respectful
existence with the natural world," say the Cochranes who
have been running old-style backwoods canoe trips in Maine

Skillful maneuvering through some rough water—
Allagash, Canoe Trips, ME.

since 1953. "We don't take civilization with us, but we don't place undue emphasis on hardship for its own sake either." Equipment features Old Town wood-canvas and durable Royalex canoes. Food is "uncommonly good" (fresh, organically-grown vegetables in season, jumbo pancakes with home-made syrup, yeast bread and biscuits), and instruction is by a family of award-winning guides whose talents run from using a setting pole in shallow rapids to baking pastries before a campfire—in a torrential rain! Trips are three to nine days on any of five rivers: St. John, Allagash, Moose, East or West Branch Penobscot. Rates: $295–$650, discounts for children. Whitewater weekends for adults or teens with experience, $200. Custom and scheduled trips. Also, Canadian river trips arranged for experienced canoeists. Arrival: Bangor, ME.

MAINE/
GEORGIA

CHEWONKI FAMILY ADVENTURES
RR 2, Box 1200 PD, Wiscasset, ME 04578. Attn.: Greg Shute. (207) 882-7323. Fax (207) 882-4074.

Okefenokee
Swamp (GA), St.
John River,
Allagash
Wilderness
Waterway,
Penobscot River
(ME)

For families, small groups and other individuals, Chewonki has scheduled canoe trips from March until Labor Day. It's a chance to learn wilderness and paddling skills in a relaxed atmosphere of genuine concern for other participants. Enter the realm of the alligator and sandhill crane in Georgia's Okefenokee Swamp for eight days of canoeing, camping on cypress covered islands and wooden platforms above the swamp (end of Mar., 8 days, $600). In the remote northwest corner of Maine paddle from Baker Lake to the village of Allagash on the magnificent St. John River, and look for a feed of fresh brook trout and fiddleheads (end of May, 9 days, $675). In July/August lake and river paddling for experienced and novice canoeists is offered on the Allagash Wilderness Waterway (11 days, $750). The end of August beginners and families follow in the historic route of Thoreau, paddling the West Branch of the Penobscot River from Lobster Lake to Chesuncook. Few rapids on this section, and moose sightings almost guaranteed (End Aug., 7 days, $525). (See also *Wilderness / Nature Expeditions, Youth*.)

Tranquility on the Allagash—*Greg Shute for Chewonki Family Adventures, ME.*

MAINE

Saint Croix and Machias rivers

SUNRISE COUNTY CANOE EXPEDITIONS
Cathance Lake, Grove Post Office, ME 04638. Attn.: Martin Brown. (207) 454-7708.

Whitewater technique is Martin Brown's specialty, including instruction in poling—a practical method of upstream and shallow-river travel. "We take pride in turning virtually anyone into a technically skilled and confident canoeist in a matter of days," he says. For more than 20 years he has stressed a high quality of instruction, northwoods guiding and canoemanship in his trips. The Saint Croix, with its easy to moderate rapids, he considers ideal for families and beginners, yet suitable for all levels of expertise. The pace is leisurely, and you make camp with time to swim, fish or just relax. Moonlight paddles highlight these trips—or early mornings in the pre-dawn mist. Most trips four to six days,

Navigating the Moisie River— *Sunrise County Canoe Expeditions, ME.*

May–October, approximately $115/day. For a rigorous whitewater clinic with an extended wilderness journey, Martin recommends the Machias River. Its Class II–III water winds through the remote interior of eastern Maine, and is known for excellent trout and salmon fishing. May–June. 4 days, $495; 7 days, $795. (See also *Youth,* and this chapter—Texas / Utah, Northwest Territories.)

MINNESOTA / ONTARIO

CANOE COUNTRY ESCAPES, INC.

194 South Franklin St., Denver, CO 80209. Attn.: Brooke & Eric Durland. (303) 722-6482.

Boundary Waters Canoe Area (MN), Quetico Provincial Park (Ont.)

For a unique wilderness experience plan a five-, six-, or ten-day guided trip in Minnesota's Boundary Waters or Ontario's Quetico Provincial Park. The Durlands schedule trips for up to nine canoeists according to their interest and abilities—laid-back, strenuous, fishing, active seniors, or families (geared to kids four and up). "There are no passengers on these trips, only crew. You'll help paddle your canoe, portage the gear and pitch in on the camp chores," explains Brooke. They provide all food, equipment (canoes, tents, sleeping bags, foam pads) and guide. Instruction and practice session before trip begins. Rates 5–10 days, $535–$895, include Duluth airport pick-up, pre- and post-trip meals and lodging. Their most popular trips are five-day, lodge-to-lodge trips, $650 for "active seniors who want soft adventure." They also specialize in setting up custom-guided trips using the participants' choice of dates and itinerary. Straight outfitting (no guide) also available June–September.

MINNESOTA/
ONTARIO

GUNFLINT LODGE & OUTFITTERS

Gunflint Trail, Box 750, Grand Marais, MN 55604. Attn.: Bruce & Sue Kerfoot. (218) 388-2294 or (800) 328-3325. Fax (218) 388-9429.

Boundary Waters Canoe Area (MN), Quetico Provincial Park (Ont.)

"We're looking for people who care about our wilderness enough to leave it a little better than they found it, folks who come to enjoy the wildlife, sit around a campfire listening to the loons or watch the Northern Lights," reflects Bruce Kerfoot. His family has been outfitting for 60 years in the BWCA and Quetico Park. Their emphasis is on minimum impact camping. Gunflint is centrally located to service over 50 canoe routes. They feature guided lodge-to-lodge trips, careful route planning, nourishing foods and top-quality equipment as well as a lodge with bunkhouses, meals, sauna and a wide range of facilities. Complete lightweight outfitting: $45–$60/day, $20–$30 for children. Special package in May and Sep. Group rates for 8 or more, early May–late Oct. Kevlar, aluminum, and Royalex canoes. Free pickup at Duluth airport. (See also *Wilderness/Nature Expeditions, Ski Touring/Snowmobiling.*)

MINNESOTA

SUPERIOR-NORTH CANOE OUTFITTERS

HC64A, Box 965, Gunflint Trail, Grand Marais, MN 55604. Attn.: Earl and Anita Cypher. (218) 388-4416 or (800) 852-2008.

Boundary Waters Canoe Area, Quetico Provincial Park

What's your preference—a base camp or moving each day? A rugged, moderate or easy trip? Walleye, northern pike, smallmouth bass or lake trout? Wildlife remoteness, scenery or waterfalls? From their base on Saganaga Lake at the end of the Gunflint Trail, Earl and Anita custom plan your trip into the Boundary Waters Canoe Area and the Quetico and Northern Light Lake wilderness areas. Ultralight equipment has become their trademark, and they now plan a special ultralight package including Kevlar canoes, Eureka Timberline tents, super-light, bent-shaft paddles and other new products—"the best," says Anita. "We're getting a lot of bookings from far-away travelers, and they especially like the ultralight gear. Also the new covered area near the lock for packing and picnicking on rainy days." With or without the rain, outdoor enthusiasts enjoy the peace and quiet of over 2 million acres of pristine wilderness. Rates average around $40/person/day.

MINNESOTA /
ONTARIO

WILDERNESS OUTFITTERS, INC.

1 E. Camp St.—AT 9394, Ely, MN 55731. Attn.: Jim Pascoe and Gary Gotchnik. (218) 365-3211 or (800) 777-8572. Fax (218) 365-6288.

Boundary Waters/Quetico Wilderness

Best known as "the fisherman's outfitter", owners Gotchnik and Pascoe have paddled, fished and explored the best routes in the vast Boundary Waters/Quetico wilderness on the

Minnesota-Ontario border. "We are an unbeatable team in finding the route that meets your requirements to perfection," they say, "and we provide quality guidance, service and equipment." In operation since 1921, Wilderness Outfitters is one of the oldest and most respected services for outdoorsmen. They set up trips with lodging in their established tent camps and outpost cabins. They offer a choice of lightweight outfitting or a deluxe ultra lightweight package and food selected for your choice of day-to-day menus. There are fly-in fishing trips, fly-in and canoe-out trips, and remote locations to fly-in or go by boat. No roads in these wilderness regions of incredible scenery and fabulous fishing. Guides are not necessary on most trips as maps are extremely accurate, even to the point of marking the best fishing spots and which fish to find where. On some trips guides go with you to set up camp and return periodically to resupply you with ice, gas, bait, etc., and to take your camp down. Special packages are offered to families and small groups. Daily rates per person range from $42 to $50 for 10-day or 3-day trips with lightweight equipment, from $49 to $57 for deluxe ultra lightweight outfitting, or $59-$70 for Quetico-Superior outfitting—the ultimate in equipment for traveling faster and further into the wilderness with less effort. Airport pickup service Duluth or Hibbing. See photo page 148.

Fishing in canoe country—*Wilderness Outfitters, Inc., MN.*

NORTH
CAROLINA

NANTAHALA OUTDOOR CENTER

13077 Hwy 19 West, Bryson City, NC 28713-9114. (704) 488-6737. Fax (704) 488-2498.

Rivers in Southern Appalachian Mountains

Since 1972, NOC has provided some of the finest outdoor education in the nation. Experienced instructors are dedicated to their sport—many are national or world paddling champions. The low student/teacher ratio helps paddlers progress rapidly and the Southern Appalachian training location provides one of the longest paddling seasons in the country—from March to October. Standard whitewater courses cover basic paddling skills; specialized courses cover river leader skills, outdoor emergency, river intensives and "Weeks on Water". Standard course rates including meals, lodging and equipment: weekend $285, 3-day $415, 4-day $535, 5-day $665, 7-day $915. Private instruction can be custom designed. NOC also offers "Samplers"—one-day introductory lessons in paddling a canoe, decked canoe, whitewater kayak or touring (sea) kayak: $65/person, including lunch and equipment. For novices wanting to work on the Eskimo Roll: half-day roll sessions, $35/person. Samplers available June through August only. Arrival: Asheville, NC or Knoxville, TN. (See also *Cycling / Mountain Biking*—Carolina Cycle Tours, *River Running, Combos.*)

OREGON / IDAHO

ORANGE TORPEDO TRIPS

P.O. Box 1111-G, Grants Pass, OR 97526. (503) 479-5061 or (800) 635-2925.

Rogue, Klamath, North Umpqua and Salmon (ID) rivers

The sport of inflatable kayaking received an enthusiastic boost from OTT in 1969 when astonished onlookers watched the first orange torpedo boats make it down the Rogue where only sturdy rafts or fishing boats had gone before. Today OTT schedules more than 250 trips on the Rogue from May to September, and 154 additional trips on the North Umpqua, Klamath and Idaho's Salmon Rivers. Their follow-the-leader system encourages first timers to give it a try, and several thousand torpedo boaters run the rivers with them each year. Many trips include nights at lodges or riverside inns rather than camping. The protected wild and scenic section of the lower Rogue with its ever-changing whitewater is both challenging and fun in the easy-to-maneuver craft. (Rogue lodge trips, 2 days/$225, 4 days/$485–$510.) On the Klamath the water is warmer and roadside maxivan support gives kayakers an option of selecting the best stretch of river. This makes it a favorite for first timers and families. (3-day lodge trips $370–$435, camping $310–$365.) OTT takes up to 12 kayakers on Klamath trips, up to 20 on the Rogue and Salmon.

PENNSYLVANIA

Delaware River

KITTATINNY CANOES

Dept. AT, Dingmans Ferry, PA 18328. Attn.: Ruth Jones. (717) 828-2338 or (800) 356-2852.

"The canoe and the Delaware were made for each other," says Ruth Jones. For over 50 years three generations of her family have owned this business—"the first and finest on the Delaware," they claim. With seven locations and two campgrounds on 120 miles of the river, they arrange both calm water and whitewater trips for families, beginners or experts. The campgrounds provide complete facilities, or overnight wilderness camping can be arranged in the Delaware Water Gap National Recreation Area. Special dates each season for instruction in calm and whitewater, kayaking, guided wildflower and wildlife tours, fall foliage trip and river cleanup an annual event for which Kittatinny has won many awards. Season: mid-April through October Weekday rates: $16–$21/day per person including equipment and shuttle; slightly higher weekends. Family group and under 12 rates. (See also *River Running*.)

TEXAS / UTAH

Rio Grande, San Juan

Leisurely paddling on the Rio Grande— *Sunrise County Canoe Expeditions, ME.*

SUNRISE COUNTY CANOE EXPEDITIONS

Cathance Lake, Grove Post Office, ME 04638. Attn.: Martin Brown. (207) 454-7708.

Canoeing the lower canyons of the Rio Grande in Big Bend country along the wild Texas/Mexico border is a springtime specialty of Martin Brown. "It's the optimum season," he says, "when the cacti are flowering and the climate is just

right—fairly hot, with an abundance of sunshine, no bugs, no rain and perfect swimming." The sheer, subtly hued walls of the lower canyons rise thousands of feet. Placid water alternates with whitewater and steep rapids, and canoeists learn Martin's technique of solo paddling and poling. Trips Mar./Apr., 9 days, $895. Another springtime specialty is canoeing the Class I–II (and some Class III) water of the San Juan where it cuts deep through the slickrock country of southeastern Utah's legendary Canyonlands, characterized by awesome redrock canyons and fascinating stratigraphic formations. Anasazi petroglyphs still adorn the cliffs, and amazingly well-preserved cliff dwellings are accessible from the river. Trips Apr. and May, 9 days, $979. (See also *Youth,* and this chapter—Maine, Northwest Territories.)

VERMONT / CONNECTICUT/ GEORGIA / NORTH CAROLINA / TENNESSEE / QUEBEC / COSTA RICA

Battenkill, Winooski, Lamoille, Missisquoi, Clyde, Black, White, West, Dumoine rivers

BATTENKILL CANOE LTD.

Box 65, Arlington, VT 05250. Attn.: Jim and Jo Walker. (802) 362-2800 or (800) 421-5268. Fax (802) 362-0159.

"There's nothing so pleasurable as floating a river in a world of slowed down time and stretched out space," say the Walkers. With this philosophy BCL plans a varied program of canoe vacations. If you want to go it alone, rent a canoe for a day or so (or bring your own) and use BCL's service for arranging lodging with meals (picnic lunches) and shuttle. With more time choose three to five days of canoeing with a small groups (14 max.), spending nights at country inns or camping out. (Trips from May–October.) Geographically the itineraries are established on rivers throughout Vermont, across the border in Quebec and two days on Connecticut rivers. A river-to-river, inn-to-inn "sampler", for example, is for those who can take five days to unwind. It includes splendid rivers, swimming holes, waterfalls, riverside picnics and evenings in tiny villages. On three-day trips you paddle a different river each day and either camp or stay at the same inn at night. Rate/person with accommodations, meals, guide and shuttle range from $60–$135/day. Canoe rentals, $45/1 day, $75/5 days. Trips in Tennessee, North Carolina and Georgia in spring and fall, and in Costa Rica in winter.

VIRGINIA

Shenandoah River

SHENANDOAH RIVER OUTFITTERS, INC.

Rt. 3, Luray, VA 22835. Attn.: Nancy Goebel. (703) 743-4159.

Just two hours from Washington, DC, this "oldest and largest outfitter in the Mid-Atlantic states" puts you on the Shenandoah River with its rugged cliffs and secluded clearings where Indians once lived. SRO is active in a "help-preserve-the-Shenandoah" campaign and offers free canoeing in exchange for two filled trash bags. For mid-week canoeists SRO offers a special rate of $25 per canoe for a three-hour flatwater trip which starts at 11 a.m. every Monday through Friday. The rate for complete outfitting is $100 per canoeist for two days. Day trips are $40/canoe, and tubing $12/person. All rates include life jacket and shuttle. Also partial outfitting and group discounts. "The peace of gently floating along, the excitement of Compton Rapids and the beauty of Shenandoah Valley make these trips a welcome break from everyday living," says a vacationer.

WEST VIRGINIA

NORTH AMERICAN RIVER RUNNERS, INC.
P.O. Box 81, Hico, WV 25851-0081. Attn.: Donnie Hudspeth. (304) 658-5276 or (800) 950-2585. Fax (304) 658-4212.

Cheat, Upper & Lower Gauley, New, Upper Youghiogheny rivers

"Kayaking is the way to go for the thrill of a one-on-one experience with the river," says kayak instructor Donnie Hudspeth, "and West Virginia can't be beat when it comes to excellent runs. It has earned the name 'America's Best Whitewater.'" NARR accommodates all types and levels of instruction. Beginner courses emphasize basic strokes, river dynamics and safety. Intermediate and advanced courses review the basics, refine techniques and upgrade skill levels. Classes available Jun.–Sep., 1–5 days, $85/day, include equipment, meals, transportation and instructor. Private instruction $170/day. "With the incredible variety of rivers in West Virginia, NARR tailors instruction to appropriate learning levels," says Donnie. (See also *River Running*.)

NORTHWEST TERRITORIES / ONTARIO / QUEBEC / YUKON

BLACK FEATHER WILDERNESS ADVENTURES
40 Wellington St., E., Toronto, Ont., Canada M5E 1C7. (416) 861-1555. Fax (416) 862-2314.

Natla-Keele, Hess, Hood, Burnside, Nahanni, Mountain rivers

Black Feather pioneered canoe expeditions on rivers in the Northwest Territory and the Yukon where the arctic summer bestows 24 hours of light and a gentle climate (days in the 70s) for your wilderness adventuring. Explore waters most of us have never heard of—the Natla-Keele, Hess, Hood, Burnside, Nahanni and Mountain rivers. For the Mountain River in Northwest Territory, for instance, fly from Norman Wells to the put-in on a tiny lake ringed with mountains, and push your way through a headwaters creek where Arctic grayling play. Then settle into your seat for a roller-coaster ride of stunning beauty through adrenalin-inducing Class II water. The river cuts through five dramatic canyons with great campsites and side trip exploring. (Jul. & Aug., 2 weeks, $2,375 US.) The Nahanni run has become a classic national park trip—spectacular falls, breathtaking canyons, exhilarating hot springs, easy paddling. (Jun.–Aug., 14 days, $2,200

An exuberant paddler—*Black Feather Wilderness Adventures, Ont.*

US.) BF's complete adventure program throughout Canada (especially in Ontario and Quebec) offers hiking, biking, rafting, sea kayaking, canoeing, canoe schools and ski touring. (See also *Backpacking | Hiking | Walking*.)

NORTHWEST TERRITORIES

SUNRISE COUNTY CANOE EXPEDITIONS
Cathance Lake, Grove Post Office, ME 04638. Attn.: Martin Brown. (207) 454-7708.

Soper River

Open canoeing was virtually unheard of in Baffin Island until Martin Brown's first descent of the Soper River in 1990. The island's dramatic glacial landscape and the valley's gorges, waterfalls and lush flowering tundra glow in the Midnight Sun. The Soper River Valley, with miles of runnable Class II water, is an oasis on the otherwise desolate island. The Soper is possibly the most northerly river in the eastern Arctic navigable by canoe. The weather in July is temperate. The bugs are few. North of the Labrador Sea and west of Greenland, Baffin Island is home to a full range of Arctic birds and wildlife, and to the proud and stalwart Inuit, renowned for their carvings, sculpture, jewelry and tapestries. For eight-day trips scheduled in July, ten participants and three guides meet in Ottawa for the flight to Iqaluit (Frobisher Bay). Travel is by air charter to a tundra strip near the river for five days (50 miles) of downriver canoeing. Local Inuit join the group the final day and escort them into the community of Lake Harbour for a charter flight back. Rate including air charter: 9 days, $2,195/person or $3,925/couple. (See also *Youth Adventures*, and this chapter—Maine, Texas /Utah.)

Whitewater canoeing on the Soper River— *Martin Brown for Sunrise Country Canoe Expeditions, NW Territories (photo page 161).*

ONTARIO

Quetico
Provincial Park

CANOE CANADA OUTFITTERS

P.O. Box 1810-A, Atikokan, Ont., Canada P0T 1C0. Attn.: Bud Dickson or Jim Clark. (807) 597-6418. Fax (807) 597-5804.

"We are centrally located on the remote northern boundary of Quetico Provincial Park and outfit into the entire 2,000 square mile area," says Bud Dickson. "Our speciality is ultra lightweight outfitting for self-guided wilderness trips." Also a special Elite package with the finest hi-tech equipment on the market. "Our knowledgeable trip planning, top notch equipment and food pack, and careful routing are the highlights of our service." It's an area of abundant wildlife and sport fishing where artifacts of the voyageurs and loggers may be found. Rates: $365/week US ultralight outfitting; $450/week Elite outfitting. Youth and non-profit groups $38/day, $266/week. CCO also provides fly-in/paddle-out service and cabin/canoe trips. Drive to main base in Atikokan, pick-up service in Thunder Bay, or have limo meet you at International Falls airport.

ONTARIO

Madawaska
River

MADAWASKA KANU CENTRE

Box 635, Barry's Bay, Ontario, Canada K0J 1B0. Attn.: Claudia Kerckhoff. (613) 756-3620. Fax (613) 756-3667. [Sep.–Jun.: 39 First Ave., Ottawa, Ontario, Canada K1S 2G1. (613) 594-5268.]

MKC provides highly personalized instruction in both whitewater kayaking and canoeing, leading to diplomas recognized worldwide. Located on the Madawaska River, by Algonquin Park, it offers the comforts of a vacation resort in

European style. Classes are small (six students), and the rivers clean, warm and uncrowded. Excellent water flow is guaranteed all summer. May–September you can take a weekend introductory package, or five-day whitewater full-fledged "immersion course," for all levels of paddling skills. Beginning with river safety and rescue, go on to learn paddling skills, eskimo roll, scouting and navigating whitewater and how to select and maintain equipment. Instructors come from around the world and make learning an enjoyable experience. They video tape students who watch playbacks each evening. Weekend clinics from $186 (basic instruction and camping) to $266 Cdn. (indoor accommodations and all meals). Similarly, 5-days from $355–$555 Cdn. Excursions to Georgian Bay, Grand Canyon or Costa Rica arranged. See front cover photo.

Learning kayaking techniques—
Madawaska Kanu Center, Ont.

ONTARIO

Ottawa River

WILDERNESS TOURS

P.O. Box 89, Beachburg, Ont., Canada K0J 1C0. Attn.: Terry Hierlihy. (613) 646-2241 or (800) 267-9166. Fax (613) 646-2996.

The warm deep waters of the Ottawa River provide an ideal learning environment for anyone who enjoys whitewater

On the Ottawa River—*Wiilderness Tours, Ontario.*

and the challenge of kayaking. "Challenging whitewater one-on-one is the prime motivation for many who take our week-long kayak course," says Terry, "but most people remember the week as a great vacation." The program centers on quality instruction in a fun and sociable atmosphere. On-river sessions focus on individual abilities. After introductory classes you progress to intermediate instruction with different rapids, whitewater reading skills and playboating techniques such as wave and hole surfing, enders and handrolls. Accommodation options range from deluxe chalets or medium-priced cabin tents, to economical two-person pup tents on wooden platforms. 5-day courses, June-August, $168/weekend US, $360 US. (See also *River Running, Combo Trips.*)

Unicorn Rafting Expeditions, Inc., Maine (page 185)

River Running

There you are, relaxed and at ease, lifejacket snugly strapped around your torso, drifting slowly down the river on a rugged inflatable raft. Off in the distance you hear a rumble. You glimpse whitewater ahead, and grab hold of the ropes that crisscross the boat as you move closer, closer, louder. Then you're crashing, rising, floating, flying, pounding and twisting through a turbulent, frothy boil. You squint, blink and hold on, pummeled by walls of spray.

Suddenly it's over. You drift smoothly on, reveling in the canyon's beauty, wondering how soon it will give you another wild ride.

That's the lure of running big water, a sport which manages to combine the thrill of a world-class rollercoaster ride with experiencing up close some of the earth's most compelling land-(or canyon)-scapes.

Because of the ever-increasing popularity of river running, nearly every waterway with enough current for a raft is serviced by an outfitter. You can find a river as mild—or as wild—as you wish.

Options abound—fröm a few hours to a week or more. From single-person Sportyaks to 4-person paddle rafts to motorized craft holding up to 16. In addition to this chapter, please see *Combos* (page 217) and *Wilderness / Nature Expeditions* (page 241) for other river runs.

Rafters are often expected to haul gear, help set up camp, bail the boat, pitch in as part-time chefs and leave the campsite in pristine condition. It is a participation sport.

Aside from the obvious joys of rafting, there are also the more subtle, yet undeniable, pleasures. On the river you are *totally* involved. As one river runner drolly notes, "While hanging on to a rubber raft for dear life, with waves breaking ten feet over your head, there is little time to mull over the cares of the workaday routine."

US WEST

Rivers in AZ,
CO, NM, UT

DVORAK EXPEDITIONS

17921 U.S. Hwy. 285, Suite AG, Nathrop, CO 81236. Attn.: Bill Dvorak. (719) 539-6851 or (800) 824-3795. Fax (719) 539-3378.

Bill Dvorak has been introducing people to the unique world of rivers for more than 20 years. He calls it "river magic"— meeting the river on its own terms—"one of life's greatest satisfactions." He has no trouble finding a suitable river to accommodate any group or individual. Using paddle- and oar-powered boats, he offers trips on ten rivers (in Utah, Colorado, New Mexico, Texas) through 29 canyons, and in three countries. Having innovated participatory paddle trips, this remains the focus of his excursions (though you can opt for being rowed). Bill has consistently run about half of his trips for youth groups and places particular emphasis on family outings at special discounts. He has also been at the forefront of providing trips for "special population" groups— those with physical or emotional problems—at reduced prices. Most trips are 2–5 days, around $85–$145/day, minimum age 5 (10 on some rivers). Half and 1-day trips $35–$85. Arkansas River combos and custom fishing expeditions arranged. (See also *Canoeing / Kayaking, Youth*.)

Time on the beach—*Dvorak Expeditions, CO.*

US WEST

American,
Tuolumne, (CA);
Middle Fork &

ECHO: THE WILDERNESS CO., INC.

6529 AG Telegraph Avenue, Oakland, CA 94609. Attn.: Joe Daly or Dick Linford. (510) 652-1600 or (800) 652-ECHO. Fax (510) 652-3987.

For 22 years ECHO has been scheduling trips on some of the best rivers in the West: Main Salmon, Middle Fork, Rogue,

Main Salmon, (ID); Rogue, (OR)

Inflatable kayak in exciting water—
Echo: The Wilderness Co., CA.

American, Tuolumne and the mighty Colorado. Trips range from 1 to 12 days in oar- and paddle-powered boats, and ECHO has introduced self-bailing, inflatable kayaks on the Rogue, Salmon and Middle Fork. Choose from a wide selection of trips—from your white-knuckle variety down the rapids to one of ECHO's special theme trips—one a bluegrass band plays mountain music around a campfire, on another the harmonics of a string quartet echo from the canyons. On a kids' and parents' trip camping skills, nature hikes, star gazing, campfire games, catching crawdads and paddling inflatable kayaks get extra billing. But on all trips river runners can be as active or sedentary as they wish. May–Oct., $92 (1-day American River) to $2075 (14-day Grand Canyon). Group and youth rates. Lodge overnights on some trips. "On a scale of one to ten, my trip was an 11" comments a California tripper on the Rogue.

US WEST

20 rivers in AK, AZ, CA, CO, ID, OR, UT, WY

O.A.R.S., INC.
Box 67, Angels Camp, CA 95222. (209) 736-4677. Fax (209) 736-2902.

Established in 1972 by George Wendt, O.A.R.S is appropriately named—no motors to destroy the serenity of any of his numerous different river trips—only oar-powered rafts, paddle boats, inflatable kayaks, sea kayaks in the Grand Tetons, and on the Colorado River, spectacular wooden dories. Choose from 1- to 18-day trips on any of 20 rivers in the desert southwest, the Pacific mountains, the northern Rockies, Alaska, Baja (Mexico), Costa Rica. You can raft all seasons with

Oar power takes these rafters through the Grand Canyon—*Liz Hymans for O.A.R.S., CA.*

O.A.R.S and not cover the same water twice. Sample rates on Grand Canyon trips: 6 days/$1,205, 13 days/$2,264. On other rivers rates range, for example, from $110 for a one-day run on the north fork of the American, to $1,570 for 12 days on the Main Salmon in Idaho, and $1,640 for 10 days on the Tatshenshini in Alaska. Says a first-time river runner from Illinois, "I drove myself to a place I'd never been to meet people I did not know to have the experience of a lifetime!" From another O.A.R.S. tripper, "Most of all, my heart was at one with the river, flowing smooth and steady." (See also *Sea Kayaking*.)

ALASKA

ABEC'S ALASKA ADVENTURES

1550-AG Alpine Vista Court, Fairbanks, AK 99712. Attn.: Ramona Finnoff. (907) 457-8907.

Kongakut, Noatak, Hulahula, Koyukuk, Alatna, Kobuk rivers

Kongakut, Hulahula, Koyukuk, Alatna and Noatak. To the uninitiated, the names seem strange; to those familiar with Alaska's Brooks Range the names conjure visions of whitewater, wilderness, floating and fishing. From Fairbanks ABEC flies participants to put-in points on these rivers whose headwaters are in the Brooks Range. Rafters of all ages and abilities choose the emerald waters of the Kongakut—a fine trip for wildlife photography. Float the Hulahula through rocky rapids and serene canyons of ice all the way to the Arctic Ocean. The Koyukuk offers a 125-mile trip through arctic wilderness, home to moose, bear and wolves, with crystal-clear streams and lakes for grayling fishing. Paddlers on the

Paddling past
aufeis on the
Kongakut River—
*ABEC's Alaska
Adventures, AK.*

Alatna are in full view of the granite spires of the Arrigetch
Peaks and hike side valleys and ridges. The Noatak mean-
ders through an expanse of parkland tundra with some easy
but exciting rapids. Journeys with Ramona Finnoff, ABEC
owner and guide for more than a decade, are memorable.
Says one veteran rafter, "I wish I could float my way through
life with you in Alaska." Trips vary in length from 8–13 days
and rates from $158–$225 per day. All departures can be
combined with backpacking treks. (See also *Backpacking /
Hiking / Walking.*)

ALASKA

ALASKA DISCOVERY, INC.
234 Gold St., Dept. A, Juneau, AK 99801. Attn.: Kari Espera.
(907) 586-1911. Fax (907) 586-2332.

Tatshenshini/
Alsek, Kongakut
rivers

AD's river adventures introduce you to some of the most
remote, dramatic wilderness areas in Alaska—in the southeast on the Tatshenshini and Alsek rivers and in the north on
the Kongakut. The Tatshenshini/Alsek trip begins with a
100-mile drive from Haines to the put-in point in the Yukon.
Exhilarating stretches of Class III whitewater are interspersed
with calmer sections as the river slices through the Fairweather
and St. Elias mountains to the confluence with the Alsek, a
region flanked by glacier-laden peaks. On layovers take an
all day hike or relax in camp. Trip begins and ends in Juneau,
first and last nights in hotel. Tatshenshini 12 days, $2,150;
Alsek 14 days, $2,700. The sun will not set on the incredible

journey to the top of North America on the Kongakut River through the Arctic National Wildlife Refuge. Trip begins and ends with hotel first and last nights, and a 300-mile flight between Fairbanks and the Arctic. You land on a small gravel bar ten miles south of the Continental Divide, and set up your first camp at the headwaters of the Kongakut. Spend the next eight days paddling in inflatable Avon rafts, and hiking in this spectacular region of unforgettable grandeur—described by AD as "incomparable in sheer magnitude of wilderness." Trip is 12 days, $2,900. (See also *Sea Kayaking, Wilderness / Nature Expeditions, Combos*.)

ALASKA

Noatak, Kongakut, Hulahula rivers

ARCTIC TREKS
Box 73452-G, Fairbanks, AK 99707. Attn.: Carol Kasza and Jim Campbell. (907) 455-6502.

Arctic Treks rafts three of Alaska's great rivers: the Noatak on the north slope of the Brooks Range, and the Kongakut and Hulahula which flow north from the Arctic National Wildlife Refuge. The rivers range from smooth water to stretches of Class II or III rapids. Each person is part of the paddle crew, so previous rafting or canoeing experience is helpful but not essential. The 12-foot Avon rafts which carry two to four people plus gear are easily maneuvered and very stable. On the Noatak you float 65 miles from its headwaters in a high valley (10 days, $2,250). "Rafting the Kongakut is the classic Arctic river experience," say Jim and Carol. This fast-paced river makes for exciting paddling past startled Dall sheep and eight-foot ice shelves, and through Class III rapids in the canyon (10 days/$2,450). On the Hulahula you

Rafters inspect overflow ice— Arctic Treks, AK.

raft exhilarating whitewater in the shadow of the highest peaks of the Brooks Range. The river's pace gentles as it breaks out of the foothills into the boundless expanses of the coastal plain, and the land comes alive with musk ox and caribou (10 days/$2,300). All trips allow for hiking and exploration. Jun.–Aug. Rates include charter flights from Fairbanks. Also custom trips. (See also *Backpacking / Hiking / Walking*.)

ALASKA /
ARIZONA /
UTAH

Canning and
Tatshenshini-
Alsek rivers
(AK); Grand
Canyon (AZ);
Westwater and
Cataract canyons,
Colorado
Plateau, Green
River (UT)

COLORADO RIVER & TRAIL EXPEDITIONS

P.O. Box 57575, Salt Lake City, UT 84157-0575. Attn.: Vicki and David Mackay. (801) 261-1789 or (800) 253-7328. Fax (801) 268-1193.

The word "Trail" in this company's name signifies their emphasis on off-river hiking. Yet their trips are for people of all ages and abilities. They also emphasize "superb boatmen who are versatile chefs and intelligent interpreters of the canyon's natural history." Trips focus on rivers of the Colorado Plateau—Fisher Towers area of the Colorado, Westwater and Cataract canyons, the Green River and Grand Canyon—with rowing trips on all; also motorized rafts on Cataract and Grand Canyon Trips. You can take five-year olds (even younger) on the rollicking fun rapids of the Fisher Towers one-day trip. On Westwater Canyon (two or three days) rapids start small and end with a wild ride through Sock-It-To-Me. The five-day run through Cataract starts with a lazy float past slickrock canyons, purple mesas, orange pinnacles and pink buttes, followed by 15 miles of rapids. The spectacular trip through the Grand Canyon—motorized rafts May–September (four, six, nine days) and a rowing trip in April and August—offers lots of off-river hiking. "You can come to know the canyon up close and personal," says David. CR&T also schedules spring hiking specials on the Green and Colorado; women's, youth and senior camping trips on the Green; and early summer runs on Alaska's Canning River and Tatshenshini-Alsek. (See also *Youth.*)

ALASKA

Tatshenshini,
Alsek rivers

MOUNTAIN TRAVEL-SOBEK

6420 Fairmount Ave., El Cerrito, CA 94530-3606. (510) 527-8100 or (800) 227-2384. Fax (510) 525-7710.

"The word is *spectacular* and it was invented for the Tatshenshini," Mountain Travel-Sobek claims. Everyone who takes the trip agrees. The river bisects the St. Elias Range. Bald eagles soar overhead, grizzly bears and bull moose stalk the banks. Ice-bedecked peaks rise more than 16,000 feet. The run begins on sparkling water with Class III rapids in a constricted canyon, then the river widens when it joins the Alsek. Here glaciers press close—awesome frozen blue riv-

Fantastic ice ridges dwarf rafters in Alaska—*Bart Henderson for Mountain Travel--Sobek Expeditions, CA.*

ers and skyscraper sized chunks of ice calve from them. You spend a day scampering across the moraine onto the living face of a glacier before floating to trip's end at Dry Bay. (10 days, Jun.–Aug./$1,640.) Mountain Travel-Sobek also runs the Alsek—a seldom traveled river and perhaps the most spectacular in the Wild and Scenic System. For the first few days you ride mighty currents, hike glaciers, scout for goat and grizzlies, then come to Turnback Canyon. Here you temporarily abandon your raft and hike to view the awesome rolling turmoil in the canyon. A helicopter portages you and the raft around the notorious Turnback. Aboard the raft again, you soon reach the confluence with the Tatshenshini for a final float between calving glaciers and soaring peaks to the take-out in Dry Bay. (12 days, Jul.–Aug./$1,995.) Both trips start in Haines with a van trip to the put-ins, and end with a charter flight from Dry Bay to Yakutat.

ALASKA

**Noatak,
Kongakut,
Hulahula,
Canning,
Sheenjek and
Wind rivers**

WILDERNESS ALASKA

P.O. Box 113063, Anchorage, AK 99511. Attn.: Macgill Adams. (907) 345-3567.

"People like to participate," says Macgill Adams. He provides both oar-powered and paddle boats on each of his scheduled and custom rafting trips for eight participants "in the timeless splendor of the Brooks Range." Ranging from 7 to 15 days, all trips allow plenty of time for day hikes. A season's schedule includes, for example, trips on the Noatak, our nation's longest wilderness river; the Kongakut, an exclusively mountainside river trip; the Hulahula through a heavily glaciated region then a gentler traverse of the coastal plain; the Wind River which flows from the southern flank of the Philip Smith mountains into the northern boreal forest; the Marsh Fork of the Canning River through all of the north slopes' ecotones (mountains, foothills and coastal plain); and the Sheenjek River in autumn when the tundra is ablaze in fall colors and the evening sky is "a perfect planetarium to watch the northern lights and zillions of stars." Day hikes on the trips focus on the flora, wildlife viewing in distinct habitats and other natural features of each region. Rates range from $137 to $307/day and include group equipment, food, guiding fees and round trip transport from Fairbanks. (See also *Backpacking / Hiking / Walking*.)

Alaska's
stupenduous
beauty—*Macgill
Adams© 1987 for
Wilderness Alaska.*

ARIZONA

**Colorado River
(Grand Canyon)**

ARA'S WILDERNESS RIVER ADVENTURES
P.O. Box 717, Page, AZ 86040. For downriver trips (800) 992-8022.

Wilderness River Adventures is a veteran river-running company with its roots in the first commercial whitewater operation in the Grand Canyon. They offer both motorized and oar-powered trips through the Grand Canyon—4–6 days from Lees Ferry to Phantom Ranch, 5-7 days Phantom Ranch to Bar Ten Ranch, 7–14 days Lees Ferry to Bar Ten Ranch. Whether you take the quicker motorized trip or spend more time in the canyon on oar-powered rafts, "What better way can you imagine to experience and appreciate the rare beauty of the Grand Canyon?" queries ARA manager Dave Neuburger. "We've got the experience it takes to make every river trip safe, smooth-running, comfortable and action-packed." Rates for motorized and oar-powered trips, Lees Ferry to Phantom Ranch $550/$908; Lees Ferry to Bar Ten $1,289/$1,786; Phantom Ranch to Bar Ten $1,131/$1,369. ARA also offers a 1-day float from Glen Canyon Dam to Lees Ferry, $38. (See also *Boats / Cruises / Scuba.*)

**Rafting through
monumental
beauty in the
Grand Canyon—**
*ARA's Wilderness
River Adventures,
AZ.*

ARIZONA

**Colorado River
(Grand Canyon,
AZ), Salmon
River (ID), Baja
California
(Mexico), Costa
Rica packages**

ARIZONA RAFT ADVENTURES, INC.
4050-A E. Huntington Dr., Flagstaff, AZ 86004. Attn.: Robert Elliott. (602) 526-8200 or (800) 786-7238. Fax (602) 526-8246.

"Participation and diversity are what distinguish us from the other outfitters who run the Grand Canyon," remarks Rob Elliott. The emphasis is on involvement: rowing, paddling, hiking, swimming the small rapids, helping in the kitchen, learning the natural history and flat-out relaxing—do as much or as little as you want. AzRA's Grand Canyon trips begin and end in Flagstaff: 8 days motorized/$1,208 and 6-14 days paddle- and oar-powered $1,086-$2,064, Apr.-Oct., with discounts for early-season trips, repeat customers and group charters. Other trips Jun.-Aug. include 6 days on the Middle Fork of Idaho's Salmon/$895+; 5-6 days on the Main Salmon/ $710+; or both trips combined, 11-12 days/$1,540+. AzRA offers a special 9-day Costa Rica package year-round/$889 air, to run rivers and explore rain forests.

Discovering the exhilaration of oar-powered rafting—
Arizona Raft Adventures, AZ.

ARIZONA

Colorado River (Grand Canyon)

GRAND CANYON DORIES
P.O. Box 216, Altaville, CA 95221. (209) 736.0805.

The spectacular dory, a compartmented rough-water, motorless boat of aluminum, Fiberglas, or taut marine plywood, has been used on the world's waterways for millenia. "It rides higher and drier than a raft, and doesn't bend or buckle in the waves or get soft when it's cold," explains George Wendt, owner. There's a guide in each boat, but participants may take the oars and learn to run the rapids or risk all on one of the two-person inflatable kayaks. George believes in small groups—16 maximum per trip. He also feels his expeditions are for people who want a longer, slower, quieter voyage than most with time to observe, understand and savor the Canyon—not only from the water, but also on land. The full

Dories below Diamond Peak in the Grand Canyon—*Martin Litton for Grand Canyon Dories, CA.*

trip takes 16 days and costs $2658. Partial trips 5–11 days, $909–$2003. All trips put in at Lees Ferry or Phantom Ranch. Take-out points vary according to trip length. Meet at and return to Flagstaff. "It would be very hard to ride a raft down the Colorado once you have been down in a dory," comments one happy traveler.

ARIZONA

Colorado River (Grand Canyon)

GRAND CANYON EXPEDITIONS CO.
Dept. AG, P.O. Box O, Kanab, UT 84741. Attn.: Mike Denoyer. (801) 644-2691 or (800) 544-2691. Fax (801) 644-2699.

On 8-day motorized raft trips and 14-day oar-powered dory and raft trips, GCE runs the entire 277 miles of the Grand Canyon from Lees Ferry to Pearce Ferry. In "first-class comfort" and safety, you negotiate nearly 200 exciting rapids, passing through one of the world's most spectacular geological exhibits. "Everyone who experiences the Grand Canyon is deeply affected by it," says Mike Denoyer. For more than 25 years, GCE has run trips for special groups including National Geographic Society, Smithsonian Institution, Chicago Field Museum of Natural History, World Cinemax and others. Special interest expeditions highlight canyon history, geology, photography, ecology, archaeology and astronomy. Rates: 8-day motorized trips/$1,595, 14-day oar-powered trip/ $2,295. Apr.–Sep. Charter rates. Arrival point: Las Vegas, NV.

They all made it!— *Grand Canyon Expeditions, AZ.* (photo next page).

ARIZONA

**Colorado River
(Grand Canyon)**

OUTDOORS UNLIMITED

*6900 Townsend-Winona Rd., Flagstaff, AZ 86004. Attn.: John Vail.
(602) 525-9834 or (800) 637-7238.*

"Hear only the splash of oars and the rumble of the river as
we guide you to places we have come to love, and enjoy the
tranquil, reflective stillness that only the wild places can
provide," John Vail writes. His oar- and paddle-powered
boats carry a guide and five participants through the Grand
Canyon of the Colorado from Lees Ferry to Lake Mead in 12
days ($1,896), 5 days Lees Ferry to Phantom Ranch ($968), 8
days Phantom Ranch to Lake Mead ($1,469). Paddle options
on these trips (everyone paddles) are slightly more. For trips
starting at Lees Ferry, rates include overnight at Marble
Canyon prior to trip, and shuttle to Las Vegas for trips ending
at Lake Mead. Discounts for charters and children under 13.
May–October. Camping equipment supplied.

*ARIZONA /
IDAHO / UTAH*

**Grand Canyon,
Westwater,
Cataract canyons,
Green, Main
Salmon rivers**

WESTERN RIVER EXPEDITIONS

*7258 Racquet Club Drive, Salt Lake City, UT 84121. (801) 942-6669 or
(800) 453-7450. Fax (801) 942-8514.*

With 35 years of experience running rivers, WRE considers
its trips fun, relaxing, exciting and full of adventure. It now
is the nation's largest rafting vacation company, guiding
5,000 guests a year through spectacular canyons. WRE takes
pride in its camping cuisine, and in the fact that 80% of its
guests are referred by others who have been on their trips.
More than half come back for a trip another year. The Colo-

Always a spectacu-
lar run—*Western
River Expeditions,
AZ / ID / UT.*

rado River System is at the heart of the expeditions. Motorized trips through the Grand Canyon take six days for the
Upper Canyon and three or four days in the Lower Canyon,
with helicopter transfer to or from the river below Lava Falls.
They schedule one 12-day rowing trip in the Grand Canyon
each season. Oar-powered trips through Westwater Canyon,
and on the Green and Main Salmon rivers and a motorized trip
in Cataract Canyon vary from three to six days. Trips scheduled
May to Sep. Rates average $78–$191 per day (higher on Grand
Canyon trips), and on some rivers are less for under 17 years.

COLORADO

Arkansas,
Gunnison, San
Miguel, Piedra,
Gore Canyon or
the Colorado

ECHO CANYON RIVER EXPEDITIONS, INC.

*45000 U.S. Hwy. 50 West, CañonCity, CO 81212. Attn.: Kim and David
Burch. (719) 275-3154 or (800) 748-2953. [Oct.–Mar.: 45000 U.S. Hwy.
50 West, CañonCity, CO 81212.]*

Choose between paddles (group participation) and oars (hang
on and enjoy!) on half- and full-day whitewater rafting adventures down the Arkansas River above and through the
Royal Gorge (Apr.–Sep./$43–$76). This stretch of the Arkansas is famous for steep drops and continuous whitewater,

and 15 years min. age is recommended; whereas the Parkdale section, with full- and half-day trips on Class III water ($19–$59) is suited for families. The Gunnison River Gorge, with its tranquil calms, intense rapids and some of the most amazing scenery in Colorado, is another ECRX specialty: May, Jun., Sep. (1 day/$95, 2 days/$210, 3 days/$310). ECRX also runs the San Miguel which rolls out of Telluride, a good early season trip, (2 days/$155–$170) and the Piedra (2 days/$250) and Gore Canyon of the Colorado River (1 day/$125). Also evening float fishing and "ducky" trips (1-man inflatable kayaks) for experienced paddlers. Weekday, group and children's discounts.

COLORADO

WILDERNESS AWARE RAFTING

P.O. Box 1550A, Buena Vista, CO 81211. Attn.: Joe or Susan Greiner. (719) 395-2112 or (800) 462-7238.

Arkansas, Dolores, Gunnison, North Platte, Upper Colorado, Animas, Piedra rivers

"We are a quality-minded organization and enjoy running personalized trips," says Joe Greiner. Wilderness Aware has run trips on Colorado rivers since 1976. They take no more than 18 participants (and as few as 4) on multi-day trips, up to ten days, and pull into camp in time for hiking and relaxing before dinner, with evenings around the fire. On half- and 1-day trips, they prefer small groups—no minimum—but can handle large groups on request. Trips vary from family whitewater and guided float fishing to rough water for the more adventurous. The Greiners have thoroughly experienced guides and use top-of-the-line Avon boats in three size classes to make every water level fun.

Ready to make camp—*Wilderness Aware, CO.*

Those who want to have a hand in the action choose a paddle raft and become part of the crew. If you prefer less action, choose an oar raft where the guide does the rowing. On Class II and III sections of multi-day trips, long and skinny inflatable kayaks are provided for exploring nooks and crannies. Wilderness Aware runs seven Colorado rivers—the Arkansas, Dolores, Gunnison, North Platte, Upper Colorado, Animas and Piedra. May through Sep. Rates: $60/1 day, $175/2 days, $259/3 days, $499/6 days, $799/10 days. Group and family discounts.

IDAHO

Snake, Middle Fork of Salmon, Bruneau, Owyhee, Main Salmon rivers

HUGHES RIVER EXPEDITIONS, INC.

P.O. Box 217, Cambridge, ID 83610. Attn.: Jerry Hughes & Carole Finley. (208) 257-3477.

Hughes River Expeditions is a small, owner-operator style business that specializes in personalized service. They offer both scheduled and custom trips on Idaho rivers—Snake, Middle Fork of the Salmon, Bruneau, Owyhee and Main Salmon. "All flow through isolated backcountry, and each offers intense natural beauty, whitewater, solitude and a variety of wildlife," promises Jerry Hughes. He considers two aspects of a river trip especially important—the food and the river equipment. Fantastic meals feature marinated steaks, salmon, game hens, Dutch-oven baking and fresh fruits. Their boats include oar rafts, paddle rafts, inflatable kayaks, McKenzie drift boats and custom-designed supply pontoons. There's time to explore long-abandoned cabins, mines and Indian sites, and their "river library" lets you bone up on pioneers. Fishing is varied and excellent. Snake River through Hells Canyon, 3–5 days, $505–$960. Middle Fork of the Salmon (Idaho's most famous wilderness river), 5–6 days, May–Sep., $1,010–$1,200. Salmon River Canyon, "a superb family river vacation," 4 days, Jul. and Aug., $785 (10% youth discount). The little-known Bruneau Canyonlands (2 dates in June, limited to 10 guests and 5 guides—"a local Idaho secret"—4 days, $1,020. Special river fishing trips also arranged. All equipment provided.

IDAHO

Snake and Salmon rivers

IDAHO AFLOAT

P.O. Box 542, Grangeville, ID 83530. Attn.: Scott Fasken. (208) 983-2414.

Enthusiastic participants talk about the wonderful food on Scott Fasken's trips on the Snake and Salmon rivers in Idaho, and knowledgeable guides who set up tents and lawn chairs on the beach for rafters who soon know the comforts of luxurious camping! "Our guests are looking for several days of rest and relaxation," Scott says. "They want to be pampered on their vacation, and that's what we specialize in." His cargo raft floats ahead of the others, and by the time guests arrive at their campsite tents, chairs and duffels are in place and a deluxe dinner is ready to serve, starting for example with hors d'oeuvres and ending with cheesecake topped with strawberries. For special family trips in the Salmon River Gorge, a large playground bag provides the kids with frisbees, baseball, turbo footballs, kites and tools for building sand castles. In July the second child in a family comes free. For a wilderness journey, the Salmon River is Scott's choice with its Class III water and big, white sand beaches. For powerful whitewater, good fishing and energetic canyon hikes he recommends the Snake through Hells Canyon. For the "ultimate adventure" he combines three days on the Snake with three days of horseback riding in the mountains about the river, a six-day combo. Trips scheduled June to early September. Rates: $400/2 days, $600/3 days, $800/4 days, $1,100/6-day combo. Meeting point: Lewiston or Boise, ID.

Oar boat guides rafters on Idaho's Middle Ford—*Jay Krajic for Middle Fork River Expeditions, ID.*

IDAHO

Middle Fork of Salmon River

MIDDLE FORK RIVER EXPEDITIONS
P.O. Box 199, Stanley, ID 83278. Attn.: Patrick and Jean Ridle. (208) 774-3659. [Winter: 1615 21st Ave. East, Seattle, WA 98112. (206) 324-0364.]

"Come float in uninterrupted solitude through lands explored by Lewis & Clark," urge the Ridles. They call their Middle Fork trip the ultimate whitewater adventure. "We provide a first class adventure with true western hospitality and personalized service, gourmet food with home-baked delights, the only champagne brunch on the river and a farewell banquet at trip's end. Guests from 6 to 85 years have enjoyed our trips." They use oar and paddle boats and inflatable kayaks. You're off the river each afternoon with plenty of time for hiking, soaking in natural hot springs, trout fishing, exploring for Shoshone petroglyphs, swimming—or just savoring the pure mountain air. Arrive in historic Stanley by car or by air service from Boise the night before your trip to get acquainted and ready for the river. Jun.–Sep., 3- and 6-day trips, $650–$1050. Children and group rates. "Very professional, well organized, great food," reports a happy guest.

IDAHO

Main Salmon, Snake, Owyhee, Grande Ronde rivers

NORTHWEST VOYAGEURS
P.O. Box 373, Lucile, ID 83542. Attn.: Jeff or Carol Peavey. (208) 628-3021 or (800) 727-9977. Fax (208) 628-3780.

Grab the paddles and assault the rapids in a variety of watercraft, including whitewater dories, oar rafts, paddle rafts, inflatable kayaks or canoes. "In the wilderness backcountry, what you thought might be an interesting sight turns out to be an overwhelming experience. There simply aren't words to describe the feeling," says Jeff. "Your senses come alive. The groups of adventurers are small, personal and above all, friendly. The company is good. The food is wonderful. The thrill is unimaginable." Jeff offers half-day to five-day trips on the Main Salmon, and three- or six-day trips on the Snake, Owyhee or the Grande Ronde. Custom fishing and river trips also arranged. "I really felt the guides cared about us as people, and I knew they were concerned about our safety and that we had the best time possible on the river, and we did," reports one recent guest. Spring/fall rates $495/3 days, $675/5 days, $790/6 days. Summers rates $550, $750, $850. (See also *Combo Trips*.)

IDAHO

Snake, Salmon, Lochsa, Moyie, Owyhee, St. Joe rivers

RIVERS ODYSSEYS WEST (ROW)
P.O. Box 579-AN, Coeur d'Alene, ID 83814. Attn.: Peter Grubb. (208) 765-0841 or (800) 451-6034.

"The rivers we float flow free, unregulated by dams, except for the Snake," explains Peter Grubb. "We start trips on the Moyie, Owyhee and Lochsa in late April when the snows melt. The Middle Fork of the Salmon has its highest water in June, with medium flows in July and August, and is nice in

Rafts beached at
campsite with a
glorious view—
*River Odysseys West,
ID.*

September when fall colors begin to show. The Snake is good
April through September." ROW's trip information fills you
in with how to get to the put-in, suggested reading and a full
description of each run. Paddle rafts and inflatable kayaks
encourage participation. Family trips are a specialty—"re-
unions with shared activities, great food, playtime and the
chance just to sit and catch up," says Peter. Established in
1979, ROW runs more Idaho rivers than other companies,
and has added walking tours of Hells Canyon to its trips.
Season: Apr.–Sep., from $150/day up for 3- to 6-day trips,
also 1-day trips, youth discounts.

IDAHO

**Middle Fork of
Salmon River**

ROCKY MOUNTAIN RIVER TOURS

*P.O. Box 520-AG, Eagle, ID 83616. Attn.: Dave & Sheila Mills.
(208) 345-2400.*

RMRT describes the Middle Fork of the Salmon as wild,
untamed, rugged and awesome as it rips through 105 miles
of inaccesible, primitive country. They use new Riken
whitewater rafts, paddle boats and inflatable kayaks, all self-
bailers. "Our tours," explains Dave, "allow time for hiking,

fishing, birdwatching and swimming, as well as discovery of the area's wildlife and historic legacy—abandoned mines, remote homesteads and Indian pictographs." Families, including grandparents, are especially welcome. Sheila whips up dishes like chicken/feta with tomato linguini, shitake mushroom lasagna and grilled salmon, recipes which are reported in her new *Rocky Mountain Kettle Cuisine II*. Start and end in Stanley. Rates: 6 days, $1195; 4 days, $775; 3 days, $825; Jun.–Sep. Children and group discounts. Private charter groups arranged.

IDAHO

Main Salmon River

SALMON RIVER OUTFITTERS
P.O. Box 1751, McCall, ID 83638. Reservations/Information: P.O. Box 32, Arnold, CA 95223. Attn.: Steven Shephard. (209) 795-4041.

Float Idaho's fabled Main Salmon in fabled comfort. This outfit's six-day, 80-mile river trip in oar boats, paddle boats or inflatable kayaks has been called by one travel expert, "the best river-rafting adventure in America." Offered only twice a month, June through September, "so as to give each group our full attention," Steven Shephard explains, the trip combines the rugged scenery of roadless wilderness with emphasis on comfortable camping and exceptionally good eating. All trips start with the first night at a riverside guest lodge. The equipment provided at camps on sandy beaches includes roomy dome tents, camp chairs and sheet-lined sleeping bags. Food that materializes from streamside ovens includes

"You will not lose weight!"—*Steven Shephard for Salmon River Outfitters, ID.*

chicken enchiladas, fresh salmon, handcranked ice cream and banana walnut buttermilk pancakes embellished with yogurt topping chunky with coconut, walnuts and dates. You will not lose weight. Several five-and six-day specialty trips scheduled through the season focus on Salmon River lore, wine tasting, folktales spun by a harpist/storyteller or trips staying each night at wilderness lodges. Rates: 5 days, $1,070; 6 days, $1,260. (See also *Wilderness / Nature Expeditions*.)

MAINE

Kennebec,
Penobscot, Dead
(ME), Hudson,
Moose (NY)
rivers

UNICORN RAFTING EXPEDITIONS, INC.

P.O. Box T, Brunswick, ME 04011. Attn.: Jay Schurman. (207) 725-2255 or (800) 864-2676. Fax (207) 725-2573.

"The Kennebec, Penobscot, and Hudson rivers are now recognized as the premier whitewater rivers in eastern America," claims Jay Schurman. "We've combined western- and eastern-style rafting and give each participant first-class, individual treatment—including gourmet meals with steaks on one-day trips and lobster on our overnight expeditions." Day-trip packages include lakefront cabins at Schurman's lodge and kids' rafting on the lower Kennebec for free. Schurman offers a wide variety of trips to suit everyone: families, singles, groups, first-timers or experienced river runners. For exploring the Maine wilderness, plus riverside camping with friendly companions, Unicorn offers two-, five-, six-day river adventures. For experienced rafters seeking a real challenge—"a highly exciting and dangerous river"— Unicorn recommends its one-day Moose River (NY) run. Still

Everybody
paddles—*Unicorn
Rafting Expeditions,
Inc., ME.*

fun but less demanding is the 1-day Hudson run. Rates for 1-to 6-day trips: $65–$565. See photo on page 164.

MONTANA

Flathead River

MONTANA RAFT COMPANY
Box 535N, West Glacier, MT 59936. Attn.: Randy Gayner. (406) 888-5466 or (800) 521-7238.

Picture yourself drifting along one of Glacier National Park's Wild and Scenic rivers. Enjoy forested canyons, meadows ablaze with wildflowers, mountains soaring skyward and the occasional splash of whitewater, with excellent opportunities for wildlife viewing: deer, moose, elk, or maybe a bear or river otter. Participate in paddling the raft if you like, or you can just relax. Trips on the North and Middle Forks of the Flathead, one to four days. Camp along the riverbanks, enjoy hearty meals with hiking and fishing stops throughout. Custom trips, any size group, large or small. Strictly fishing trips also available. Half-day rates $29; 3–1/2 days, $310; 12 and under child rates. (See also *Backpacking / Hiking / Walking, Combos*—Glacier Wilderness Guides.)

Drifting a Wild & Scenic river in Glacier Nat'l Park—*Montana Raft Company, MT.*

NEW YORK/ VIRGINIA

Hudson, Moose (NY), Cheat (WV) rivers

WHITEWATER WORLD, LTD.
Rt. 903, Jim Thorpe, PA 18229. Attn.: Paul Fogal. (717) 325-3656.

Whitewater World has complete rafting facilities on three great rivers in New York State and West Virginia. "Each river offers its own brand of raw adventure in a remote wilderness setting," says Paul Fogal. "Either they offer rumbling, frothing, surging currents; slam-bang rapids that thunder through towering gorges; or unexpected swirls, rises and plunges…" You can raft the Hudson River Gorge in the Eastern Adirondack

Slam-bang
rapids—*Whitewater
World, Ltd., PA.*

Mountains starting near Indian Lake, NY in April, May, September or October; day rate, $70. Or choose the Moose River in early spring. In northern West Virginia the Cheat River offers still more excitement with its 35 separate, diverse rapids. "It has more rapids in its 12-mile stretch than any other river in the East," notes Fogal. April and May, day rate, $63. Youth rates, group discounts for 15 or more.

*NORTH
CAROLINA*

NANTAHALA OUTDOOR CENTER

13077 Hwy 19 West, Bryson City, NC 28713-9114. (800) 232-7238. Fax (704) 488-2498.

Nantahala,
French Broad,
Ocoee,
Chattooga,
Nolichucky
rivers

NOC offers rafting on whitewater rivers in the southern Appalachians. No experience required for any of the guided trips. Near Great Smoky Mountains National Park, the Nantahala River offers a delightful Class II and III taste of whitewater for beginners and families. Experienced paddlers can rent rafts ($12–$16/person) and inflatable "ducks" ($27 for one person, $40 for two). Guided trips ($19–$25/day. Another ideal river for family rafting is the French Broad, which winds through a gorge in Pisgah National Forest. (Half-day trip/$29–$32, full day/$37–$47.) A favorite of many, the Ocoee is exciting, with big waves and almost constant action ($29–$37). NOC runs trips on two sections of the wild and scenic Chattooga River: Section 3, easy-to-moderate, popular with youth groups and families ($45–$59); and Section 4, one of the most thrilling and difficult whitewater runs in the Southeast ($56–$76). A spectacular free-flowing river, the Nolichucky rivals the excitement of any river in the East during spring high water ($48–$64). Guided "duck" trips offered when water levels drop in late spring and summer. Weekday and group discounts. (See also *Cycling / Mountain Biking*—Carolina Cycle Tours, *Canoeing / Kayaking, Combos*.)

PENNSYLVANIA

KITTATINNY CANOES

Dept. AT, Dingmans Ferry, PA 18328. Attn.: Ruth Jones. (717) 828-2338 or (800) 356-2852.

Delaware River

"Run the rapids of the Delaware in crystal-clear water beneath spectacular cliffs," urges Kittatinny, located in the Pocono Mountains a few hours from Philadelphia, New York or Connecticut. You're on your own in a paddleraft—just right for families, youth groups and scouts since no rafting experience is necessary. Choose your stretch of river along 120 miles where Kittatinny has locations, and camp at their two fully equipped campgrounds. They offer shuttle service, family specials and barbecues for 20 or more paddlers during a season lasting from mid-April through October. Rates depending on number in group range from $16–$21 per person weekdays, slightly higher weekends. (See also *Canoeing / Kayaking*.)

UTAH

ADRIFT ADVENTURES

P.O. Box 577, Moab, UT 84532. Attn.: Myke Hughes. (801) 259-8594 or (800) 874-4483. Fax (801) 259-7628.

Cataract & Desolation/Gray canyons

Myke Hughes runs everyone's favorite rivers in Utah's Canyonlands. Choose Cataract Canyon of the Colorado River through Canyonlands National Park for a three- or four-day motorized or a five-day oar-powered trip—especially wild and exciting in May and June. with spring run-offs ($399–$599 including charter flight). A four-day run through Desolation and Gray canyons of the Green River is a popular family adventure ($415). Labyrinth Canyon of the Green offers a wilderness wonderland for rafting or canoeing—no rapids on the 45-mile section past sandstone cliffs and sculptured landscapes (3 days, $395). Also, half- and full-day trips on the Colorado ($26–$35). Discounts on all trips for kids. Arrival: Grand Junction or Salt Lake City. (See also *Combos*.)

UTAH/ COLORADO

ADVENTURE BOUND, INC.

River Expeditions, 2392 H Road, Grand Junction, CO 81505. Attn.: Tom Kleinschnitz. (303) 241-5633 or (800) 423-4668. Fax (303) 241-5633.

Westwater, Desolation, Cataract, Lodore; Green & Yampa rivers; Dinosaur Natl. Monument

In business since 1963, Adventure Bound offers river enthusiasts five of the most popular trips in the West—Westwater Canyon (Colorado River), Green River Wilderness (Desolation and Gray canyons), Cataract Canyon (Colorado River), each with Grand Junction, CO as the starting and ending

A tranquil moment in Dinosaur National Monument—*Adventure Bound, UT.*

point. Also the Lodore Canyon (Green River) and the Yampa and Green rivers, both trips winding through the Dinosaur National Monument with meeting point in Steamboat Springs. Most trips are scheduled three to five days, May to September, with charters April and October/November. Westwater is a one- or two-day trip. Rates average $85/day. Adventure Bound uses oar, paddle and large pontoon boats, and inflatable kayaks—important for mixing experienced rafters with those new to the sport. Emphasis is on fulfilling individual goals—hiking a side canyon, kayaking the rapids, swimming the river, socializing, unwinding or immersion in the region's rich history, wildlife and geology. "A good combination of safety, excitement and fun with guides who are competent and personable,"writes a participant.

UTAH

Yampa and Green rivers

DINOSAUR RIVER EXPEDITIONS

P.O. Box 3387, Park City, UT 84060. Attn.: Tim Mertens. (801) 649-8092 or (800) 247-6197. Fax (801) 649-8126.

Trips on the Yampa and Green rivers, both within Dinosaur National Monument, are the specialty of this outfitter, in

Whitewater on the
Yampa—*Dinosaur
River Expeditions,
UT.*

business since 1979. "We are a small, dedicated company," says Tim, "and keep our trips small, normally under 18 people, so we can pay a lot of attention to each one. Our guides are experts on the flora, fauna, geology and history of this part of the country." DRE schedules one trip a week, from three to five days, and includes a chartered scenic flight from Vernal to the river put-in. Meet at the DRE office in Vernal about 9 a.m. on the day of the trip for transport to the Vernal Airport for the flight. At the end of each trip DRE takes you back to the Vernal office. Oar-powered inflatable rafts from 14–18 feet carry three to four participants. One or two inflatable kayaks (rubber duckies) on each trip add fun in smaller rapids and challenge in large ones. Trips May–Sep., $395/3 days, $495/4 days, $595/5 days, including scenic flight to put-in. Children's rates (8–12) available. DRE also offers a two-day whitewater trip including a scenic ground tour to the put-in, as well as one day jeep tours, mountain bike tours and guided horseback trail rides. (See also *Fly Fishing*—Old Moe Guide Service.)

UTAH/IDAHO

Green, Yampa,
Colorado, (UT)
Middle Fork of
Salmon (ID)

DON & MEG HATCH RIVER EXPEDITIONS
Box 1150, 55 E. Main, Vernal, UT 84078. Attn.: Don and Meg Hatch. (801) 789-4316 or (800) 342-8243. Fax (801) 789-4126.

In 1929 Bus Hatch pioneered the first commercial whitewater business in the U.S. Over 60 years later, the Hatch family is still running rivers. Trips through Cataract Canyon of the Colorado, which slices its way through Canyonlands Na-

Still fun after 60 years of river running—*Brad Hatch for Don & Meg Hatch River Expeditions, UT / ID.*

tional Park in Utah, start and end in Grand Junction with transport to the put-in and a flight back from Hite Marina; four & five days, $550 to $650. A fully packaged 6-day trip on the Middle Fork of the Salmon (Idaho) includes air charters from Boise to trip's start in Stanley and return from town of Salmon at trip's end, $1150. Hatch recommends as ideal for beginners and families the Dinosaur trip on the Yampa and Green rivers, starting and ending in Vernal (Utah), 3, 4, & 5 days, $395 to $600. His daily Dinosaur excursion from Vernal he calls the best one-day trip in the country, $55. Oar- and paddle-powered rafts as well as inflatable kayaks are provided on all trips; April–September. "Know-how, experience and quality" are stated traditions of the Hatch family.

UTAH

Desolation Canyon

HONDOO RIVERS & TRAILS

P.O. Box 98, Torrey, UT 84775. Attn.: Pat or Gary George. (801) 425-3519 or (800) 332-2696.

"The greatest fun in river running is rowing or paddling your own boat," says Pat George who leads each of Hondoo's trips through Desolation Canyon of the Green River in Utah. With warm water and rapids that are gentle at the Sand Wash put-in, increasing in turbulence as you continue downstream, Pat considers this the perfect stretch of water for novice and intermediate kayakers. On seven-day trips, the Aspen Kayak School provides instruction ($730). Hondoo also offers six-day oar-powered raft trips ideal for families, with inflatable kayaks and paddle boats for those who want them ($660).

Off-river activities add to the fun of running the Green, Pat points out—hiking and exploring side canyons, and seeing historical and archaeological sites. Trips begin and end in the town of Green River, and rates include a pre-trip motel night and flight to the put-in. (See also *Pack Trips, Wilderness / Nature Expeditions, Cattle Drives*—Pace Ranch.)

A paddle raft in Desolation Canyon—*Hondoo Rivers & Trails, UT.*

UTAH

Colorado & Green rivers

SHERI GRIFFITH EXPEDITIONS

P.O. Box 1324, Moab, UT 84532. (801) 259-8229 or (800) 332-2439. Fax (801) 259-2226.

Soft on risk, yet high on adventure! The challenging whitewater of the Cataract and Westwater canyons of the Colorado River and the deep, historic Desolation Canyon of the Green are the settings for Sheri Griffith's two- to five-day journeys. Promising both thrills *and* pampering and using paddle and oar boats, the trips are designed for adventure seekers and canyon lovers. For Colorado River trips min. age is ten, Green River is five; (for 5-16 year-olds, rates are about 1/3 less.) (Cataract trips, 3–5 days, $542–$694. Westwater, 2–3 days, $278–$393. Green, 4–5 days, $397–$694. Scheduled May–Aug.) "Have you ever wanted to send the kids to camp and you go too?" Sheri asks. One of her specials is a five-day family trip on the Green River. "Families play together and learn together," she says. "Rafting is a team sport." Special trips include some for women only, sharing comradeship, adventure and education; personal and professional development seminars for adults; and a Cataract luxury trips with a canyonland sunset as your waiter flambés your dessert! (See also *Combos.*)

A luxurious twist—elegant riverside dining—*Sheri Griffith Expeditions, UT.*

UTAH

Cataract, Westwater, Desolation canyons

TAG-A-LONG EXPEDITIONS

425 North Main St., Moab, Ut 84532. Attn.: Bob Jones. (801) 259-8946 or (800) 453-3292. Fax (801) 259-8990.

"Variety…beginner to veteran, there's a Tag-A-Long expedition just right for you," says Bob Jones. For major class whitewater enthusiasts Cataract Canyon during high water season offers guests a "Grand Canyon" class whitewater experience in just three or four days—and for only a third the cost (4 days/$680, 3 days/$595). For the best in a brief adventure offering major class whitewater action, join our Westwater Canyon *Rapid Escape*. "Regardless of the water level, you'll go face to face with some of the Colorado's finest whitewater," assures Bob (2 days/$350). Combine the Westwater and Cataract Canyon expeditions, add a half-day land exploration of Arches National Park and an overnight and hot shower at a Moab Motel—that's *Rapids, Rapids, Rapids* (6 days/$980). For novice or experienced paddlers, master your own inflatable kayak or join our guided raft and shoot the magnificent rapids of the Green River through Desolation Canyon. Perfect for families, first-timers or experienced boaters, you enjoy rapids every day—some 50 in total (5 days/$585). New! *Wilderness Accent Expeditions* offer extended explorations with a special focus on geology, natural history, desert biomes and ancient to present Indian culture and ceremony. Each *Wilderness Accent Expedition* is led by an expert in the field, from naturalists to archaeologists. All Tag-A-Long expeditions begin and end in either

Water, water everywhere—*Tag-A-Long Expeditions, UT.*

Moab or Grand Junction, CO.; discounts for children; half-day and one-day rafting also offered. (See also *Van / Jeep / Rail, Ski Touring.*)

WEST VIRGINIA / TEXAS

New, Gauley, Rio Grande rivers

CLASS VI RIVER RUNNERS, INC.
P.O. Box 78, Ames Heights Road, Lansing, WV 25862. (304) 574-0704 or (800) 252-7784. Fax (304) 574-4906.

"America's most condensed area of challenging and diverse whitewater" is Class VI's description of West Virginia's New and Gauley rivers. With rapids named "Mash" and "Heaven Help You," you know you're in for some big water. "We run small, personal trips in paddle-powered rafts, oar boats, self-bailers or non-self-bailing rafts. The choice is yours. Our guides are highly qualified and our meals are the best." You can go rafting, paddle a ducky, fish, swim, do-it-all on beautiful rivers that offer something for everyone. Rates: New River, 1 day / $34-$88, 3-6 days / $90 per day; Upper or Lower Gauley, 1 day / $79-$161. A 2-day trip on the Gauley ($192-$244) includes all river equipment, four hearty meals and 100 major rapids. "It's man against the elements in their rawest form," writes a three-time veteran of Class VI trips. "One reaps a rare sense of satisfaction." Class VI has added a Kids Care program—excellent day care at very affordable prices—so they can have as much fun as you'll be having out on the river. Also offers custom trips including float fishing, horseback riding/rafting combos, kayak clinics, plus three- to nine-day Rio Grande River trips, November to April, $225-$699.

WEST
VIRGINIA

NORTH AMERICAN RIVER RUNNERS, INC.
P.O. Box 81, Hico, WV 25854-0081. Attn.: Frank Lukacs. (304) 658-5276 or (800) 950-2585. Fax (304) 658-4212.

Cheat, Upper & Lower Gauley, New, Upper Youghiogheny rivers

"A quality river trip at a reasonable price," says President Frank Lukacs, "is what NARR is all about." In addition to state-of-the-art equipment, North American has one of the most intensive guide training programs in the East. NARR runs one- and two-day trips in four to ten person rafts through spectacular mountain gorges on some of America's best whitewater. There are runs through awesome Class III to V water—the Cheat Canyon Apr.–May, the churning, continuous Upper Gauley and the turbulent Lower Gauley, Sep.–Oct., and the immense New River Gorge May–Oct. Also the Upper Youghiogheny, not a beginner's river, Class V–VI water, weekdays Apr.–Oct. Daily rates start at $52. (See also *Canoeing / Kayaking*.)

A cozy camp—
Canadian River
Expeditions, B.C.

BRITISH
COLUMBIA /
ALASKA /
YUKON

CANADIAN RIVER EXPEDITIONS
40-3524 W. 16th Ave., Vancouver, BC, Canada V6R 3C1. (604) 738-4449. Fax (604) 736-5526.

Chilcotin, Tatshenshini, Alsek and Firth rivers

"There's tremendous diversity in the wilds of BC, Alaska and the Yukon," explains John Mikes who has outfitted trips in this region for more than 20 years. "On our river expeditions we see enormous glaciers, towering mountains, forests, wildlife, fjords, tundra and lots more. It's an incredible classroom on ecosystems and biology." He uses oar-powered rafts for river travel. His 12-day Tatshenshini and Alsek expeditions start and end in Whitehorse and include three layover days to explore, hike, climb onto glaciers and soak in the superb scenery ($2,295). The Alsek run includes an exciting helicopter portage of Turnback Canyon. To get to the put-in for an 11-day Chilcotin-Fraser expedition ($2,325), you travel from Vancouver by bus, ferry, yacht and seaplane to Chilko Lake, high in the coastal mountains, then raft 200 miles through the heart of BC, ending with a funky train ride back to Vancouver. Still another of Mikes' special trips is an 11-day Firth River and Herschel Island expedition in the Northern Yukon National Park ($2,650). He calls it a "wildlife spectacular." You'll see dozens of moose, muskoxen, grizzlies, foxes, Dall sheep and other wildlife and with luck 10,000 or more caribou on their annual migration. Trips Jun., Jul., Aug. for 11–20 participants; min. age 10. (See also *Wilderness / Nature Expeditions.*)

ONTARIO

Ottawa River

WILDERNESS TOURS

Box 89, Beachburg, ONT., Canada K0J 1C0. Attn.: Terry Hierlihy. (613) 646-2291 or (800) 267-9166. Fax (613) 646-2996.

Spectacular scenery and big wild rapids characterize the majestic Ottawa River. It offers a unique combination of warm water and powerful rapids all summer long. Just 75 miles west of Ottawa, this whitewater paradise is in easy driving distance of major northeast population centers. Day trips through the river's untamed wilderness with its big

Running the Ottawa River—
Wilderness Tours, Ontario.

waves, haystacks and hydraulics guarantee wet smiles. Whitewater mini-vacations cover two diverse routes with new rapids each day. During May–June high water the trip combines paddle rafting with 38' Colorado-style motorized boats. In the summer the traditional guided trip is offered, along with a unique guide-your-own raft program— with six paddlers per raft and guides alongside in kayaks. The company also offers jet boating on the Niagara River as well as the Lachine River in Montreal, Quebec, a ski tour in April to British Columbia and wild jungle rafting in Costa Rica in November. Rates for Ontario-based tours average $60–$80 US per day, with accommodations at $11 US per tent to $85 US per chalet. "I truly appreciate when an organization has tremendous people skills," says one recent participant. "The people were nothing short of perfect and the three days we were there can only be described as ecstasy and continuous, non-stop enjoyment and thrills." (See also *Canoeing / Kayaking, Combos*.)

QUEBEC

Great Whale River

EARTH RIVER EXPEDITIONS

P.O. Box 182A, Accord, NY 12404. Attn.: Eric Hertz. (914) 626-2665 or (800) 643-2784. Fax (914) 626-2665.

In the James Bay region of northern Quebec a magnificent wilderness is under siege from hydro-electric development. As guests of the Whapmagoostui Band of the Cree nation, you can run the beautiful Great Whale River, sleep in tepees under the Northern Lights, share native American customs and learn first hand their struggle for survival. This an other surrounding rivers are critical habitat not only for animal species such as Beluga whales, caribou, wolf, rare fresh water seal and water fowl, but for the Cree way of life as well. Recent trips have introduced key players in New York politics to the magnitude of the environmental impact from the massive hydro project for the New York Power Authority. A flight from Montreal and a float plane to the put-in bring you to the start of five days rafting the river. Nights are spent at native Cree camps where your Cree guides prepare fresh trout and other Cree foods. You begin to comprehend the land, the culture and their 5,000-year bond, and experience Grand Canyon-size rapids amid stunning sub-arctic scenery of granite, stunted trees and brilliantly colored lichen. The Great Whale chief talks with your group about the hydro-electric project back at Whapmagoostui the last day. Spend the night at homestays with the Crees, and fly to Montreal the following day. Scheduled Jul. and Aug., 7 days, $1,300. (See this chapter—Mexico and Quebec.)

QUEBEC

Magpie River

EARTH RIVER EXPEDITIONS
P.O. Box 182A, Accord, NY 12404. Attn.: Eric Hertz. (914) 626-2665 or (800) 643-2784. Fax (914) 626-2665.

In the pristine wilderness of northern Quebec the Magpie River flows through miles of forests, granite gorges and spectacular falls before emptying into the St. Lawrence. In self-bailing paddle boats you run Class IV rapids, explore remote lakes and gorges, watch for moose, bear, osprey and eagle and bask in the canyon's solitude. On nine-day trips, start at Montreal, fly north to Sept-Isle and to a fishing camp at the put-in on Magpie Lake. For the next six days explore a region few people have seen and sleep in the magical light of the aurora borealis. A highlight is Magpie Falls, hurtling 100 feet in a thunderous crescendo. Take out above the Magpie-St. Lawrence junction and drive back to Montreal. Scheduled in Aug., 9 days, $1,900. (See this chapter—Mexico, and Quebec.)

Between a rock and a soft place—*Barry Tessman for Earth River Expeditions, Quebec.*

MEXICO

Lacanja and Usumacinta rivers

EARTH RIVER EXPEDITIONS
P.O. Box 182A, Accord, NY 12404. Attn.: Eric Hertz. (914) 626-2665 or (800) 643-2784. Fax (914) 626-2665.

Even the logistics of reaching the remote Lacanja River in the state of Chiapas are an adventure. Eric Hertz meets his groups of 15 paddlers in Mexico City where you transfer to a flight south to Villahermosa for overnight in a hotel. Next day it's a five-hour drive to the village of Lacanja, where you camp on the riverbank. Then, in specially designed four-man inflatable kayaks, you begin a week-long river journey on Class III and IV water through what Eric calls "a jungle paradise lost in time." Deep azure pools, lush vegetation and runnable sliding waterfalls give "the feeling of floating through a giant hanging garden." The jungle canopy sometimes covers the entire river, with the roar of macaws, toucans, parrots and howler monkeys breaking the great silence. On a side hike you inspect the Mayan ruin of Bonampak (790 A.D.) containing detailed murals with hieroglyphic texts. The river, once a canoe route to transport Mayan princesses, joins the larger Usumacinta where you are met by motorized dugout canoes for moving 20 miles downstream to the takeout to a van back to Villahermosa and flights to Mexico City and home. Trips scheduled in spring, 10 days, $1,400. (See this chapter—Quebec.)

Alaska Discovery, Inc., Alaska (page 202)

Sea Kayaking

We've heard a lot about sea kayaking as a recreational activity in recent years—first in the Pacific Northwest, now on the east coast, the Caribbean, Alaska, coastal waters everywhere. This awareness has come after many years of familiarity with river kayaking.

It's not that the sea touring kayak is a newer boat design than the river kayak. Actually the sea kayak is a direct descendent of the original craft used by Eskimos for hunting walrus in the frigid north.

"The touring kayak is designed to function as a vehicle in a variety of conditions, whereas the river kayak is designed for quick maneuvering and for certain kinds of paddling," explains Cliff Vandenbosch who offered the first sea kayaking trips on the coast of Maine ten years ago. "The sea kayak is to ocean travel what the cross-country ski is to snow travel. In coastal waters it will travel in a straight line with few corrections. It is not as maneuverable as the river kayak, but because it holds its course it is easier for paddling in ocean waters. Paddling a river kayak in the ocean is a lot more work, and it's not as stable."

The touring boat is up to 20 feet long—twice as long as the river kayak—and allows room for two paddlers and their gear. Most sea kayaks are equipped with foot-controlled rudders. Paddling expertise is not difficult to acquire, and trip operators teach you the basics during the course of your journey. The pace of most guided trips is slow, allowing for easy learning.

The increase in guided services for ocean kayaking is reflected in the trips described in these pages. You can paddle the crystal waters of inlets and lagoons in the Bahamas, or the rugged coastline of Cape Breton Highlands in Nova Scotia. Drink in the aesthetic qualities of Maine's coastal waters where land and sea meet, and where mountains rise from the water.

Kayak with whales on the British Columbia coast and explore wilderness coves of Vancouver Island. Paddle to tidewater glaciers and spawning streams of salmon in Alaska. Or choose an inland journey in Wyoming on Jackson Lake amid the beauty of the Tetons.

ALASKA

Glacier Bay, Admiralty Island, Hubbard Glacier, Icy Bay

ALASKA DISCOVERY, INC.
369 S. Franklin St., Juneau, AK 99801. Attn.: Kari Espera.
(907) 586-1911. Fax (907) 586-2332.

Alaska Discovery began kayak touring 20 years ago. They now offer four canoe/kayak itineraries, May through August, two from Juneau, two from Yakutat. Exploring Glacier Bay (7 days/ $1,500) starts and ends in Juneau with first and last nights in hotel, floatplane charters, five days of touring in two-person kayaks (paddling 25-40 miles) and four nights of wilderness camping in meadows of beach flats. "It's a chance to see humpback whales, bird life, marine mammals, mountains, glaciers." On another seven-day trip starting with a flight out of Juneau you paddle 17-foot Grumman canoes in Admiralty Island ($1,250, includes first and last night hotel stay). Explore the salt-water beaches of the east shore. Kayak explorations from Yakutat begin with spectacular bushplane flights. On the nine-day Hubbard Glacier and Russel Fjord trip ($1,550) you tour in two-person Klepper kayaks below the St. Elias Mountains and camp on beach flats. Watch for seal, porpoise and otter. Huge icebergs calve from the dynamic glacier. On a 12-day kayak excursion in Icy Bay ($2,150) drift among icebergs and watch seals and small porpoise. Two nights at most camps, with time to hike into the hills and close to the Malaspina Glacier. For all excursions first and last nights in hotels are included. (See also *River Running, Wilderness / Nature Expeditions, Combos*.) See photo page 200.

ALASKA

Kanai Fjords, Katmai National Park

HUGH GLASS BACKPACKING CO.
P.O. Box 110796, Anchorage, AK 99511. Attn.: Chuck Ash.
(907) 344-1340. Fax (907) 344-4614.

"Our quality-of-service philosophy and the areas we take you to are what set us apart from other Alaskan wilderness companies," says owner Chuck Ash. "We operate our floats through roadless wilderness on the finest waters in Alaska." A kayak trip in the Kenai Fjords is a journey back in time to the end of the last ice age. The route takes you to the face of the tidewater glaciers, among seal-capped ice floes and to the spawning streams of salmon; 5–7 days, $950–$1,195. Or paddle the clear, protected waters of the Bay of Islands in Katmai National Park after two days of hiking and bear viewing in Brooks Camp; 7 days, $1,295. Shuyak Island, at the northern end of the Kodiak Island group, is a magnificent spot for whales, sea lions and puffins as well as the otters and eagles found in all areas; 7 days, $1,350. Most trips are suitable for novices. Guides are experienced Alaskan wilderness travelers.

An island of seals
in the Kenai
Fjords—*Hugh*
Glass Backpacking
Co., AK.

"Emphasis is on interpretation of natural systems, companion-
ship and enjoyment." adds Chuck. (See also *Backpacking/Hiking
/ Walking, Wilderness / Nature Expeditions and Fly Fishing—*
Brightwater Alaska.)

FLORIDA/
CARIBBEAN

BOTTOM TIME ADVENTURES

*P.O. Box 11919, Ft. Lauderdale, FL 33339-1919. Attn.: A.J. Bland.
(305) 921-7798 or (800) 234-8464. Fax (305) 920-5578.*

The Bahamas

From November to May BTA schedules four- to seven-day
sea kayaking trips to the near islands in the Bahamas or to the
Berry Islands, a 90-mile chain which A.J. Bland calls "the
most exquisite kayaking grounds in the western hemisphere."
Inlets, lagoons and protected channels are all ideal for ocean
kayaking. You paddle crystal waters (inches from starfish,
bone fish, eagle rays) or through mangrove-lined inlets,
home to countless birds. These trips are for novice to advanced kayakers, and each day's paddle is at your own pace.
If you opt for snorkeling over vividly colored reefs, exploring
a deserted island, shelling (said to be the finest in the Bahamas), windsurfing or sunbathing, the launch will pick you up
for return to the *Bottom Time II*, your live-aboard yacht. The
three-deck 90' catamaran provides a/c double cabins for 28
as well as kayaks, guides and chef-prepared meals. "A kayak

puts you close to the birds and fish as never before," comments A.J., "and every evening you'll toast another golden sunset." Rates: $795/4 days to $1,095/7 days including meals, accommodations, guides and kayaks.(See also *Cycling / Mountain Biking, Wilderness / Nature Expeditions, Boats / Cruises /Scuba.*)

MAINE

COASTAL KAYAKING TOURS, INC.

P.O. Box 405, 48 Cottage Street, Bar Harbor, ME 04609. Attn.: Cliff Vandenbosch. (207)288-9605 or (800) 526-8615.

Acadia National Park

You'll get a nice taste of sea kayaking on daily guided paddling tours along the coast of Acadia National Park, but better yet are the *Island Camping Outings* for two to five days. Designed for participants rather than passengers, they put you in waters with miles of protected coastline and countless offshore islands—"the finest sea kayaking New England has to offer," according to Cliff Vandenbosch who has paddled thousands of miles in these and other coastal areas. "Our trips are open to paddlers of all abilities," he says, "and for those wishing to learn about sea kayaking they are ideal. Our experienced guides provide expert instruction throughout the trips." In groups of eight kayakers and two guides, you paddle a state-of-the-art expedition kayak equipped with foot-controlled rudder. Camping equipment and fresh or frozen foods are supplied, and fresh clams, mussels or mackerel in season. A two-day trip gives you a night of island camping—a mini-wilderness getaway. On a three-day trip you start south of Acadia to put the summer breeze at your back for a beautiful journey along the coast. On the five-day expedition you get into more remote areas with some openwater crossings. On all trips there's time for close-up views of wildlife—porpoises, seals, shore birds, an occasional whale and for beachcombing in the summer sun. Rates: 1/2 day, $43; full day, $65; 2 days, $175; 3 days, $359; 5 days, $599; May–Sep.

WYOMING

O.A.R.S., INC.

Box 67, Angels Camp, CA 95222. (209) 736-4677. Fax (209) 736-2902.

Grand Teton National Park

Sea kayaking does not necessarily require an ocean shoreline locale. O.A.R.S. offers sea-kayaking expeditions in Wyoming's Grand Teton National Park. With one- and two-person sea kayaks designed after the craft used by the Aleuts for hunting walrus in the frigid north, kayakers start with a short period of instruction. Soon they are enjoying the freedom of paddling on the Snake River and around Jackson Lake, with the beauty of rugged alpine peaks reflected in deep clear water. Moose graze in the marshes, and hawks and eagles fly overhead. This is a "catered" camping trip—with ice, fresh foods (nothing dehydrated), camping gear and fresh water carried by motor-powered rafts. Guides take care of the cooking and campsites and lead nature walks, paddling explorations and hikes in remote canyons with rushing creeks, waterfalls and feeding ponds for moose and elk. Each day kayakers pack their bags and tents and help load the rafts, then paddle five or ten miles to their next camp, with time for a swim, hike, volleyball or horseshoes before a "gourmet" camp dinner is ready. The 5-day (4-night) trip departs from Jackson every other Monday, mid June to late Aug.; $645/person. (See also *River Running*.)

BRITISH COLUMBIA

NORTHERN LIGHTS EXPEDITIONS LTD.

6141 NE Bothell Way, #101, Seattle, WA 98155. Attn.: David Arcese. (206) 483-6396.

Inside Passage

Kayaking the Inside Passage in British Columbia has been Northern Lights' specialty for a decade. David Arcese describes one trip: "On a clear, moonless night the water sparkled with luminescence, meteors showered overhead. We drifted silently with the current, then heard the unmistakable sound of whales blowing and slapping their tails. Soon more than 30 whales were in the darkness around us. We paddled with them—finally turning back toward the light of our campfire on the beach." The expeditions are both enlightening and awe-inspiring for participants, who need not be experienced kayakers. Besides orcas, they encounter bald eagles, salmon, seals, porpoises, and paddle through narrow passages past

Encountering orcas close-up—*Northern Lights Expeditions, BC.*

abandoned native villages and magnificent mountains. David considers the Inside Passage the ultimate destination for sea kayaking. "Kayakers choose it for the same reason rafters choose the Grand Canyon, or climbers the Himalayas," he says. More than 30 departure dates for 6-day trips, mid-Jun. to mid-Sep./$795. Meeting point is Port McNeill, B.C.

BRITISH COLUMBIA

WESTERN WILDCAT TOURS

P.O. Box 1162, Nanaimo, B.C. Canada V9R 6E7. Attn.: Roseanne Van Schie. Phone & Fax (604) 753-3234.

Vancouver Island, Inside Passage

Travel Vancouver Island by sea kayak and explore wilderness coves, sheltered inland passages, placid lagoons, crashing surf and sandy beaches that are home to orcas, otters, sea lions and numerous species of seabirds. This region offers a deluxe smorgasbord of paddling possibilities. "Our goals are to guide you safely and expertly through some of the wildest wilderness areas of Vancouver Island," says Roseanne. In Hot Springs Cove beaches cry out to be visited by people floating by. There's time ashore for exploring or relaxing by hot tubing west coast style at seaside hot pools that soothe away the years. Or sail on the *Golden Dolphin*, a classic '84 motor yacht, with kayaks on board so you can paddle at your leisure around Desolation Sound and Gulf Islands. *Paint and Paddle trips* include artists John Hookyand Linda Montgomery who assist paddlers in creating their own interpretations of the beauty of quiet islands, Gulf Island trips along the southeastern shore of Vancouver Island offer spectacular

View from your kayak on Vancouver Island—*Western Wildcat tours, B.C.*

scenery, low rainfall and protected passages. Cruise the course of history at legendary Nootka Sound on the west coast of Vancouver Island. Here you will paddle in the shadow of steep fjords to the ancient Nootka village of Yuquot, "Windy Place", where you camp in sheltered coves and watch eagles ride the wind above the sea. All trips focus on indigenous peoples and an option is a ceremonial feast and legends program, complete with drumming, dancing and a six-course salmon dinner at the Cowichan Native Heritage Centre. Scheduled trips of four to seven days or custom itineraries are available May–September for up to eight paddlers. Rates range from $110–$275 per day. (See also *Backpacking / Hiking / Walking*.)

NOVA SCOTIA

Cape Breton
Highlands, Bras
d'Or Lake, St.
Peter's Canal,
Mabou River

KAYAK CAPE BRETON

RR 2, West Bay, Nova Scotia, Canada B0E 3K0. Attn.: Eberhard Witt. (902) 535-3060.

"Who will forget suddenly encountering whales and watching them emerge next to our kayaks?" questions Eberhard Witt. He offers four- and five-day guided tours and one-day clinics. Former owner of a kayak shop in Germany, he uses high quality equipment and considers safety and relaxation to be key elements of his adventures. Most scenic and challenging of his guided tours is a five-day trip along the rugged coastline of Cape Breton Highlands; open mostly for experienced kayakers. You camp in sheltered coves and dine on fresh-caught fish. His four-day Bras d'Or Lake trip is ideal for beginners and intermediates. They glide past the shoreline and through St. Peter's Canal to the ocean. Another four-day tour follows the meandering Mabou River to the ocean and gives paddlers views of fascinating rock formations and bird colonies, and a chance to explore uninhabited Henry Island. All trips are for 3–8 paddlers, from $350 for 4 days to $490 for 5 days Cdn., scheduled Jul.–Sep. One-day kayaking clinics, May–Oct. are $60–$80/day.

Windjammer Barefoot Cruises, Ltd., Florida (page 211)

Windjammers

You help to cat the anchor and sail from the harbor under power. Then, with the power off, all is quiet except for the lapping of waves against the hull, and you heave ho on the mainsheet to hoist the sail. Later, under the captain's not-thoroughly-trusting eye, you take a trick at the wheel. But for the moment it's delicious to feel the sun and wind and listen to the splash of the water as you sail effortlessly out to the open sea.

In the two- or three-masted Tall Ships of yesteryear with a dozen or so other sailors, or in one-masted boats closer to 25 feet, you can cruise the Caribbean from one isle to another, sail the New England coast and put in at old whaling ports, ply the inland freshwaters of Lake Michigan or explore the West Coast from California to the San Juans and British Columbia.

Windjammers were the engineless sailing ships first built to haul cargo in the 1800s, now thoroughly refurbished or newly built. Passenger cabins on most have two to four bunks, electric lights, and hot-and-cold running water with hot showers and tiled heads nearby. A sailing skiff provides extra activity at anchor, and a launch transports those who want to go ashore to visit villages or to sunbathe and swim at a sandy beach.

If your dream is to be captain of your own sailboat or bareboat charter, a stint at a sailing school will turn you into a qualified skipper in short order. You can master the basics in classroom sessions combined with on-the-water experience over several weekends or an intensive week. The course itself seems less like school and more like a carefree sailing vacation, and it turns you into a knowledgeable skipper ready for endless sailing on your own.

(For barefoot and crewed charters in the Caribbean and the Pacific Northwest, please see chapter starting on page 135. For a current list of windjammers in New England, contact the Maine Publicity Bureau, 97 Winthrop Street, Hallowell, ME 04347, (207) 289-6070.)

MICHIGAN

**Lake Michigan
Cruising**

TRAVERSE TALL SHIP CO.

*13390 S.W. Bay Shore Dr., Box A, Traverse City, MI 49684. Attn.:
Captain John Elder. (800) 968-8800 or (616) 941-2000.*

Sail aboard a traditional tall ship to such destinations as
Beaver Island, Harbor Springs, legendary Mackinac Island,
and many other islands, bays and charming coastal villages.
"The words *undiscovered paradise* are not misused when de-
scribing some of these destinations," says Captain Elder. The
114' *Manitou* offers classic three- and six-day windjammer
cruises through the crystal-clear waters of northern Lake
Michigan and Lake Huron. When anchored, passengers enjoy kayaks, rowing dinghies or exploring the islands and
pristine lakeshores. "Whether you help the crew or just relax
you're sure to discover some of the Great Lakes' best kept
secrets," the captain adds. The *Manitou* sleeps 24 in 12 double

**The two-masted
Tall Ship** *Malabar*
**sails Lake
Michigan**—*Traverse
Tall Ship Co., MI.*

cabins. Rates, including meals, range from $349 to $799, Jun.–Sep. Hop aboard the *Manitou's* sister ship, *Malabar*, for a two-hour afternoon cruise or the popular sunset sail and "floating bed-and-breakfast" overnight, sailing on beautiful West Grand Traverse Bay. The *Malabar* sleeps 16 in eight rustic cabins at $175/couple including a hearty breakfast to satisfy sea-going appetites. The *Manitou* and *Malabar* are two of the largest sailing vessels on the Great Lakes.

NEW
ENGLAND

**Southern New
England Coast**

OUT O' MYSTIC SCHOONER CRUISES
7 Holmes St., P.O. Box 487, Mystic, CT 06355. (203) 536-4218 or (800) 243-0416.

The *Mystic Whaler*, a replica of the "sharpshooter" schooners of the 19th century, and the *Mystic Clipper*, designed after the famous Baltimore Clippers, are two-masted, gaff-rigged schooners, 100' and 125' long respectively. They sail the coastal waters of lower New England with approximately 50 passengers enjoying the sea and sky and the escape from hectic days ashore. Three- and five-day sneak-aways put in at various island and coastal ports—Sag Harbor, Greenport, Block Island, Newport, Cuttyhunk, Martha's Vineyard and others. A three-day swashbuckling pirate sneak-away focuses on a hunt for buried treasure, while those with less time take a half-day luncheon cruise, all-day or overnight cruises or a dinner sail on weekend evenings. Informality is the keynote—wear dungarees, sneakers, a bathing suit or shorts—and spend your time lolling in the sun, reading a good book or helping the crew with setting sails, steering and handling lines. Comfortable cabins are equipped with bunks and hot and cold running water wash basins. Rates range according to season and class of cabin; average $75 for 1 day, $400 for 3 days/nights, $575 for 5/days/nights.

CARIBBEAN

**British Virgin
Islands, West
Indies**

WINDJAMMER BAREFOOT CRUISES, LTD.
1759 Bay Road, Miami Beach, FL 33139. Attn.: Glenn Dean. (305) 672-6453 or (800) 327-2601. Fax (305) 674-1219.

"You don't have to be an old salt to enjoy Tall Ship cruising. Your land legs will become sea legs a knot or two out of port," say Glenn Dean. "For over 40 years, WBC has been windjammin' the Caribbean and the Atlantic at the wheels of the magnificent Tall Ships of the past." With designated ports of call but no fixed schedule, WBC recommends the adventure of wind-filled sails, sun-dripped days and moon-filled nights wild with stars. Discover hidden coves and secret cays. Plenty of time for beachcombing, snorkeling, shopping, sight-seeing or just relaxing. Its fleet of tall ships departs every Monday on 6-, 13-, or 14-day trips in the British Virgin Islands or the

West Indies, one-class service, $600–$1,625. (See also *Boats / Cruises / Scuba*.) See photo page 208.

See photo page 208.

US EAST/
CARIBBEAN

Annapolis, St. Petersburg, Marathon (FL Keys), St. Croix (U.S. Virgin Islands

ANNAPOLIS SAILING SCHOOL
P.O. Box 3334-ATG, Annapolis, MD 21403. (800) 638-9192.

Sailing is fun and easy for all ages, and this school encourages a learning vacation at one of four locations. The school has taught more than 90,000 people how to sail, cruise and qualify for bareboat charters since 1959 when it became America's first sailing school. With 22 sailing vacation courses at various levels, its beginner courses get any landlubber off to a good start. For example: "Become a Sailor in One Weekend" ($185), and a 5-day "New Sailor's Vacation Course" ($375). For sailing-minded families the school recommends combining a weekend beginner course with a 5-day supervised flotilla cruise. They also package hotel accommodations with a sailing vacation. Schools are located in Annapolis, St. Petersburg, Marathon (FL Keys) and St. Croix (U.S. Virgin Islands).

Students enjoy sailing instruction on St. Croix's tropical breezes—
Annapolis Sailing School, MD.

US EAST/
CARIBBEAN

Captiva Island (FL), Port Washington, City Island (NY), Newport (RI), Tortola, St. Lucia

OFFSHORE SAILING SCHOOL
16731-110 McGregor Blvd. Ft. Myers, Fl 33908. Attn.: Steve and Doris Colgate. (813) 454-1700 or (800) 221-4326. Fax (813) 454-1191.

Founded in 1964, OSS offers an opportunity to combine learning to sail with a first-class vacation experience. "Sailing is fun, easy to learn, safe and opens a whole new world of travel," Steve Colgate emphasizes. An America's Cup and Olympic sailor, he designs the OSS curricula, writes the textbook and guarantees that at the end of a week's vacation you'll be sailing. Branch locations in Captiva Island in Florida, Tortola and St. Lucia in the Caribbean, Newport in Rhode Island, Port Washington and City Island in New York make it easy and enticing to choose a learn-to-sail vacation. With four students per instructor, OSS courses emphasize thorough preparation, well-planned classwork and many hours of "hands-on" sailing aboard stable Olympic Class 27-foot Solings. Rate of $975 for 6 days includes accommodations, course and all course materials. In New York, 3–4 days course tuition/$450–$495. OSS also teaches courses in bareboat cruising preparation, advanced sailing and racing, and offers flotilla cruises throughout the world.

Learning to sail is easy and fun—
Offshore Sailing School, FL.

STILL MORE

Roads Less Traveled, Colorado (page 221)

Combos

Your pack trip has ended and you wish you could board a raft and run a river. After that you'd like a jeep and camping trip. Or perhaps some backpacking and kayaking, plus a little fly fishing.

Combo trips now are getting easier to arrange. Outfitters not only have expanded their services to include other types of adventure. They also have coordinated their itineraries with other trip operators in the same region. The result is a growing number of scheduled or customized combos for fun-loving vacationers who want to pack a variety of experiences into their holidays.

In the Appalachians, for example, you can combine cycling, whitewater rafting, kayaking and climbing. In Minnesota, pedal a bike along the Lake Superior shore and paddle a canoe in the Boundary Waters Wilderness. In Ontario, you raft the Ottawa River for two days then spend several days exploring woodland meadows and rolling hills on horseback.

In Utah you can travel by horse in the Arches National Park or the LaSal Mountains then raft the Colorado—or trek through colorful canyonlands on foot or mountain bike or by jeep. In New Mexico start in Santa Fe for wilderness hiking, cycling and river rafting.

A mountain sports week in Colorado offers riding instruction pedalling a bike, climbing a rocky ridge and rafting a river.

Run a river in Idaho by raft or canoe then explore mountain trails on bikes or by horseback. Ride into Montana's Glacier National Park by horse and raft out on the Flathead River.

On a half dozen river runs in Alaska's Brooks Range and Gates of the Arctic National Park it is possible to book a backpack expedition at either the start or the end of the river run. On a photo expedition in Admiralty Island and Glacier and Icy bays, you travel by float plane, sea kayak, canoe and yacht to capture on film the humpback whales, bears, eagles, sea lions and glaciers.

Hopefully, multiple vacation days will keep up with multiple trip planning.

US EAST / WEST

OUTWARD BOUND

Backpack / canoe /
climb / sail / raft

384 Field Point Road, Greenwich, CT 06830. (203) 661-0797 or (800) 243-8520. Fax (203) 661-0903.

Hands-on learning in real life situations challenge adventurers on Outward Bound's courses. A wide selection of wilderness activities build teamwork, trust and concern for others. And they enhance awareness that the natural world needs our care. Combo possibilities are varied. In Texas raft the mighty Rio Grande, and backpack through desert mesas and canyons in the Chihuahuan Desert. In Utah climb in the La Sal Mountains and Canyonlands, then run whitewater rapids. Challenges in Oregon's Cascades include whitewater rafting, backpacking, mountaineering, rock climbing and rappelling. Other multi-element courses include canoeing, backpacking and mountaineering in Washington's North Cascades, sailing and mountaineering in Washington's San Juan Islands, backpacking and rafting in Alaska's Gates of the Arctic National Park, whitewater rafting, hiking and rock climbing on the Green, Yampa or Colorado rivers in Colorado and Utah, or canoeing, rafting and sportyaking in Colorado, New Mexico or Utah. Eastern based trips include backpacking, rock climbing, and canoeing in the Southern Appalachians of North Carolina, canoeing and sailing in Florida's Everglades and Keys, sailing, canoeing and backpacking in Penoboscot Bay and Northwoods, Maine, or in Maryland In Minnesota combine canoeing, backpacking and rock climbing. Trips in Texas are scheduled fall and winter; in other regions between April and October. Trips run 6–29 days. Rates: $545–$2695.

ALASKA

ALASKA DISCOVERY, INC.

Admiralty
Island, Icy Strait,
Glacier Bay—
Canoeing / sea
kayaking / bear
and whale
watching /
hiking / beach
camping

234 Gold St. Dept. A, Juneau, AK 99801. Attn.: Kari Espera. (907) 586-1911. Fax (907) 586-2332.

This adventurous combo includes canoeing, sea kayaking, bear watching, beach camping, hiking, observing salmon runs and whales and traveling by charter floatplanes and boats in southeast Alaska. Meet your group at a Juneau hotel, then fly to Admiralty Island Wilderness Monument for two days of canoeing, beach camping and bear watching at Pack Creek. With the salmon running expect lots of bear and eagle action. Fly to Gustavus at entrance of Glacier Bay National Park for a gourmet dinner and overnight at a cozy country inn, then cruise Icy Strait to spot (and hopefully photograph) whales, sea lions, sea otters and seals. The day ends with a flight to a remote beach inside Glacier Bay for four days of kayaking and hiking before return to Juneau. Rate of $2,500 includes all charter costs and first and last nights at Juneau hotel on this ten-day (nine-night) trip. (See also *Sea Kayaking, River Running, Wilderness / Nature Expeditions*.)

ALASKA

Backpack / trek / canoe / raft / fishing—Brooks Range, Gates of the Arctic, ANWR

SOURDOUGH OUTFITTERS

P.O. Box 90, Bettles, AK 99726. Attn.: Gary Benson. (907) 692-5252. Fax (907) 692-5612.

The Brooks Range is a wilderness that Sourdough has been exploring since 1973, and they are still finding new routes into unexplored areas. Every summer at least one exploration trip is offered—you can help rewrite the maps. Trekkers can hike in the headwaters of the Noatak amidst ancient mountains and hanging glaciers, then canoe the Noatak River through spectacular scenery. If you do this trip in late August you will see the caribou migration. You can backpack into the Arrigetch Peaks exploring glacially carved granitic spires and alpine valleys where Dall sheep and grizzly bear are found. End the trip by canoeing the Alatna River. Another combination starts by backpacking in the Gates of the Arctic and then canoeing down the North Fork of the Koyukuk. Backpackers who want a challenge can backpack in the headwaters of the Killik River. For those who enjoy whitewater, run the Ivishak River. Most Brooks Range rivers are Class I and II and can be run with canoes. For those who enjoy world-class fishing, Sourdough offers a sheefishing trip on the Kobuk River where a 15-pound fish is considered small. Sourdough is a firm believer and practitioner of low impact camping and wilderness preservation. Trip lengths range from 4 to 20 days. Rates for guided trips are $190 to $225 per day. Unguided trips also offered, rates vary. (See also *Dog Sledding*.)

ARIZONA / IDAHO / MINNESOTA

Cycling, hiking, rafting, canoeing

TIMBERLINE BICYCLE TOURS

7975 E. Harvard, #J, Denver, CO 80231. Attn.: Dick and Carol Gottsegen. (303) 759-3804.

TBT offers wilderness experiences that combine hiking, rafting and canoeing with cycling to create extraordinary adventures. Its *Grand Canyon Biker/Hiker* assembles in Flagstaff, AZ, and begins with a five-day cycletour through beautiful Oak Creek Canyon to Sedona and on through the Prescott and Coconino national forests. The group then van shuttles to the Grand Canyon's South Rim for two days of hiking into the heart of the canyon (7 days, $875). Another trip begins in Missoula, MT, with two days cycling through the Bitterroot Valley into Idaho. Bicycles are left behind as the group next embarks on a four-day whitewater rafting adventure on the Salmon through the River-of-No-Return Wilderness to Riggins

Cycling the White Rim Trail in Canyonlands Nat'l Park—*Timberline Bicycle Tours, CO.*

and rendezvous with bicycles for three final days of cycling through the Bitterroots for return to Missoula (9 days, $1,295). Another fascinating combo focuses on the Arrowhead Country of northern Minnesota, where Timberline joins five days of cycling along the North Shore of Lake Superior (through the Superior National Forest) with four days of canoeing in the pristine Boundary Waters Wilderness (9 days, $995). (See also *Cycling / Mountain Biking*.)

COLORADO

**Climb / ride / bike / raft—
Sangre de Cristo Mountains, Arkansas River**

ADVENTURE SPECIALISTS, INC.

Bear Basin Ranch, Westcliffe, CO 81252. Attn.: Gary Ziegler or Amy Finger. (719) 783-2519. [Dec.–Apr.: 515 W. San Rafael, Colorado Springs, CO 80905. (719) 630-7687.]

For the adventure seeker looking to pack as much outdoor experience into five or six days as possible, Adventure Specialists has the perfect combination. Their "Mountain Sports Week" starts at a rustic ranch for a day of basic climbing and two days of horse riding instruction and riding the range on horseback. You spend the next two days on a hi-tech bike, and finish with a day rafting the Arkansas River; six days, $650. A five-day "Surf and Turf" package has you on horseback, riding and fishing for three days, then two days of rafting the Arkansas; or replace horseback riding with mountain biking; 5 days, $650 or $525 biking. All trips May–September, with pick-up/return in Colorado Springs. (See also *Hiking with Packstock, Pack Trips*.)

COLORADO

Four Corners

FOUR CORNERS CENTER FOR EXPERIENTIAL LEARNING

1760 Broadway, Grand Junction, CO 81503. Attn.: Maria O'Malley. (303) 858-3607. Fax (303) 858-7861.

Rock climb or rapell on sandstone cliffs. Canoe down the Colorado River or run the whitewater on a raft. Ride horseback or test your mettle with solo camping overnight. The potpourri of activities programmed in the Four Corners region by this service also includes kayaking, hiking, mountain biking, wildlife observation and nature study. "We design each trip to meet group needs," Maria explains. Their programs are customized for small groups (8–12, occasionally more). Participants report: "The day was extremely successful even though some in our group had never been rock climbing"..."The sunset barbecue after the well organized mountain bike ride was superb"..."The quality of your program and your warmth and endless patience are impressive!" Director Don West has spent over 30 years in experiential education (with Outward Bound and others). "Bring your enthusiasm, be ready to learn, grow and have fun," urges Maria. Programs scheduled March to November for up to 14 days. Rate: $195 per day includes air-conditioned van transport, camping equipment and many meals. Package rates with lodging and meals on request. (See also *Trail Rides, Cycling / Mountain Biking*.)

COLORADO /
NEW MEXICO /
UTAH

Hike / Raft /
Mountain Biking

ROADS LESS TRAVELED

P.O. Box 8187, Longmont, CO 80501. Attn.: David Clair. (303) 678-8750 or (800) 488-8483.

"Our goal is to share the magic and beauty of the backcountry by day, and at night the comforts of a fine inn, remote guest ranch or mountain hut." says David. "To sense the nature that surrounds you, and to see the remnants of bygone mining days or the wildlife that scampers by, you need to venture onto quiet, unpaved roads." This he offers on imaginative itineraries that combine hiking, biking and rafting with overnights at huts, inns, B&Bs or remote ranches or lodges. Bike 'n hike trips, for example, follow trails into the red-rock canyons of Bryce and Zion national parks, or from hut to hut on a stretch of the Colorado Trail and the Holy Cross Wilderness. Explore the footpaths of Rocky Mountain National Park and an extensive network of cycling trails on a five-day inn tour, or start in Santa Fe for five days of hiking an unspoiled wilderness, cycling old forest roads and rafting through vibrant canyons. All itineraries are graded for athletic beginners, intermediates or beginners in ability. Guides are local to the area. Food is almost entirely fresh. "By the end of the first day the only word that kept popping up was 'Wow!'" says a typical participant. Rates average $160–$190 per day. Trips for up to 13 participants, Apr. to Oct. (See also *Cycling / Mountain Biking*.) See photo page 216.

IDAHO

Horseback / raft / mountain bike

NORTHWEST VOYAGEURS

P.O. Box 373, Lucile, ID 83542. Attn.: Jeff or Carol Peavey. (208) 628-3021 or (800) 727-9977. Fax (208) 628-3780.

Peddlers and paddlers, adults or families, can have it both ways on special mountain biking-rafting trips. Begin riding on easy trails at 5,000 feet in McCall through pine-covered hills, hidden alpine meadows and forests to Burgdorf Hot Springs. Stay overnight in a cabin, then ride down to the Salmon River Canyon, a descent of 3,500 feet, to Vinegar Creek. Camp beside the river before packing your gear in waterproof bags for two days of whitewater rafting. Cover 40 miles by raft from Vinegar Creek, or try an inflatable canoe. After two days of rafting and camping mount your bike and ride up to the high breaks of the Salmon River canyon, then go deeper into the wilderness and just let it swallow you up. "These four-day combination trips are world class vacations in every respect," says Jeff. "Your satisfaction is guaranteed 100%." Rates for bike-raft trips are $595. Horse-raft trips also offered at $650. In January a trip to Costa Rica combines cultural interaction, sea kayaking, snorkeling, nature walks alive with monkeys and exotic birds, horseback riding through

Riding horseback to the river put-in—F. Mignerey for Northwest Voyageurs, ID.

tropical forests and rafting. Rate: $3,495 for 21-day trip, including round trip airfare; Jun. through Aug. (See also *River Running*.)

MAINE

Kennebec, Penobscot, Dead rivers

NORTHERN OUTDOORS, INC.

P.O. Box 100, The Forks, ME 04985. Attn.: Wayne and Suzie Hockemeyer. (207) 663-4466 or (800) 765-7238. Fax (207) 663-2244.

The Hockemeyers were the first to launch commercial rafting trips in New England 17 years ago. They soon discovered that their fun-loving guests wanted a whole range of outdoor activities. Their river trips quickly expanded from the Kennebec to the Penobscot and Dead rivers, and they have added horseback riding, paddle tennis, mountain biking, canoeing, kayaking and fishing to the program, as well as a swimming pool, hot tube, sauna and restaurant—and snowmobiling in the winter. Accommodations range from campsites and cabin tents to cabins, lodge rooms and logdominiums. They also have added a whole range of affordable packages to suit varied preferences. For example, a five-day family package offered May to October, including breakfast and dinner, a day of rafting and choice of non-guided activities, costs $45 per person per day with cabin tent accommodations, or (98 with logdominium rooms. (Children under 12 take a halfway rafting trip at half price.) Various other guided activities such as riding or another raft trip are added to the package price at a discount. Another popular option is the Friday-to-Sunday-weekend package. The 100-acre resort in the Maine woods has become the largest outdoor adventure center in New England.

MONTANA

Glacier National Park, Flathead River, Bob Marshall and Great Bear Wilderness-Hike / raft / ride/ wildlife photography

GLACIER WILDERNESS GUIDES

Box 535N, West Glacier,MT 59936. Attn.: Randy Gayner. (406) 888-5466 or (800) 521-7238.

Hiking and rafting is a combo which gives you the best of both worlds. GWG offers five- to eight-day trips for hiking inside Glacier National Park then rafting the wild and scenic Flathead River, with a motel night in between. Rate: $435–$660. Or ride horseback through the Bob Marshall and Great Bear wilderness areas for 3 and a half days, followed by two and a half days floating the Flathead back to civilization, six days, $750. On Watchable Wildlife Tours, each day in a different area, overnights are scheduled at various motels and day hikes are planned for photographers or hikers to observe black and grizzly bears, moose, bighorn sheep and mountain goats. Rate for 5 days, 6 nights, $825–$955. You can make custom arrangements on all GWG trips to fit vacation schedules. (See also *Backpacking / Hiking / Walking, River Running*—Montana Raft Co.)

NORTH
CAROLINA

Southern Appalachian Mountains— cycle / raft / kayak / climb / hike

NANTAHALA OUTDOOR CENTER
13077 Hwy 19 West, Bryson City, NC 28713-9114. Attn.: Betsey Lewis. (704) 488-2175.

NOC offers a variety of combos—from a weekend package of cycling and whitewater rafting on the Chattooga (a scheduled trip open to individual reservations), to a custom week for a group learning adventure. For the latter program, clients which include colleges, schools, church groups, clubs, corporate groups and families select from activities such as rafting, kayaking, canoeing, rock climbing, cycling, hiking and the ropes course. These are the "tools" to enhance problem solving, communication, stress management skills or whatever goals are of primary interest to a specific group. Depending upon the group, goals may range from strengthening the team concept to a week of challenging family fun. Instructors are experienced professionals. They develop for each group a challenging and safe activities program in a fun environment. For a corporate group, for example, the end result is gaining insights that make a difference in how they operate back at the office. All programs are flexible, designed for individual group needs. (See also *Canoeing/Kayaking*, *River Running*, *Cycling / Mountain Biking*—Carolina Cycle Tours.)

UTAH

Canyonlands, La Sal Mountains, Colorado River— raft/ride/jet boat/ jeep/bike/hike

ADRIFT ADVENTURES
P.O. Box 577, Moab, UT 84532. Attn.: Myke Hughes. (801) 259-8594 or (800) 874-4483. Fax (801) 259-7628.

With his headquarters in Moab, in a region that offers everything to outdoor people, it was inevitable that Myke Hughes would add combo extensions to his rafting trips on the Colorado River. So far he has evolved six combos. One that fits almost any itinerary is a morning of horsebacking in the Arches National Park, followed by an afternoon of rafting ($60). Or spend half a day in a jet boat and the other half jeeping ($69). Ride for two days in the cool LaSal Mountains and follow with four days rafting Cataract Canyon ($750). A three-day run in Cataract combines with two days of jeeping through Canyonlands back to Moab ($695). Or pedal a mountain bike for three days and spend three more rafting Cataract ($690). Still another combo involves any of the river trips mixed with two days at Pack Creek Ranch to swim, hike or ride (add $295 to rafting cost). Discounted children's rates for most combos. May–Sep. (See also *River Running*.)

UTAH

Canyonlands, Cataract Canyon,

KAIBAB MOUNTAIN BIKE TOURS
P.O. Box 339, 391 South Main Street, Moab, UT 84532. (800) 451-1133. Fax (801) 259-6135.

"Imagine three days of mountain biking in the most awe-

Maze District, LaSal Mountains

some part of Canyonlands, then hiking to the mighty Colorado for two days of excitement rafting Cataract Canyon, while never leaving the wilderness!" says Brett Taylor, founder of Kaibab. His company combines the best of mountain biking with the best of river rafting in southeastern Utah. Choose a five-or seven-day combo in Canyonlands National Park, biking in the Maze District then running Cataract Canyon. A scenic flight over the canyons is included in the tour. "It was marvelous! Great!" says a recent participant. "The guides are knowledgeable and concerned and give excellent instruction, and the food was outstanding. We want to do it all over again." Another option offers five or seven days of biking in the LaSal Mountains outside Moab, followed by the unforgettable rafting trip down Cataract. Trips scheduled May through Sep., $825–$1,069. (See also *Cycling / Mountain Biking*.)

UTAH

SHERI GRIFFITH EXPEDITIONS

Colorado & Green rivers, Canyonlands National Park— bike/raft/ride

P.O. Box 1324, Moab, UT 84532. (801) 259-8229 or (800) 332-2439. Fax (801) 259-2226.

The challenge of guiding one's own fat-tire bike through miles of pristine canyon country is matched with the adrenaline-pumping thrill of rafting Cataract Canyon of the Colorado on one of Sheri Griffith's combos. Modern mountain bikes are light, agile and fun to ride on the miles of dirt roads and jeep trails for novice and experienced riders alike. Bike three days, raft four, Apr.–Sep., $1,099, vehicle supported. Another combo includes riding horseback for several days— in the cool of the La Sal Mountains in summer, or in canyons where Butch Cassidy and his outlaws used to hide in spring and fall. Then spend a night in Moab, and raft Cataract Canyon on the Green River. Trips depart from Moab every Sunday. (See also *River Running*.)

ONTARIO

WILDERNESS TOURS

Raft/trail ride/ mountain bike/ windsurf

Box 89, Beachburg, ONT., Canada K0J 1C0. Attn.: Terry Hierlihy. (613) 646-2291 or (800) 267-9166. Fax (613) 646-2996.

Wilderness Tours encourages trail riding at their 600-acre Outdoor Center as the perfect complement to all their whitewater trips as well as to five-day "Learn-to-Adventure" packages. On these you raft both the main and middle channels of the Ottawa River for two days, then spend three days exploring woodland meadows, rolling hills and valleys on horseback or on mountain bikes. Besides the more rugged outdoor activities, options include windsurfing, volleyball, relaxing in hot tubs or just soaking up the sun on a sandy beach. Learn-to-Adventure rate, 5 days, $360 US. (See also *Canoeing/Kayaking, River Running*.)

Brent Wallace for Nimmo Bay Resort Ltd., British Columbia (page 239)

Fly Fishing

Dropping your line in the right fishing hole is no doubt the secret to great fishing for the estimated 50 million North American anglers who make this activity one of the most popular forms of recreation. Sure you need to know what you're doing, what sort of tackle is best for the conditions you're encountering, how the weather affects your chances. But nothing helps if the fish aren't biting. After all, what sort of fish stories would that give you to tell?

The fishing outfitters selected for this chapter know where those whoppers are lurking in the depths. You can choose to float wild rivers in Alaska and reel in rainbows, grayling or Arctic char. Some Alaska lodges boast the accessibility of 18-80 pound king salmon.

In Montana's Bob Marshall Wilderness savvy locals rave about the fly fishing on the Sun River. Walk/wade trips on Montana's Gallatin, Firehole, Gibbon, Madison and Yellowstone rivers, drift boat fishing for large browns and rainbows on the Madison, Jefferson, Yellowstone, Henry's Fork and Missouri rivers, or float tube fishing on alpine lakes are challenging and rewarding—if you know where to go and what to do when you get there. And in the lively waters of Idaho and Canada are sites skilled fishing guides can lead you to for uncommonly good fishing.

Whether you're an avid fly fisherman or a novice, experienced guides help you find the most reliable locations and select the right nymphs or dry flies for reeling in the big ones. Whether you're looking for the ultimate in catch-and-release fly fishing along the streams and rivers of the West, or for a king-size Alaskan halibut for the dinner grill, these operators, outfitters and lodges—many of which are designated as "preferred lodges" by Orvis, a company that sets high standards for fishing, accommodations, equipment and amenities—base their business on knowledge of the waters that reliably produce great fishing year after year. When you put your fishing fortunes in these able, calloused hands you're virtually guaranteed extraordinary angling success. And *you'll* know the truth about the stories you return with.

<table>
<tr><td>

ALASKA

**Upper and Lower
Kenai River**

</td><td>

ALASKA WILDLAND ADVENTURES

*P.O. Box 389, Girdwood, AK 99587. Attn.: Kirk Hoessle. (907) 783-2928
or (800) 334-8730.*

Where else can you fish for world-famous king salmon, red
or silver salmon, plus dollies and rainbow trout and huge
halibut—all in one great, action-packed week? Alaska
Wildland's answer to the question indicates that the pro-
grams they offer anglers are unique and productive. June and
July are the months for their five-day package featuring king,
rainbow and halibut, with headquarters at their comfortable
riverside lodge on the Kenai River. They have operated the
sport fishing lodge since 1977. The program begins with
three days of drift boat fishing for king salmon on the Lower
Kenai, then a day on the Upper Kenai for rainbow trout, red
salmon and Dolly Varden. On the fifth day you charter out of
Seward for halibut fishing on the spectacular seacoast. (Rate
for 5 days $1,895. Program can be split into 2 or 3 days—2
days $695, 3 days $995.) Closeness to Anchorage—about 100
miles south—eliminates the cost of bush planes for trans-
porting fishermen and supplies, and helps to keep package
rates down, Alaska Wildland points out. The guest/guide
ratio is three to one. Guests are picked up in Kenai on Day 1
and returned to Anchorage at end of trip. (See also *Wilderness
/ Nature Expeditions, Boat Charters / Cruises.*)

</td></tr>
<tr><td>

ALASKA

**Alagnak,
Goodnews and
Talachulitna
rivers**

</td><td>

BRIGHTWATER ALASKA

*P.O. Box 110796, Anchorage, AK 99511. Attn.: Chuck Ash.
(907) 344-1340. Fax (907) 344-4614.*

Chuck Ash has been guiding and outfitting fly fishermen
since 1975 on some of Alaska's finest wild rivers, floating by
raft in remote wilderness accessible only by bushplane. "You'll
be living on the water and can fish whenever you like," says
Chuck. Groups of four fishermen and two guides camp on
riverbanks each night. He offers three trips to choose from,
June to September, with bush flights included in rates. The
Alagnak River trip in the Bristol Bay area is in the heart of
Alaska's trophy wilderness fishing for rainbow trout, gray-
ling and char plus five species of Pacific salmon; $1795/week
from King Salmon. Goodnews River trips on the northwest
side of Bristol Bay offer the same species; 8 days, $1,995 from
Dillingham. Talachulitna River trips, five or seven days, start
by bush plane from Anchorage, with good rainbow and
grayling and runs of king and silver salmon. All you need are
bedroll and fishing gear, with rentals available. (See also
*Backpacking / Hiking / Walking, Sea Kayaking, Wilderness /
Nature Expeditions*—Hugh Glass Backpacking Co.)

</td></tr>
</table>

In Alaska's remote
wilderness—*Chuck
Ash for Brightwater
Alaska, AK.*

ALASKA

**Kenai, Alaska
Peninsula,
Homer**

GREAT ALASKA FISH CAMP & SAFARIS

*HCO Box 218, Sterling, AK 99672. Attn.: Laurence John (800) 544-2261.
Fax (503) 452-7429.*

"When you come with us to the Kenai, expect trophy class
fishing, a world-class staff and the best in equipment and
facilities," Laurence John writes. His comfortable lodge and
cabins, with the Kenai Wildlife Refuge at the back door, face
two of Alaska's famous fishing and migratory salmon streams.
"Over the years writers and TV producers have tried to
document our intimate safaris," he says, "but have discovered that the ultimate experience has nothing to do with 'Big
and Fancy' but rather with small, personal, meaningful and
memorable." All trips base out of the lodge, in front of which
we have set six world's records. In season anglers catch 18–
80 lb. king salmon on the Kenai River and 10–15 lb. silver
salmon. From the lodge you fish for rainbow, dolly varden,
halibut and lake trout May through September, kings May 15
through July 31, sockeye June through August and pink
salmon—over two million of which enter the Kenai during
their runs. Wild river float trips on the Alagnak and Lake
Creek for groups of four and six "can't be beat for pure
wilderness and super fishing." Flyouts for sockeye and sil-
vers on the Alaska Peninsula fulfill expectations. July and
September trips to Katmai for fishing along with the brown

bear provide considerable excitement. Halibut runs out of Homer and a lake boat on Skilak and Hidden lakes for lake trout add to the wide range of fishing experiences at Great Alaska. (See also *Wilderness / Nature Expeditions*.)

ALASKA

**Aniakchak
National
Monument**

PAINTER CREEK LODGE
7111 Spruce St., Anchorage, AK 99507. Attn.: Joe Maxey. (907) 344-5181. Fax (907) 344-6172.

Aniakchak National Monument on the Alaska Peninsula is one of the most remote and least fished areas in Alaska. Eight-pound arctic char and three-pound grayling are common, as well as rainbow trout, Dolly Varden and five species of salmon. Fly from King Salmon (by commercial flight) to the lodge and take day trips from there by jet boat or bush flight. Or fly out to one of several basecamps for a few days of fishing, and float to another camp. A floatplane picks you up after several days of reeling in big ones. These waters have little or no pressure from anglers. The nearest fishing lodge is over 100 miles away, and it is entirely likely that you will not see another fisherman during your stay. "We have the ability and equipment to get you to those truly secret spots where the fishing is fabulous and the scenery spectacu-

One of the secret spots—*Painter Creek Lodge, AK.*

lar," says Joe. Accommodations at the lodge are somewhat basic in cabins with four beds and private bath. Each deluxe wilderness camp trip is limited to four anglers, two guides and two rafts. Sport fishing at lodge, 4 days, $1,500; with flyouts $1,750. Week at lodge $3,000. Wilderness adventures customized, $125–$300/day. Season: May–September.

COLORADO

Flat Tops
Wilderness Area

ELK CREEK LODGE

P.O. Box 130, Meeker, CO 81641. Attn.: Bill Wheeler. (303) 878-4565 or (303) 878-5311.

"This is an exclusive fly fishing getaway offering rustic elegance at its finest with the friendly warmth of western hospitality," says Bill Wheeler. Set in the Flat Tops Wilderness Area, five miles of completely private Elk Creek flows from the mountains past the lodge and into the White River, where guests can fish another six miles of privately owned water for brook, brown, rainbow or a pure strain of wild cutthroats lurking in Trappers Lake, also owned by the Wheeler family. The most requested program at this Orvis endorsed lodge is a five-day package including two days of flyout service for drift boat fishing in the incomparable Green River in northeast Utah. The beautiful canyon has been called "the best tailwater fishery in North America," with 10,000 trout per mile, a lot of big trout and excellent dry fly fishing. The lodge provides flyout service to other premier western rivers and trail rides to fish high alpine lakes. There is an Orvis fly fishing school and a fully equipped Orvis tackle shop at the lodge. Rates range from $1,200–$2,500 per week, including airport transfers from Steamboat Springs, Aspen, Eagle, Vail or Grand Junction. A private air shuttle is an option.

COLORADO

Blue and
Colorado rivers

ELKTROUT LODGE

P.O. Box 614, Kremmling, CO 80459. Attn.: Colleen Paine or Marty Cecil. (303) 724-3343. Fax (303) 724-9063.

Is your secret dream a river you can wade mile after mile and cast at will, without ever encountering another fisherman? Elktrout Fly Fishing Lodge combines creature comforts, attentive staff and outstanding meals with ten miles of completely private trout water open only to guests. The lodge owns or leases 2 miles of the Blue River, 5 miles of the Colorado River, several miles of Pass Creek and Troublesome Creek and 12 ponds. It's like owning your own trout stream where all the classic mayfly, caddis and stone fly hatches run throughout its long fishing season, from mid-May to mid-October. Two-pound rainbows and browns are common in the rivers while private ponds produce four-pounders and up. As an Orvis "high standards endorsed fishing lodge" Elktrout offers beginning to advanced casting instruction and complete on-the-water guide service. Each day guests fish new water—the Colorado one day, picturesque creeks, fast moving waters or magnificent spring-fed ponds the next. "All of us thoroughly enjoyed the lodge," wrote one recent guest, "the friendly and competent staff, beautiful scenery and the dedication to sportsmanship and conservation in everyone's thoughts and actions." Rate: $350 per day includes food, lodging, guide, fishing; 3-day packages are $945, 6-days $1,680.

COLORADO

FRYINGPAN RIVER RANCH

32042 Frying Pan River Road, Meredith, CO 81642. Attn.: Jim Rea.

Fryingpan River, Roaring Fork River

(303) 927-3570 or (800) 352-0980.

Thirty-one miles upriver from Basalt, at 8,800 feet just below the Continental Divide, the Fryingpan Ranch is located on the Fryingpan River, one of America's Gold Medal trout streams. Above the ranch are eight miles of pristine water full of wild trout and surrounded in spectacular scenery. A mile below the ranch anglers fish in meadows and beaver ponds, as well as in the nearby Roaring Fork River. There are many high lakes and smaller streams around the ranch, including Nast Lake, less than 100 yards from the lodge. It's filled with brook trout just the right size for a small boy or a small boy who accidentally grew up. Skilled guides help you sharpen your skills, let you learn the waters within easy reach of the ranch and provide congenial companionship. The ranch is one of only three Orvis-endorsed fishing lodges in the state. Rates range from $915 per person (two rods) for a three-day stay to $1,835 for seven days (two rods), lodging, meals, guiding and all ranch activities included. Non-fishing guests are also welcome at the ranch. Pickup at Aspen airport is provided. (See also *Pack Trips*.)

IDAHO

RENSHAW OUTFITTING, INC.

P.O. Box 1165, Kamiah, ID 83536. Attn.: Lynda Renshaw.

Clearwater National Forest, Selway Bitterroot Wilderness

(208) 926-4520, 935-0726 or (800) 452-2567. Fax (208) 935-0726.

You don't spend 40 years as Idaho's longest continuously licensed outfitter without finding a few good fishing holes, and Jim Renshaw has found some dandies near his permanent basecamp on Weitas Creek, in Unit 10 of the Clearwater National Forest. "The creek is loaded with 10- to 14-inch native rainbow and cutthroat trout," Jim declares. "An excellent fly fishing stream!" It is an easy five mile ride on horseback for up to six people from the trailhead to the camp, which is equipped with floored tents, wood heat, cots with foam pads, hot showers, lights, even ice cubes for your drinks and plenty of excellent home-style food. "Prime fishing months are June through August," says Jim. Rates: $650 per person for a 7-day trip. Daily riding is involved on another 7-day pack trip moving to several different campsites in the Selway Bitterroot Wilderness, and the fishing there also is great. 7-days, $900. (See also *Pack Trips*.)

MONTANA

Bighorn river

EAGLE NEST LODGE
P.O. Box 470, Hardin, MT 59034. Attn.: Nick Forrester. (406) 665-3799.

Fly fishing for trophy trout on the Bighorn, a river well suited for monster rainbows and brownies, is the specialty at Eagle Nest Lodge. Cool temperatures and steady flows with almost a year-round succession of hatches produce well-fed and active fish. "Our goal is to provide the discriminating sportsman with the very best trophy trout fishing," says Nick Forrester. "Our guides put you in the right place with the right pattern at the right time. They can teach beginners, help intermediate casters improve their technique and maybe even show an expert a thing or two." With no spring runoff, you can expect the best dry fly action May through September for Blue Wing Olives, Midges, Pale Morning Duns, caddis flies and Tricos. Nymphs are productive nearly year round. The log lodge is hidden away in a cottonwood grove and is the first

Trophy trout fishing for discriminating sportsmen—*Eagle Nest Lodge, MT.*

to earn a double endorsement from the Orvis Company. For a wilderness experience for fishing seven alpine lakes, hiking, riding and camping, Forrester recommends his cozy basecamp in the nearby Cloud Peak Wilderness/Big HornMountains. Lodge rates: 4 days/5 nights including guides, boats, meals and lodging, $1,600. Basecamp $170/person/day including guides, horse, tents and sleeping bag.

MONTANA

Paradise Valley

HUBBARD'S YELLOWSTONE LODGE
Box 662, Emigrant,MT 59027. (406) 848-7755. Fax (406) 848-7471.

Hubbard's is located on the shores of springfed Merrell Lake in the heart of Montana's Paradise Valley, blue ribbon trout water which is home to some of Montana's finest. This Orvis-endorsed lodge offers the tranquility of being away from it all, yet with the comforts of first-class lodging and dining close at hand, and rainbows up to eight pounds in the cool lake waters. Guests have exclusive access to the lake. Scuds, leeches and damsel fly nymphs are year round staples, and nymph fishing throughout the season is explosive. Summer months offer excellent dry fly fishing when trout feed on a variety of midges, caddis flies, mayflies and terrestrials. According to one expert fisherman: "Sitting and waiting near pods of feeding trout is the best technique on Merrell Lake. An unforgettable experience. If the fish are not feeding actively on the surface, simply retrieve black, olive or red marabou wooly buggers. If you have any fly fishing experience at all, you should pick off a four- to five-pounder or two a day." Fishing trips can also be arranged on Yellowstone, in Armstrong's, Nelson's or Deputy's spring creeks, or on blue ribbon streams flowing through Yellowstone Park. Guided packages: 6 nights lodging, 5 days fishing, $1,580–$1,940/person; 4 nights and 4 days fishing, $1,190–$1,390. Day float trips $150, horseback accessed fishing $125 per day.

MONTANA

Bob Marshall Wilderness

KLICK'S K BAR L RANCH
Box 287, Augusta, MT 59410. Attn.: Nancy Klick. (406) 467-2771.
[Winter & spring: (406) 562-3589.]

Fly fish for wild 12"–20" rainbow trout on medium size freestone streams for comfortable wading and fishing. The two forks of Montana's Sun River meet right at this legendary ranch on the edge of the Bob Marshall Wilderness. Bring wading gear, dry fly dressing, insect repellent, sun screen, sunglasses, a hat and a rain jacket; mountain showers are a possibility. A 15-year veteran fly fisherman at the ranch suggests a light-weight, 8–9 foot graphite rod with a 1 7/8 CFO 111 reel and 4–6 weight line. Among his favorite flies are Royal Wolf #16 and Humpy #16. Another angler who has fished here for many Julys likes dry flies such as Royal Trude #14, or Nymphs like Wooly Bugger #8–10. From Augusta it's a half-hour drive to Gibson Lake where you continue by jet boat to the ranch. Stay in a cozy, rustic, one-, two- or three-room cabin the first night, then saddle up next morning for a fishing pack trip to wilderness sites such as Bear Lake. "It's a beautiful nine-mile ride," says Nancy Klick. "I've done well on a size 14, 16 black gnat or a small black ant, casting far enough in front of cruising fish so they can't see the fly land on the water. Some fish will feed within 18 inches of the shore." Rates for these horseback-fly fishing trips in the Bob Marshall Wilderness are $110 per day, 6 day minimum including lodging, meals (some of which you catch), guide and horse—all but fishing gear and personal items. Also 84° natural warm water pool at lodge. (See also *Pack Trips*.)

MONTANA

**Gallatin,
Firehole,
Gibbon,
Madison,
Yellowstone,
Jefferson,
Henry's Fork,
Hebgen and
Missouri rivers,
Quake Lake**

LONE MOUNTAIN RANCH

Box 160069, Big Sky, MT 59716. Attn.: Bob and Vivian Schaap. (406) 995-4644. Fax (406) 995-4670.

"Our location is ideal for fishing the blue ribbon streams that make southwest Montana and Yellowstone famous," says Bob Schaap. "Our professional guides know local waters and help make fishing for trout an exceptional adventure." The adventure includes *walk/wade trips* on the Gallatin, Firehole, Gibbon, Madison and Yellowstone; *drift boat fishing* to outwit large browns and rainbows on rivers like the Madison, Jefferson, Yellowstone, Henry's Fork and Missouri; *float tube fishing* on

Hebgen, Quake Lake and alpine lakes, some of which are accessed by horseback; and *specially designed trips* for fit people that involve riding or strenuous hiking. Bob recommends June for high water and challenging fishing, July and August for superb dry fly fishing, and September and October for tangling with some really big browns—a season when the ranch's fly fishing package of five or more guided trips per week comes with a 10%–15% discount for ranch guests. Regular rates for two anglers run about $255 per day, and $175 per angler per day for horseback fishing. The ranch is an Orvis Endorsed Lodge and provides a complete retail fly fishing shop featuring Orvis products. (See also *Ski Touring / Snowmobiling*.)

NEW MEXICO

San Juan Mountains

THE LODGE AT CHAMA

P.O. Box 127, Chama, NM 87520. Attn.: Frank Simms Vice Pres./Gen. Mgr. (505) 756-2133. Fax (505) 756-2519.

Anglers from around the world gravitate to the luxurious Lodge at Chama for the top-rated fishing experience on its 32,000 acres in the San Juan Mountains of northern New Mexico. The highcountry lakes produce 16- to 25-inch heavy-bodied rainbows, brown and cutthroats that test fishing skills. "Fishermen marvel at the strength, beauty and endurance of our trout," comments manager Frank Simms. Some lakes are reserved exclusively for catch and release fly fishing. For the angler who prefers stream fishing there are miles of crystal-clear waters full of brown, rainbow and brook trout. Among special features at the outstanding lodge are

hearty gourmet fare, a spa with hydro-therapy whirlpool and sauna, spacious rooms and spectacular views of the mountains. Rate of $375/day includes fishing and guide service, hiking, horseback riding, sporting clayys, ranch tours, wildlife viewing, transportation on the ranch, lodging and meals.

UTAH

Green River

OLD MOE GUIDE SERVICE

P.O. Box 3387, Park City, UT 84060. Attn.: Terry Collier. (801) 649-8092 or (800) 247-6197. Fax (801) 649-8126.

From its source high in Wyoming's Wind River Range, the Green River runs south into Flaming Gorge Reservoir. The river flows crystal clear from the dam, offering consistent temperatures and excellent year-round fishing. Abundant rainbow, cutthroat, brown and brook trout make this clear stretch of the Green some of the best fishing anywhere in the West, and the best way to enjoy this world-class river is by guided fishing/float trips. These trips are led by experienced river guides who lead participants to great trout fishing, incredible scenic beauty, excellent Dutch oven cooking and wildlife. Fishing floats of one to four days on a 29-mile stretch of the Green begin just below the Flaming Gorge Dam in Utah, continuing to the Colorado state line through Brown's Park—perfect for novice or skilled fishermen. Catch and release is encouraged. Overnight camping or customized trips can be arranged to meet the most challenging angling inclinations. Guided fishing float trips for one to two people are $275 per boat, per day. Overnight trips are $190 per person, per day. (See also *River Running*—Dinosaur River Expeditions.)

ALBERTA

Canadian Rockies

MCKENZIE'S TRAILS WEST

Box 971, Rocky Mountain House, Alberta, Canada T0M 1T0. (403) 845-6708.

"All our fishing trips are by horseback only and take place in the Rocky Mountain Wilderness in conjunction with our pack trips," the McKenzies explain (See Pack Trip chapter.) On the six-day trip there are good fishing opportunities for golden trout which will weigh in at about one to one and a half pounds, and cutthroat trout which will go up to four pounds. On the 12-day trips, there is more of a variety—cutthroat and golden trout and also rainbow trout, lake trout and Arctic grayling. We break camp every other day, packing all our gear with us as we go and camping at sparkling fresh water streams and lakes. It's the ultimate trip for fishermen, and great for the husband who enjoys fishing and the wife who enjoys riding (or vice versa). (See also *Pack Trips*.)

BRITISH
COLUMBIA

Chilko River,
Tsuniah Lake

MCLEAN'S RIVER RIDGE RESORT

Chilko Lake, P.O. Box 2560, Williams Lake, BC, Canada V2G 4P2. Attn.:
Ryan Schmidt. (604) 398-7755. Fax (604) 398-7487.

Trophy rainbow trout are native to the Chilko River with its turquoise blue, crystal clear waters, deep pools, rapids, ledges and slow-moving broad spots. The best dry-fly fishing is in July and August. The glacier-fed river, nestled in B.C.'s Coast Range, 180 miles north of Vancouver, is one of North America's premier trout streams. Wet flies work throughout the season, from June 11 to October 15. In August a major salmon run enters the system. Fish for average 1.5–3.5 lb. rainbows, or 4–9 lb. trophies, from flatbottom jet sleds by drifting the river, anchoring in front of pools, or wading the ledges in your own chest waders or state of the art float tubes. These are provided along with accommodations for 12 guests in the log lodge or private cabins, with three meals a day, experienced guides and even free fly-fishing lessons. All trips are custom-arranged. Rates: 3 days, $495 (US); 4 days, $695 (US); 7 days, $1,095 (US). Add $300 for round trip charter flights from Vancouver to a private landing strip on Chilko Lake. (See also *Pack Trips*.)

Pulling rainbow
from the Chilko
River—*McLean's*
River Ridge Resort,
B.C.

BRITISH
COLUMBIA

NIMMO BAY RESORT LTD.

*P.O. Box 696, Port McNeill, B.C., Canada V0N 2R0. (604) 956-4000 .
Fax (604) 956-2000.*

Mount Stephens

"This is an extremely competent operation, combining superb fishing in beautiful places with an intense concern for the environment," says the Speaker of the Canadian House of Commons (a passionate outdoorsman). Floating at the foot of Mount Stephens, this gracious coastal resort constructed of red and yellow cedar and fragrant fir offers an experience difficult to duplicate elsewhere. Nimmo Bay specializes in heli-fishing tours they call "the angling odyssey", and for seekers of fish in Homeric proportions, this could be the ticket to immortal, epic fishing tales. Your helicopter pilot is an expert mountain flyer with thousands of hours. He knows where the fish are, and exactly how best to catch (and release) them with single barbless hooks. The fishery accessibly by helicopter covers 30,000 square miles of coastal and mainland wilderness, and you can fly fish or spin cast for wild winter or summer run steelhead trout, all species of Pacific salmon, rainbows, cutthroats, dolly varden or char. You can reel in lunkers to your heart's content, then fly over breathtaking panoramas of glaciers, snow-capped peaks and virgin forests, and when you set down again in the next spot, the fishing is even better than before. At the end of the day there's a unique waterfall hot tub for soothing your fished-out bones. Trips of four to five days include meals, accommodations, helicopter and pilot/guide, fishing gear and lures, hip and chest waders, round-trip helicopter service from Port Hardy to the lodge and many more luxurious amenities. Rates: 4 days $2,775 US; 5 days $3,700 US. See photo page 226.

BRITISH
COLUMBIA

TEEPEE HEART RANCH

*Box 6, Big Creek, British Columbia, Canada V0L 1K0. Attn.: Hans Burch.
(604) 392-5015 or 398-1061.*

**Chilcotin-
Cariboo country**

Sherwood Lake in the beautiful Taseko Mountains of the coast range is a two-day ride over intermediate trails from the Teepee Heart Ranch. In this remote and scenic spot the ranch maintains a fishing camp with tepee tents where fishing is at its best. Tennessee Walking horses are the mounts for these trips, and any non-fisherpeople can spend their days riding magnificent trails, or just relaxing at the basecamp. Six-day rides are scheduled mid-June to early July, and in mid-August for six to ten riders. Rate approximately $140/day Cdn. per rider includes all but sleeping bag and personal items. The Teepee Heart Ranch is 85 miles west of Williams Lake. (See also *Cattle Drives / Roundups / Horse Drives, Pack Trips*.)

Copper Canyon Lodges, Mexico (page 260)

Wilderness / Nature Expeditions

Some of the most extraordinary journeys in North America are described in this chapter. They focus on experiencing the wilderness in a variety of ways. Some require the stamina for hiking and somewhat rugged rafting and camping. Others are designed for those who prefer the ease and amenities of comfortable lodges with transport by vehicle, charter flights or boats. Participants on many of these journeys are well over-fifty, and some expeditions are ideal for families.

On a barrier island off the coast of Georgia a comfortable lodge awaits birders and naturalists who want to observe migratory birds, bottlenose dolphins and loggerhead sea turtles.

In Alaska join small groups to experience the majestic scenes and wildlife of Glacier Bay, Katmai and Denali national parks, the glaciers and marine life of the Kenai Fjords and the native cultures. In Prince William Sound join a sailboat flotilla to observe glaciers, rain-forests, sea lions, harbor seals and whales. At a lodge in the Wrangell-St. Elias National Park, 100 miles from the nearest road, your time is divided between rafting, exploring on horseback, fishing or camping on a glacier. Sled dogs, veterans of the Iditarod, pull you back to the airplane landing zone.

In Baja California travelers pet 35-ton whales. In the Four Corners region they travel from one magnificent scene to another by small aircraft, meeting ground vehicles and rafts at strategic points for closeup exploration.

On an extraordinary journey by charter flight with daily land excursions, study Baffin Island and Greenland—the culture, history, carvings, crafts and people. On ice floes off the Nova Scotia coast see thousands of baby harp seals. In the far north, view polar bears in their natural habitat (water) from small boats. Far to the south, in the Bahamas, swim with dolphins.

ALASKA

**Exploring
Admiralty &
Chichagof
islands**

ALASKA DISCOVERY, INC.

234 Gold St., Dept. A, Juneau, AK 99801. Att: Kari Espera. (907) 586-1911. Fax (907) 586-2332.

Observing the bears off Admiralty and the whales off Chichagof Island are the focus of two five-day camping adventures in southeast Alaska. They are separate trips, but on some dates can be combined. A charter flight takes you from Juneau to the Admiralty Island shore where you travel in two-person Grumman canoes, paddling 15-20 miles altogether while exploring beaches and observing bird and marine life. You spend two days at a brown bear preserve to see them in their natural habitat, then fly back to Juneau. First and last nightss hotel stays are included. For the exploration off Chichagof Island, the trip begins and ends in Juneau with all charter costs and first and last night in hotel. A cabin cruiser takes you across Icy Strait to Chichagof, where you have your first lesson in a stable, two-person kayak. Spend days paddling (no more than 6–12 miles), beachcombing, hiking, and photographing humpback whales, sea lions, sea otters and seals. A thrill you won't forget is hearing a humpback whale at night sounding from 100 yards offshore. (See also *Sea Kayaking, River Running, Combos.*)

ALASKA

**Arctic Nat'l.
Wildlife Refuge,
Gates of the
Arctic**

ALASKA RIVER ADVENTURES

1831 Kuskokwim St., Suite 17, Anchorage, AK 99508. Attn.: George Heim. (907) 276-3418. Fax (907) 258-2211.

"The vast wilderness at the top of the world teems with life during the summer," states George Heim. "It's a time of total

**Alaska's Rivers are
Wild & Scenic—**
*Alaska River
Adventures, AK.*

daylight when you can see caribou migrations, nesting birds and fields of wildflowers." George's trips into the Arctic National Wildlife Refuge and the Gates of the Arctic are planned for floating rivers, but usually they include as much hiking as rafting. "Sometimes we stay in camp to sleep in midday," he says, "then do our trekking between 10 p.m. and 5 a.m. when there's magical light for photos." Rafting the Aichilik River, incredibly dramatic as it flows northward through cathedral-like walls into the Arctic Ocean is a nine-day trip which offers the possibility of watching caribou, sheep, wolves, grizzlies, musk ox and birds before starting down a river. Scheduled in late June, $2,995 including air charters. Customized trips July and August. (See also *Dog Sledding*.)

ALASKA

ALASKA WILDERNESS SAILING SAFARIS
P.O. Box 1313, Valdez, AK 99686. Att: Nancy Lethcoe. (907) 835-5175.

Valdez

Naturalist guided flotilla sailing and kayaking in Prince William Sound is the specialty of Jim and Nancy Lethcoe. Both are Ph.Ds and authors who write about the glaciers, geology and natural history of the region, as well as cruising and the Exxon Valdez oil spill. Their fleet consists of four boats— 30', 37', 40' and 44'—which are chartered with skip-

Ready to join others for flotilla sailing—*Alaska Wilderness Sailing Safaris, AK.*

pers (usually Jim and Nancy) or without by experienced sailors. Anchoring together, all go ashore in dinghies or double inflatable kayaks (provided with each boat) to join the Lethcoes on nature walks which focus on a rainforest, the tidal zone of beaches, receding and advancing glaciers, whales (Orca, Humpback and Minke), Steller sea lions sleeping or socializing, harbor seals frolicking on icebergs or sea otter mothers shepherding young pups. Cruises are planned for three or six days, and guided activities are tailored to the interests of the guests. Each crew provides its own food. To start these sailing safaris, take the 8 a.m. Stan Stephens tourboat from Valdez to Growler Island, a six-hour trip. The Lethcoes meet you here, and after a salmon bake your flotilla of boats starts its cruise. Sailboats sleep two to six adults. Rates without skippers range from $280-$400/person for 3-day cruises, and $700-$1,000/person for 6 days. For skippered cruises they are $450 for 3 days, $1,125 for 6 days. Rates include berth, guided activities, interpretative materials, dinghy, kayaks, and (on skippered trips) licensed skipper and meals. Children 12 and under half price.

ALASKA

Kenai Wilderness, Denali National Park—natural

ALASKA WILDLAND ADVENTURES
P.O. Box 389, Girdwood, AK 99587. Attn.: Kirk Hoessle. (907) 783-2928 or (800) 334-8730.

How can you plan an exploratory trip in so vast a land as Alaska? Wildland's answer is to "experience it"—one region at a time with only a few other explorers. "Your trip should

history safaris

Exploring Denali National Park Refuge—*Alaska Wildland Adventures, AK.*

provide quality and an intimate introduction," says director Kirk Hoessle. From its woodland base with comfortable rustic cabins on the Kenai River (south of Anchorage) Wildlands links experiences together in 10- to 12-day natural history safaris for small groups (never more than 18). Varied itineraries combine experiences such as rafting or fishing the Kenai River, several days of comfortable tent camping, cruising the Kenai Fjords with its glaciers, puffins, sea otters and seals, a flight to a mountain lake to catch Arctic grayling amid a spectacular view, observing caribou or grizzlies and other wildlife. A special eight-day *Senior Safari* features a float on the Kenai River, a cruise in the Kenai Fjords and viewing and photographing wildlife in Denali National Park—adventurous travel yet non-exertive activity. "Our safaris are designed to introduce the beauty, wildlife and raw energy of this last frontier—all in guided comfort," Hoessle adds. Safari rates average $250-$280 per day with weekly scheduled departures. (See also *Boats / Cruises / Scuba, Fly Fishing, this chapter—Denali Backcountry Lodge.*)

ALASKA

Denali National Park— wilderness lodges

CAMP DENALI & NORTH FACE LODGE

P.O. Box 67, Denali National Park, AK 99755. (907) 683-2290. [Winter: Box 369, Cornish, NH 03746. (603) 675-2248. Fax (603) 675-9125.]

Two uncommon wilderness lodges are set in the geographic heart of Denali National Park with panoramic views of majestic Mt. McKinley. Both are reached by vehicle from the Park entrance over a 90-mile Park road, a five and a half hour trip during which a naturalist/guide introduces you to the Park's flora, fauna, and geology. The two lodges, a mile apart, are similar yet quite different. Camp Denali provides 18 well-appointed guest cabins, central shower, dining room, living room, and library. "Rustic elegance" describes its ambience—a place for those wanting a three- to five-night indepth experience and taste of wilderness life. North Face provides modern rooms for 35 people with the atmosphere of a small country inn, featuring 2- or 3-night stays "with a touch of country class." The region is a naturalist's paradise—mammals, bird life, wildflowers and scenery that is a textbook example of the effects of mountain uplift and glaciation. At each lodge self-guided and naturalist-guided hiking, photography, flightseeing, canoeing, biking, rafting, fishing, gold panning and interpretive programs maximize your visit. Rates: Camp Denali, $225/night, North Face Lodge, $250/night, children under 12 years 25% less. See front cover photo.

ALASKA

Denali National
Park

DENALI BACKCOUNTRY LODGE

*P.O. Box 189, Denali Park, AK 99755. (907) 683-2594 or (800) 841-0692
year round. Fax (907) 683-1341. [Sep. to June: P.O. Box 810, Girdwood,
AK 99587. (907) 783-1342 or (800) 841-0692. Fax (907) 783-1308.]*

Managed by Alaska Wildland Adventures (see listing above),
this lodge is located deep within Denali National Park at the
end of Park Road—92 miles from the park's east entrance.
Included is a half-day coach ride through the park offering a
chance to see grizzlies, moose, caribou, Dall sheep, wolves,
fox, golden eagles and other bird life, as well as Mt. McKinley—
the tallest peak in North America. The 24 comfortably ap-
pointed cabins, each with private bath, and spacious lounge
and dining/lounge areas, provide cozy headquarters for
exploring the region. The lodge naturalists introduce you to
the fragile ecosystems in this sometimes harsh environment,
and to the equally spectacular boreal forest and sub-arctic
tundra. Hike a nearby ridge for a spectacular view, explore
on a mountain bike, try your hand at gold panning or fishing
for grayling, go on a guided (or unguided) hike or by van to
a scenic spot. With a concern for wildlife and the rare ecosystems, guests divide into small groups for various activities.
Open from early June to mid-September for one- to four-
night stays. Minimum of two nights recommended. (See also
Boats / Cruises / Scuba, Fly Fishing and this chapter—Alaska
Wildland Adventures.)

ALASKA

Kenai Peninsula,
Katmai, Denali
National Park

GREAT ALASKA FISH CAMP & SAFARIS

*HCO Box 218, Sterling, AK 99672. Attn.: Laurence John. (800) 544-2261.
Fax (503) 452-7429.*

"Our guided safaris for only six travellers are the ticket if you
want to experience Alaska for yourselves—in an intimate
atmosphere with just the right degree of challenge," advises
Laurence John. He recommends nature walks and wildlife
viewing for seniors, active safaris for most, and adventuresome trips for those who want to push it a little. On a ten-day
Greatland Safari in safari vehicles you explore the Kenai
Peninsula, Katmai and Denali National Park. The trip includes rafting the Kenai River, sea kayaking or cruising in the
protected waters of Kachemak Bay Maritime Wildlife Refuge, and paddling the calm waters of the Swan Lakes Canoe
Trail. In Denali you go flightseeing, photograph a majestic
bull caribou, view other animals, pan for gold and raft a river.
For those who want more adventure, the Wilderness Safari
provides sleeping in tents and more kayaking, rafting and
mountain biking. Other specialties include the Bears of Katmai,
a safari and fishing combination, adventure camps on Skilak

Lake with fishing, rafting and hiking, and various other combinations customized for groups. All trips base out of Laurence's deluxe lodge, its back door swinging open to the Kenai Wildlife Refuge and the front door to two of Alaska's famous fishing and migratory salmon streams. Seminar facilities. Rates for ten-day safaris: around $260/day, 10% less for Senior Safari and Under Canvas trips. (See also *Fly Fishing*.)

ALASKA

Hike, trek, raft, canoe, sea kayak in 5 national parks & Noatak River

HUGH GLASS BACKPACKING CO.
P.O. Box 110796, Anchorage, Ak 99511. Att: Chuck Ash. (907) 344-1340. Fax (907) 344-4614.

"There is an inner peace, a tranquility, to be found in the wilderness that is attainable in but few other settings," remarks founder Chuck Ash. The regions for his trips are the Wrangell-St. Elias, Lake Clark, Kenai Fjords, Gates of the Arctic and Katmai national parks, the Noatak River National Preserve and the Arctic National Wildlife Refuge. All are true wilderness areas accessible only by bush plane. Trips, led by experienced Alaskan guides, involve hiking/trekking, rafting, canoeing or sea-kayaking. Emphasis is on scenery, natural history and enjoyment. Pass from alpine tundra to bottom-land spruce forest, viewing volcanic peaks, pristine waters, majestic fjords and glacial mountains. Observe how bear, wolves, moose, lynx, fox, salmon, trout, eagles, songbirds, waterfowl and wildflowers are all interlocked in a timeless embrace. Trips: 5-10 days. Average cost: $125/day. Start from Bettles, Anchorage or King Salmon. (See also *Sea Kayaking, Backpacking / Hiking / Walking, Fly Fishing—* Brightwater Alaska.)

ALASKA

Katmai and Denali national parks, and Kenai Peninsula— brown bear watch

NATURAL HABITAT WILDLIFE ADVENTURES
One Sussex Station, Sussex, NJ 07461. Attn.: Ben Bressler. (201) 702-1525 or (800) 543-8917. Fax (201) 702-1335.

The *Brown Bear Watch* the end of July offers a chance to observe not only bears but other animal life as well as unmatched scenery during 13 days of travel in the Kenai Peninsula and Katmai and Denali national parks. Viewing porpoises, whales, sea lions, puffins and sea otters while cruising the Kenai Fjords, and spotting moose in the Kenai Wildlife Refuge, are highlights of your first few days of travel. Next, the brown bears of Katmai are the focus of your stay at Brooks Lodge in Katmai National Park. From the safety of protective platforms at Brooks Falls you watch them just a few feet away, fishing for lively salmon swimming upstream to spawn. They pay little attention to you as they concentrate on their difficult task. Exploring Denali National Park absorbs the

"Fisherman"
unaware of
photographer—
Natural Habitat, AK.

final days of your trip. It starts with rafting on the Nenana
River, then driving to the heart of the park for two nights at
North Face Lodge. Wildlife viewing focuses on grizzly bear,
Dall sheep, moose and caribou with options for hikes, fishing, cycling and canoeing. Extremely knowledgeable guides
and naturalists enhance this exploration. All transport in
Alaska, naturalist guides, accommodations and meals are
included in rate of $3,795. Group limited to 16. (See this
chapter for trips in Manitoba, Nova Scotia, Baja.)

ALASKA

**Wrangell/St.
Elias National
Park**

ULTIMA THULE OUTFITTERS
*Box 109, Chitina, AK 99566. Attn.: Paul & Donna Claus. (907) 344-1892
(phone & fax) or (907) 345-1160 (radiophone).*

A bush pilot flies you 350 miles from Anchorage to a remote,
modern lodge in the 13-million-acre vast and beautiful
Wrangell/St. Elias National Park. The lodge is 40 miles from
the closest neighbor, 100 miles from the nearest road. "Flying
is a necessity here," says Paul Claus, a veteran bush pilot.
"Everything we do is by air." In winter you might land on a
glacier for a day of skiing or ice climbing, or fly to a point
where you can mush through this vast paradise on a dogsled
behind winning Iditaraod dogs, or fly over the region to see
dall sheep, caribou or moose. Evenings at the lodge include
a sauna and viewing the Northern Lights from a dogsled or
the ice skating rink. In summer spend a night camping in
comfort on a glacier, and next morning hitch the dogs up to
sleds for a run to the airplane landing zone you could also fly

to a sand bar for a day's rafting on a wild river, or fly to a trailhead for exploring on horseback, and catch a salmon or grayling or dolly. Each day opens a new adventure, with guides and planes provided to take guests in whatever directions they choose. Rates of $500-$600/night per person include flights, all activities, meals, lodging. Children under 12 half price, under five free, babysitting free. "We love the majestic wild country which surrounds our year-round home," Paul adds. For most of us, it's the ultimate Alaskan adventure.

COLORADO

Canyonlands,
Dinosaur
National
Monument,
Colorado
Rockies,
Canadian Arctic

**Bird watching near
Santa Elena
Canyon**—*Cloud
Ridge Naturalists,
CO.*

CLOUD RIDGE NATURALISTS

8297 Overland Road, Ward, CO 80481. Att: Audrey Benedict. (303) 459-3248.

This organization offers a range of field seminars for exploring the West's special places. Dinosaur tracks and traces, butterfly ecology and behavior, alpine wildflowers and desert rivers—these and other phenomenon are enjoyed by small groups of 12-20. No seminar requires a background in science—only an interest in learning. Knowledgeable instructors have first-hand research or working experience with their subjects—and the enthusiasm to make it fun. Trips are graded for families—easy (mostly vehicle travel), moderate and strenuous. They range from Utah's Canyonlands to the Canadian Arctic. Scheduled May-Oct., 2-10 days, rates aver-

age $50-$60/day except the 10-day Arctic trip, $2,900. Fine lodging or pretty campsites selected. "We strive to be the best—at whatever we do!" declares director Audrey Benedict.

GEORGIA

Barrier island birding

LITTLE ST. SIMON ISLAND
P.O. Box 1078-AG, St. Simons Island, GA 31522. Att: Debbie McIntyre. (912) 638-7472.

Birders may spot up to 200 species on the sand beaches, and in the saltwater and freshwater marshes, tidal flats and pine and oak forests of this privately owned, unspoiled barrier island off the Georgia coast. The pace is restful. Among the other sights and sounds: bottlenose dolphins, bellowing alligators and loggerhead sea turtles who come ashore in the summer to lay their eggs. Explore the 10,000-acre secluded and undeveloped island in the company of professional naturalists. This intriguing hideaway offers the luxury of charming accommodations, excellent meals, pool swimming, miles of uninhabited beach, horseback riding, canoeing and other activities to enjoy in small groups (up to 24). Rates: $150-$200/person, 2-night minimum, including room, meals, activities. Full island reservations available for groups. No charge for island ferry with reservation. Open Feb.-Nov.

He's smiling at you!—*Bill durrence for Wilderness Southeast, GA.*

GEORGIA

Smoky Mountains, Everglades, Okefenokee

WILDERNESS SOUTHEAST
711-AG Sandtown Rd., Savannah, GA 31410. (912) 897-5108. Fax (912) 897-5116.

"Nature provides the setting and Wilderness Southeast handles everything else—well-planned itineraries, competent, personable naturalist guides, high quality camping gear and

Swamp, barrier islands— educational camping

great food," says Fulfillment Director Gussie Motter. Since 1973, this non-profit "school of the outdoors" has specialized in educational wilderness expeditions in the Okefenokee Swamp, the Everglades, the Golden Isles off the coast of Georgia and South Carolina, and, more recently, Belize, Costa Rica and the Amazon Basin. Learn about alligators and life under the lily pads as you paddle through the primeval splendor of the Okefenokee Swamp. Sea kayaking expeditions explore the 10,000 Islands area of the Everglades or the wild barrier islands of the Georgia coast. Other programs allow you to observe the ancient nesting ritual of the loggerhead sea turtles, or swim with the endangered West Indian manatee. Diverse tropical ecology programs offer riverboat explorations and/or chances to hike and snorkel in Belize and Costa Rica and the Amazon Basin. WSE also offers special opportunities for teens. Most rates range from $70 to $100/day with discounts for families.

MAINE

Family adventures in Maine, Quebec, Baffin Island, Georgia, Florida

Sea kayaking the Maine coast—
Chewonki Family Adventures, ME.

CHEWONKI FAMILY ADVENTURES
RR 2, Box 1200 PD, Wiscasset, ME 04578. Att: Greg Shute. (207) 882-7323. Fax (207) 882-4074.

Does your family enjoy canoeing, hiking, sea kayaking, camping? Do your friends have similar interests? For a group of approximately ten participants Chewonki will provide leaders and all equipment for tailor-made trips for canoeing Maine rivers, sea kayaking along the coast, hiking at Katahdin or in Baffin Island, canoeing the George River in Quebec or (in Feb./Mar.) Georgia's Okefenokee or Florida's Everglades. You are involved in each aspect of the trip but supply only

your clothing, packs and sleeping bags at average rates of $80/day. "Building a close, small, joyful community is a satisfying and important part of the adventures we offer to families," Don Hudson, Director of Chewonki Foundation, explains. "The activities are varied and rewarding." Chewonki is a non-profit educational foundation that offers environmental education programs throughout the year. Trips are planned according to the skills, length of time and interests of a family or group. "The food is perfect and leaders' knowledge of camps, natural history and pre-planning is excellent," writes one participant. "Chewonki runs fabulous vacations." (See also *Canoeing / Kayaking, Youth.*)

MINNESOTA

BWCA, Quetico
Provincial
Park—lodge/
camping trips

GUNFLINT LODGE & OUTFITTERS

Gunflint Trail, Box 750, Grand Marais, MN 55604. Att: Bruce & Sue Kerfoot. (218) 388-2294 or (800) 328-3325. Fax (218) 388-9429.

With emphasis on learning the skills of wilderness living, the Kerfoots send small groups of eight or nine into the vast Boundary Waters Canoe Area on the Minnesota/Canada border. One seven-day outing involves four nights at lodges and two camping, and another is a complete camping and canoeing trip. A lodge-to-lodge canoeing trip is "somewhat patterned after the treks in the Himalayas—the guests do not carry anything but day packs, and afternoon tea awaits them at each day's destination," explains Bruce. Spend a night at Gunflint Lodge, next night camp out, then arrive at Chippewa Inn in Canada. Camp again on the return to Gunflint Lodge for two nights. This seven-day camping/canoeing trip stresses wildlife, birds, photography, fishing, wilderness cooking and camping skills. It's a nature-oriented fun trip, not a test of endurance. Free Duluth airport pickup/return. Jul.-Sep. trips. (See also *Canoeing / Kayaking, Ski Touring / Snowmobiling.*)

NEW MEXICO

Four Corners
region by air/
vehicle/raft

SOUTHWEST SAFARIS — FLIGHTSEEING

P.O. Box 945, Dept. AG, Santa Fe, NM 87504. Att: Bruce Adams. (505) 988-4246 or (800) 842-4246.

Bruce Adams has solved the problem of how to cover the vast distances of the spectacular American Southwest. Since 1974, Southwest Safaris has used aircraft to transport visitors from one magnificent, often inaccessible, scene to another. After landing—at the Grand Canyon, Monument Valley, Mesa Verde, Canyon de Chelly, Arches, Canyonlands, Bryce Canyon, Oak Creek Canyon or the San Juan River—tour members climb on board a ground vehicle or raft and continue their backcountry exploration of the Four Corners Region. Southwest Safaris offers 1-day tours as well as over-night expeditions. All trips emphasize the study of geology, archaeology, ecology and western history. As sculpted mesas and volcanic mountains, painted deserts and petrified forests, gooseneck canyons and unmapped Indian ruins pass beneath the wing, safari members travel back through geologic time. Bruce's FAA-approved natural history tours are offered year-round; rates from $299. Arrival: Santa Fe, NM.

TEXAS

THE FOOTHILLS SAFARI CAMP AT FOSSIL RIM

P.O. Box 329, Glen Rose, TX 76043. (800) 245-0771. Fax (817) 897-3785.

Texas Hill Country

Early morning quiet is interrupted by the howl of a wolf in the distance. Soon other wolves join in and their songs fill the air. Deep in the heart of this wilderness center in Texas Hill Country, two hours southwest of Dallas, you view some of the world's most endangered, threatened and exotic animals, while staying in deluxe, air conditioned tents with private baths and eating meals such as grilled filet mignon or sesame chicken with wild mushrooms. The schedule is flexible at this first authentic safari camp in America. You experience the excitement and romance of a tented African safari where your neighbors are antelopes, gazelles, red wolves and cheetahs and 1,000 other free-roaming animals representing 32 species that are kept on the 3,000-acre property. Encounter herds of wildebeest, oryx or zebra on early morning and sunset game drives led by professional naturalists across rolling hills and African-like savannahs. Naturalist guides assist you with a closer look at the plight of species nearing extinction; you see at first hand what can be done to preserve the animals, and take close-up photos. Evenings you gather around a bonfire to swap stories or star-gaze through the powerful telescope. Hiking tours are also arranged as well as custom trips for groups. Rates include all essentials except clothing and personal gear: 3 days/$375–$450, 4 days, $562.50–$675.

UTAH

HONDOO RIVERS & TRAILS

P.O. Box 98, Torrey, UT 84775. Att: Pat or Gary George. (801) 425-3519 or (800) 332-2696.

Henry Mts., Awapa Plateau, San Rafael Swell, Green River, naturalist trips

If you want to sight canyon-country critters and photograph them, grab your binoculars and telephoto lenses and head into Utah's backcountry with Hondoo Trails. Naturalists lead these trips. The focus is on large mammals—elk, buffalo, bighorn sheep and antelope. With basecamp headquarters, ride each day on horseback or by vehicle to prime habitats. In June observe elk in Utah's high plateaus. From July to September buffalo roam in the Henry Mountains. August is the month for spotting antelope in Awapa Plateau. Bighorn sheep graze in the canyonlands in September. These five-day basecamp excursions are $550-$670. In April and October

Gary leads an expedition in the San Rafael Swell to observe wild horses (5 days, $610). A five-day seminar and canyon-country vehicle tour is scheduled May, August, September, $660. Another rock art seminar combined with rafting the Green River, camping and staying several nights as guests at the Ute Indian's Florence Creek Lodge in June and July, 7 days, $840. Arrival point Grand Junction, CO. Trips depart from Torrey (town of Green River) with pre-trip motel nights included in rates. (See also *Pack Trips, River Running, Cattle Drives*—Pace Ranch.)

BRITISH COLUMBIA/ YUKON

Chilcotin, Alsek, Tatshenshini, and Firth rivers

CANADIAN RIVER EXPEDITIONS
40-3524 W. 16th Ave., Vancouver, BC, Canada V6R 3C1. (604) 738-4449. Fax (604) 736-5526.

River running is far more than paddling and action. It provides a natural history classroom, especially in these regions noted for wildlife, birds, glaciers, waterfowl and diverse ecosystems. Experts who explain it all accompany each of CRE's river trips. Silently drifting oar-powered rafts optimize wildlife viewing. On just one trip on the Tatshenshini 30 grizzlies were spotted, and on another 14 new species of birds were added to the CRE Bird List. The Chilcotin-Fraser trip is a backcountry introduction to incredible diversity of landforms and ecosystems—from lush fjords and coastal islands, 13,000-foot peaks and enormous glaciers to mountain lakes, forests, grasslands, sage and cactus. The Upper Alsek is a place to observe moose, beaver, songbirds, terns

13,000′ peaks in the St. Elias Mountain—*Canadian River Expeditions, BC/Yukon.*

and waterfowl and an amazing variety of ecosystems as the river carves its way through the St. Elias Mountains. Along the Firth River in late June and early July, with 24-hour daylight, wildflowers explode in color and scores of bird species are seen nesting. This also is the region to encounter the migration of the Porcupine Caribou herd, with over 100,000 animals fording the river. Running these rivers opens new comprehension of the natural world. (See also *River Running*.)

MANITOBA

NATURAL HABITAT WILDLIFE ADVENTURES
One Sussex Station, Sussex, NJ 07461. Attn.: Ben Bressler.

Hudson Bay—
polar bear watch
(201) 702-1525 or (800) 543-8917. Fax (201) 702-1335.

Every fall the tundra surrounding Churchill on Canada's Hudson Bay becomes a stopover for hundreds of the largest, most dangerous and most respected of all creatures—the polar bear, uncontested king of the Arctic. In winter the bears make their home on the pack ice. In summer they are forced into a migratory circle, set adrift on rudderless rafts of broken ice that eventually land near Churchill. The *Polar Bear Watch* in October and early November offers animal enthusiasts, photographers and adventure travelers of all ages the rare chance to actually mingle with some of these extraordinary creatures as they live, wild and free, in their own habitat. Viewing is done from tundra buggies with oversize tires and safe, outside viewing platforms. Usually six to ten bears are seen daily, but there may be as many as 50. The people of Churchill are committed to helping the bears migrate safely through their town. Side trips include a visit to an Eskimo museum, with chance to build an igloo or meet with foremost authorities on polar bears, Arctic wildlife and the northern lights. Rates include round trip air Winnipeg/Churchill, all transfers, accommodations, meals and naturalist guides for 6-9 days, $1,745-$2,595. (See this chapter for trips in Alaska, Nova Scotia, Baja.)

NOVA SCOTIA

NATURAL HABITAT WILDLIFE ADVENTURES
One Sussex Station, Sussex, NJ 07461. Attn.: Ben Bressler.

Gulf of St.
Lawrence—seal
watch
(201) 702-1525 or (800) 543-8917. Fax (201) 702-1335.

Travel by helicopter to land on the ice floes in eastern Canada's Gulf of St. Lawrence where you can actually embrace newborn pups! On this *Seal Watch* excursion in March you experience a thrill which many say has changed their lives, and your participation will help protect one of the world's most endearing animals. "It's like dropping into another world," says one participant. Says another, "The feeling I received was overwhelming peace, contentment, happiness and love.

Getting acquainted with a cuddly Harp Seal pup—*Natural Habitat, Nova Scotia.*

Never have I felt closer to God and heaven." Participants meet in Halifax for a short flight to the Magdalen Islands and a hotel overnight. Next morning naturalist guides provide expedition suits and assign helicopters for flights to reach the seals (10-45 minutes). You set down a few hundred yards from the herd and in small groups approach the snowy-white pups. In winter some 250,000 Harp Seals enter the Gulf to bear their young, nurse them, then abruptly leave them to make their own way. Only during three weeks in March can you visit these cuddly animals who have been slaughtered for years for their pelts—a practice recently banned in Canada. The consequent loss in the region's economy is partially restored by tourism to see the seals. Naturalist/scientist presentations, photo workshops, nature hikes, cross-country skiing or snowshoeing are offered participants. Rates for five- or six-day trips with one to four flights to the ice floes range from $1,595-$2,495. (See this chapter for trips in Alaska, Manitoba and Baja.)

NORTHWEST TERRITORIES/ GREENLAND

ARCTIC ODYSSEYS

P.O. Box 37-A, Medina, WA 98039. Attn.: Skip and Susan Voorhees. (206) 455-1960 or (800) 252-7899. Fax (206) 453-6903.

Natural history treks

Among the most adventurous of explorations are those offered by Arctic Odysseys, a pioneer in leading travellers into the vast and spectacular Arctic. They use Twin Otters on their Arctic travels—the ideal aircraft for viewing the region because of its low airspeed and short takeoff and landing capability. From March through May they schedule a nine-day dog sled trip, departing weekly from Ottawa. You are outfitted with caribou fur pants and jacket and seal kamiks and travel by dogsled the next six days with Inuit guides to explore southwest Baffin Island, spending nights in tents or igloos. Seals, walrus, polar bears and land mammals inhabit the region. Through July and August another nine-day trip from Ottawa features the wildlife and culture on Baffin Island. In August an eight-day trip departs from Winnipeg to the Northwest Territories to view and photograph polar bears 700 miles north of Churchill in the natural setting bears favor—water. Bear-viewing is done from boats. Nights are spent at lodges. Another August trek, the most extensive of Arctic Odysseys' itineraries, departs from Ottawa for eleven days of exploring in Northwest Territories and Greenland. Stops in Baffin Island include Iqaluit, Cape Dorset, then to Resolute Bay on Little Cornwallis Island, Grise Fjord on Ellesmere Island, Beechey Island, Pond Inlet and Bylot Island. Then on to Jakobshavn on Greenland's "Iceberg Coast" before return to Iqaluit and Ottawa. It's a journey filled with surrealistic beauty, views of wildlife and marine mammals, historic places, villages, carvings, crafts, museums, native peoples and unbelievably spectacular scenes. "You'll see the Arctic as it really exists," promise the Voorhees. Among their recent guests are prestigious museum groups. Rates: $372–$472/day for 9-day trips, $541/day for 11-day trip, including transport, most meals, accommodations, guide services.

Polar bear viewing from a small boat—*Susan Voorhees for Arctic Odysseys, NW Territories.*

QUEBEC

Longue-Pointe-
de-Mingan

MINGAN ISLAND CETACEAN STUDY

*106, rue Bord de la Mer, Longue-Pointe-de-Mingan, Quebec, Canada
G0G 1V0. Attn.: Richard Sears. (418) 949-2845. [Winter: 285, Green, St.
Lambert, Qc, Canada J4P 1T3. (514) 465-9176.]*

Get away to the sea and immerse yourself in an educational
adventure. This non-profit research organization invites the
public to participate in the ecological studies of marine
mammals. It is a rare opportunity to take part and contribute
to this ongoing research conducted by the first people to
carry out extensive research of cetaceans along the Quebec
North Shore. Educational programs are offered June-Octo-
ber to help finance the research and enhance the public's
awareness of marine mammals in their natural habitat. The
program focuses on local populations of blue, humpback,
finback and minke whales, as well as white-sided and white-
beaked dolphins. Sessions of five to ten days are based at the
coastal village of Longue-Pointe-de-Mingan, where you are
introduced to rookeries of seabirds such as Atlantic puffins,
Arctic terns, razorbills and eider ducks, among others. Sail
each morning on 24-foot inflatable boats, greeted by birds,
grey seals and harbor porpoises. "We are certain that experiencing the graceful breach of a 40-ton humpback whale, a
close encounter with an 85-foot blue whale, or being en-
gulfed in a herd of 300 white-sided dolphins will leave a
lasting impression," says Richard. Guests can actively participate in research or simply observe and photograph the
marine mammals and birds. "It's your vacation," Richard
adds. "You decide." Rate: $145 US per day, Jun. to Oct.

YUKON/
NORTHWEST
TERRITORIES/
ALASKA

Canoe, backpack,
raft, dog sled, ski

ARCTIC EDGE

*Box 4850-AG, Whitehorse, Yukon Territory, Canada Y1A 4N6. Attn.:
Dave Loeks. (403) 633-5470. Fax (403) 633-3820.*

"We specialize in expedition-style travel by canoe, backpack,
raft, dog team and skis in the mountain regions of our home
area," writes Dave Loeks. His "area" is the Far Northwest—
the rivers and mountains of the Yukon, Northwest Territories and Alaska. From April to November you can explore by
canoe the rivers flowing out of the remote Ogilview-MacKenzie
Mountains—pristine, dramatic, incredibly scenic. In the North
Yukon National Park observe grizzlies, bald eagles, caribou
and Dall sheep. Come in the arctic spring when 12-18 hours
of warm sunlight makes for fast traveling by dog team or skis
over a settled snowpack in Yukon backcountry. These are
neither survival trips nor soft adventures, but "for people
who will swing a paddle, shoulder a pack and participate in

the tasks of a wilderness journey." Most trips 12-21 days, scheduled and custom, average rates $150-$200/day US + air charters.

FLORIDA/
CARIBBEAN

BOTTOM TIME ADVENTURES

P.O. Box 11919, Ft. Lauderdale, FL 33339-1919. Attn.: A.J. Bland. (305) 921-7798 or (800) 234-8464. Fax (305) 920-5578.

The Bahamas

Swimming with dolphins has been a specialty with BTA for 12 years in a remote area of the northern Bahamas. "We do not feed or entice these magnificent wild creatures for their affections," A.J. Bland explains. "They visit with us of their own free will, and apparently for the pure fun of interacting with us. On each trip they have been there to greet us. Often they swim within inches of our masks, enticing us to follow them to sea. They are eager swimmers and seem to enjoy encounters with humans who are accomplished swimmers." Olympic Gold Medalists who have visited the dolphins speak of establishing eye contact and feeling really one with them—interacting "more intimately than I ever thought possible," reports one. BTA schedules the unique trips April–September on the *Bottom Time II*, its 90' catamaran which sleeps up to 28 in double cabins and provides chef-prepared meals, licensed guides and crew. Videos and stills from each day's encounters are reviewed in group discussion. Rate: $1,395 for 7 days. Also charter and group rates. (See also *Cycling / Mountain Biking, Boats / Cruises / Scuba*.)

The delight of swimming with dolphins—*Bottom Time Adventures, Florida / Caribbean.*

MEXICO

**Baja Peninsula,
San Ignacio
Lagoon**

**Petting a 35-ton
whale**—*Amistad,
Mexico.*

AMISTAD, INC.
*107 Stillmeadow Lane, Hot Springs, AR 71913. Att: Gene Sparling.
(501) 525-0964.*

Gene Sparling invites people to share the awe-inspiring experience of meeting 35-ton whales who gently surface next to your boat to be petted and touched, maintaining eye contact with you. The mothers commonly push their babies to the boats to encourage contact. This "friendly activity" has taken place only since the 1970s, though the Pacific Grey Whales have bred in these waters of the San Ignacio Lagoon off Baja's west coast for thousands of years. Gene's guides are local people, and knowing them enriches the trips. The week's adventure starts in Loreto with accommodations there the first night (also the last). Next day drive to San Ignacio (167 miles) and on to Laguna (36 miles) for camping and spending two to six hours in a 22' fishing boat each day for whale watching. Beachcombing, birding, siestas and meeting the locals fill the day. Scheduled and custom trips, Feb.-Apr., 7 days $1,150. Gene offers another adventure October through April in Canyon San Pablo to see prehistoric cave paintings—thousands of them—traveling by backpack or with burros, 7 days, $1,150.

MEXICO

Copper Canyon

COPPER CANYON LODGES
*1100 Owendale Dr., Suite G, Troy, MI 48083. Attn.: Judy Almeranti.
(313) 689-2444 or (800) 776-3942. Fax (313) 689-9119.*

Mexico's Copper Canyon is four times the size of our Grand Canyon and half again as deep. It is an intricate maze of rugged canyons carved by great rivers—a remote region of pine forests, sculpted rocks, rushing streams, waterfalls and magnificent canyon walls rising 7,600 feet. And it is the home of the Tarahumara Indians, renowned as the world's greatest runners. An ultra-scenic five-hour ride on the Chihuahua al Pacifico Railway from Chihuahua City to Creel begins a nine-day guided excursion which makes it possible to explore the spectacular region in comfort. At the Copper Canyon Sierra Lodge, where rooms are heated by wood stoves and lit by kerosene lamps, you hike to a waterfall, painted cave and hot springs and view canyons just three miles from the Continental Divide. On Day 4 you take the seven-hour drive descending 7,000 feet to the sub-tropical town of Batopilas, where the cobblestone streets are swept each morning,and mule trains arrive from neighboring villages to pick up supplies and tropical flowers grow in profusion. The restored Riverside Lodge with its gardens, Victorian furnishings and fine chef is your comfortable base for exploring the town and its environs. By Day 8 you are back in Creel and boarding the train for return to Chihuahua City. Rates for 9-day tour including all but gratuities: $1,150-$1,300, dbl. occupancy. See photo page 240.

MEXICO

Baja Peninsula, Magdalena Bay, Sea of Cortez— whale watch

NATURAL HABITAT WILDLIFE ADVENTURES
One Sussex Station, Sussex, NJ 07461. Attn.: Ben Bressler. (201) 702-1525 or (800) 543-8917. Fax (201) 702-1335.

This *Whale Watch* expedition in January takes you to the warmth of the Mexican sun. The annual journey made by thousands of Pacific Gray whales from the rich feeding grounds of Alaska's Bering Sea to the lagoons in Mexico's Baja Peninsula may be the most impressive of all animal migrations. Their travels take them 6,000 miles to the warm and calm waters of Magdalena Bay, a favorite spot for breeding and birthing. It is here where humans can encounter these magnificent animals. Sail on a 14-passenger motor yacht, the *Don Jose* or a smaller skiff to observe 50-foot Grays from within an arm's length. They are not afraid of humans. Sometimes there is a chance to actually pet them, a truly unforgettable experience. Baja is also home to other marine life. Humpback, Blue and Killer whales are frequently seen throughout the Sea of Cortez. Bottlenosed dolphins swim alongside the bow of the boat. California sea lions allow people to swim with them off Espiritu Santo Island. Accommodations are in double cabins on the *Don Jose* on these eight-day trips. 1993 trips depart from Los Angeles or Tucson at rate of $2,175 including round trip air to La Paz, Mexico. 1994 trips will depart from La Paz at rate of $1,995. (See this chapter for trips in Alaska, Manitoba, Nova Scotia.)

Jack Montgomery for Chewonki Expeditions, Maine / Canada (page 266)

Youth

What do you know about horsemanship—riding, packing, feeding, hobbling? What experience have you had camping—selecting and pitching camp, fire building, fire protection? Are wildlife tracking and sign identification among your skills? Do you know a lot about map reading and orienteering? Or camp chores? These are among the skills which young coed groups learn at ranch camps in summer.

Other teenage programs focus on backpacking, rock climbing, rappeling, canoeing, kayaking, exploring caves, whitewater rafting and "reading" a river.

Highly qualified river running outfitters give participants a chance to learn rafting skills as well as technical kayaking and canoeing. When you're involved with rivers and off-river hikes, minimum impact camping and ecology as well as the region's geology and history take on new importance.

Wilderness camping leads naturally to a comprehension of orientation and survival when you're learning the techniques from expert guides. A bonus is the confidence your new-found knowledge brings.

Building a wooden sea kayak is something you accomplish on the Maine coast. It better be good. You'll put to sea in it on a coastal expedition.

Young adults from late teens to early 30s are eligible for van-camping trips in the U.S., Mexico, Canada and Alaska. These are inexpensive explorations with experienced tour leaders and include whitewater rafting, horseback riding, mountain biking, sun bathing and a lot of fun. Anyone with most of the summer free can make an entire loop around America and across the border to the Canadian Rockies.

A lot of young adults and teenagers like vacations with other young adults. And they welcome a chance to add to their skills and knowledge during vacation time. The ideas reported here are for those with an inquisitive and adventurous spirit.

US / CANADA /
MEXICO

TREKAMERICA

P.O. Box 470, Blairstown, NJ 07825. Attn.: Cynthia Rowlands. (908) 362-9198 or (800) 221-0596. Fax (908) 362-9313.

Camping tours

No matter which itinerary you choose, TrekAmerica guarantees to take you into the heart of North America. Whitewater rafting, horseback riding, mountain biking or sun bathing on the beach, on seven-day to nine-week camping adventures. Explore the U.S., Canada, Alaska and Mexico in an exciting, inexpensive and fun way. Highlights include Disneyland, national parks, Niagara Falls—hundreds of attractions from coast to coast. Tour leaders are experienced professionals who really know their country. Although many passengers have never camped before, they find it comfortable and enjoyable, the best way to discover the "real America". In the cities stay in nice, centrally located budget hotels. All camping equipment, except sleeping bag, provided. Minimum age if you choose a scheduled tour is 18. Design you own trip and group of 13, and there are no age restrictions. Prices start under $500. (See also *Van / Jeep / Rail*.)

Van campers expressing their feelings toward their surroundings—*TrekAmerica, NJ.*

COLORADO

C BAR T RANCH

P. O. Box 158, Idledale, CO 80453. Attn.: Roger Felch. (303) 674-6477 or 674-5149.

Wilderness camping/riding

"Catch your horse and saddle him! Mount up and move out!" The challenge of outdoor living in the Rocky Mountains lies ahead for coed groups of ten for three-, four-, and seven-week sessions. After gathering in Denver, the group drives to the base ranch in the foothills for several days of learning

Riding and camping in high mountains—*C Bar T Ranch, CO.*

wilderness camping skills and riding. Each participant learns to handle, care for and feed his or her own horse. Then it's off to the high mountains for riding, packing, fishing and camping. Trails lead through remote parts of the millions of acres of national forest lands in Colorado and past remnants of old frontier mining towns and historic markers. Hearty meals are prepared over the campfire. "It's a unique opportunity to enjoy nature's magnificence while cultivating a healthy respect for the rigors of wilderness living," says Roger Felch. For boys and girls 11–17, Jun.–Aug.; 3 weeks, $1,350; 4 weeks, $1,700; 7 weeks, $2,800.

COLORADO

DVORAK EXPEDITIONS

Raft/kayak/canoe in Arizona, Colorado, Idaho, New Mexico, Texas

17921 U.S. Hwy. 285, Suite AG, Nathrop, CO 81236. Attn.: Bill Dvorak. (719) 539-6851 or (800) 824-3795. Fax (719) 539-3379.

Through instructional clinics, more than 1,500 students have learned whitewater techniques from this highly qualified outfitter. Among the trainees are youth groups from camps, churches, scouts and schools. "We specialize in training on wilderness rivers," Dvorak states, "and we take pride in turning out well-rounded boaters." In June a 22-day whitewater skills camp specifically designed for 12- to 19-year olds offers the most comprehensive course. They learn technical kayaking, rafting and canoeing skills, the ability to read the river, the

Learning the skills in a kayak—*David Blehert for Dvorak Expeditions, CO.*

principles of minimum impact camping and the history and geology of the rivers they run. Other clinics range from one to six days on the Green, Gunnison, Colorado, Dolores and Arkansas rivers; for example—1 day/$80; 6 days/$875; 22 days/ $1595. Rates include equipment required for course and transportation to put-in. Arrival: Grand Junction, CO. (See also *River Running, Canoeing / Kayaking.*)

MAINE/ QUEBEC/ NEW FOUNDLAND

Canoe, kayak, hike, sail & wilderness camping

CHEWONKI EXPEDITIONS

RR 2, Box 1200 PD, Wiscasset, ME 04578. Attn.: Dick Thomas. (207) 882.7323. Fax (207) 882-4074.

The Chewonki Foundation offers a variety of three- to seven-week adventures for ten participants between the ages of 14–18 years. Two leaders accompany each expedition and stress natural history and wilderness skills. A three-week program on Lake Umbagog on the Maine/New Hampshire border focuses on whitewater kayaking and wilderness living. The Thoreau Wilderness trip combines 4–15 weeks of canoeing the St. John, Allagash and Penobscot rivers with tendays of hiking around Mt. Katahdin in Baxter State Park. During another seven-week program, participants spend about three weeks building a wooden sea kayak which they then use for a three and a half week expedition along the coast of Maine.

A three-week sailing trip in traditional wooden sailing/ rowing boats stresses the skills of seamanship, camping on unspoiled islands and exploring the Maine coast. A similar expedition travels in seagoing kayaks. Two five-week canoe trips take participants into the central and northern Quebec wilderness; a three-week hiking expedition follows the Appalachian Trail in Maine; and canoeists paddle through northern Maine on a three-week expedition. Rates: about $1,900 for 3 weeks; $3,150 for 7 weeks. (See also *Canoeing / Kayaking, Wilderness / Nature Expeditions*.) See photo on page 262.

Young sailors learn to read charts—
Chewonki Foundation, ME.

MAINE

Eastern Maine Rivers

SUNRISE COUNTY CANOE EXPEDITION
Cathance Lake, Grove Post Office, ME 04638. Attn.: Martin Brown. (207) 454-7708.

Paddling with the guides at Sunrise County Canoe Expeditions not only builds canoeing skills, it also builds self-confidence and self-reliance and provides a lot of fun. Exploring and living on the northwoods lays the groundwork for ventures in future years. In fact, some of the older teens have the opportunity to work as apprentice guides, later obtaining their guides' licenses. Everyone learns about fly fishing, biology, orienteering and survival as well as safety precautions. Each group is kept small, and each handles its own campfire meals and camp chores. As for canoe voyaging, these registered guides consider it an art. Whitewater technique is their specialty, and excellent coaching produces skillful paddling within a few days. Solo paddling and poling are included in the instruction. For ages 12–16, two- and three-week sessions in Maine and Quebec are scheduled each summer. Rates average $375/week; $1,195/2 week camp, $275 additional weeks. (See also *Canoeing / Kayaking*.)

UTAH

Desolation and Gray canyons

COLORADO RIVER & TRAIL EXPEDITIONS
P.O. Box 57575, Salt Lake City, UT 84157-0575. Attn.: Vicki and David Mackay. (801) 261-1789 or (800) 253-7328. Fax (801) 268-1193.

To explore Desolation and Gray canyons on the Green River from an ecological, historical or recreational perspective, CRTE has developed a series of Earthway Education Expeditions by expanding the length, focus and participatory elements of their river trips. Geared toward the specific interests and demographics of the group, the basic intent is to teach students about ecology through information collected in the field. For high school kids who are interested in biology, ecology and outdoor activities, a seven-day "Ecology & Conservation" youth camp is offered. Activities involve off-river hiking, paddling, field work, camp chores, fireside discussions and star gazing as well as orienteering, knot-tying and low-impact camping. Campfire reading and discussion help develop a personal conservation philosophy. Scheduled June 22–28. Rate: $425. Also scheduled are a Senior Citizen's Camp on "Outdoor Skills & Ethical Views," Aug. 22–28, $645; and a Women's Camp on "The River as Metaphor," June 6–12, $645. Rates include round trip transportation from town of Green River. Maximum of 15 participants. (See also *River Running*.)

VIRGINIA

Backpack/rock climb/canoe/ kayak/mountain bike

WILDERNESS ADVENTURE
Box 460, New Castle, VA 24127. Attn.: Gene or Pat Nervo. (703) 864-6792 or (800) 782-0779. Fax (703) 389-9866.

"Everything we do is an adventure," says Gene Nervo, a retired Marine colonel. "It's exciting and challenging. This is not a typical summer camp." He started the adventure program three years ago with 32 participants from 10 to 18 years old. They now number nearly 300 per season, divided into co-ed age groups of 10–12, 13–15 and 16–18 years, with no more than 14 in each group. Each week's session is a backpacking trip, moving from one camp to another with different activities at each—rock climbing and rapelling at one, canoeing and kayaking at another, or caving, mountain biking (for the older campers) or maneuvering an obstacle course. Evenings are for campfires and sleeping under the stars. The emphasis is on "comfortable" survival in the wilderness while having fun along with gaining self-confidence and learning a lot about teamwork. The youth/counselor ratio never exceeds five-to-one. For 15–18 year-olds studying French, six of the one-week sessions include students from France. Rates start at $495 per week, with discounts for additional sessions. A shuttle service picks up and drops off participants at the Roanoke airport ($20 each way), or in Washington, DC ($40 each way). Says the parent of one participant, "Every inch of our son's body had bruises and insect bites, but every inch of his mind and spirit was filled with joy and enthusiasm. We're not sure why, but that's okay."

WYOMING

**Wind River
Mountains**

SKINNER BROTHERS, INC.
Box 859, Dept. AG, Pinedale, WY 82941. (307) 367-2270 or (800) 237-9138. Fax (307) 367-4757.

"What better place to perfect your wilderness skills than in the footsteps of the great Explorers, Indians and Mountain Men!" say the Skinner Brothers. They offer a variety of co-educational youth adventures and challenge for the well-seasoned outdoor camper, as well as those wishing to improve their skills or just enjoy a western adventure. From rock climbing, whitewater rafting, backpacking, horseback riding to fishing. They offer it all to fit one- to eight-week summer programs. Campers live in tepees, have their own horse and learn that "there is nothing better for the inside of a kid than the outside of a horse." They ride majestic mountain trails, fish and camp in the beautiful Wind River Mountains. Enrollment is limited. The Skinners are famous for their worldwide adventures. Programs Jun. to early Aug. (See also *Mountaineering / Rock Climbing, Pack Trips*.)

IN SNOW

Denali Dog Tours, Alaska (page 274)

Dog Sledding

"Hi! Ho!" yells the musher, and your team of huskies lurches forward through the snowy white silence across open tundra, along historic mining trails and over icy rivers.

Dogs have been pulling sleds in Alaska for hundreds of years. The Eskimos used them to hunt seal and walrus. During Gold Rush and surveying years they hauled freight and carried heavy loads of mail to bush communities.

Today outfitters employ teams of nine or so huskies to haul 10- to 12-foot sleds which are lashed together with halibut sinew. With no nails the sleds have the flexibility to slide across ice and lumps of frozen earth.

Huskies heed the same commands used in the mule-skinner days—"ha" (turn left), "gee" (right), "ho" and "hi" (let's go). They pull a loaded sled at five to seven mph on a good trail. Little has changed since the first great wilderness traveler passed this way.

Many sled dogs are veterans of the famous Iditarod, an annual two-week, 1,049-mile epic dogsled race from Anchorage to Nome which was started 20 years ago. It is a race with the elements where howling winds can make for minus 40-degree temperatures and cause white-outs. Despite all the obstacles, each year some 75 mushers are infected with Iditarod fever to the extent of handing over the entry fee (more than $1,000) for a shot at the $50,000 prize.

If you will travel to Alaska around the end of February, you can be on hand for the start of the Iditarod Race, then fly to a lodge on the Yenta River to watch the teams come by. You'll be treated to your own dogsled ride on the famous trail before returning to Anchorage.

On most dogsled trips you cover less than 35 miles each day. The hard-working huskies bed down for the night outdoors, burying themselves in the snow with faces protected by tails. After a snowy night if your huskies appear to have broken away, worry not. Soon little mounds will rise up in the snow, and under each mound, a dog.

ALASKA

Iditarod Dogsled Race

ALASKA RIVER ADVENTURES

1831 Kuskokwim St., Suite 17, Anchorage, AK 99508. Attn.: George Heim. (907) 276-3418. Fax (907) 258-2211.

On a unique package which George Heim offers the end of February, you arrive in Anchorage for the start of the Iditarod Dogsled Race across 1,000 miles of wilderness to Nome. After the race begins you fly to Riversong Lodge on the Yenta River to watch the teams come by, stay on for two days and have a dogsled ride on the Iditarod Trail, then return to Anchorage. Rate for 3-day package, $550. Can be customized for your preference. (See also *Wilderness / Nature Expeditions.*)

ALASKA

Denali National Park

DENALI DOG TOURS

Box 30, McKinley Park, AK 99755. Attn.: Will & Linda Forsberg. (907) 683-2644, 683-2294 or 683-2660.

The Forsbergs spend 5 months each year covering trails throughout the Interior with their dogs. They hunt for their food supply and net salmon for their huskies. Their Park concession gives them the sole right to haul climbers' gear from Wonder Lake to the lower ice fall on the Muldrow Glacier of Mt. McKinley. They do their hauling trips February to April. See photo page 272.

ALASKA

Brooks Range

SOURDOUGH OUTFITTERS

P.O. Box 90, Bettles, AK 99726. Attn.: Gary Benson. (907) 692-5252. Fax (907) 692-5612.

Travel by dog sled into the majestic mountains of Alaska's Brooks Range. The trips originate in Bettles and follow a winter trail up the Wild River, into the valley of the North Fork of the Koyukuk River and up to the Gates of the Arctic. This area was a blank spot on the map 50 years ago—known only by the natives and a few miners. It is a region of spellbinding beauty—rocky peaks jutting out of an unmarked snowpack, their crowns seeming to touch the wavering Northern Lights. The early morning sun turns the mountains subtle shades of pink and beckons you deeper into their world. You will overnight in heated tent camps or cabins. Everybody runs their own dog team and sled. Arctic gear such as parka, bunny boots, mittens, sleeping bag, etc. are also supplied. Everyone is expected to help with the camp chores, care for the dogs, gather firewood and melt snow and ice for water. Participants should be in good physical condition and have a good sense of adventure. Six- and eight-day trips are offered mid-February through mid-April, and November if there are good snow conditions. Rate: $200–$225 per person per day. (See also *Combos*.)

Running your own dog team in the Brooks Range— *Nevada Wier, Sourdough Outfitters, AK*. (photo page 274).

MINNESOTA

Boundary Waters Canoe Area

BOUNDARY COUNTRY TREKKING
Gunflint Trail HC 64, Box 590, Grand Marais, MN 55604. Attn.: Ted Young. (218) 388-4487 or (800) 322-8327.

Experience the adventure of mushing your own dog team through the spectacular Boundary Waters Canoe Area. Heading BCT's program is one of America's foremost mushers, Arleigh Jorgenson. On your arrival, he or one of his experienced dog sledders will conduct an orientation and then serve as guide and instructor on the trip. Share in the excitement of harnessing the dogs, the thrill of mushing the team, and the care and feeding of the dogs at camp. Spend nights in remote cabins and/or "yurts"—Mongolian domelike, canvas covered structures equipped with bunks and a wood-burning stove. Two people share each sled and team. Sleeping bag, all meals and car shuttles are provided. Scheduled 3-day trips in Feb. and Mar. start at $660/person. A 2-day seminar for the novice is offered in Dec., up to 10 participants, $360. Custom trips for groups of 4–8. A special 7-day adventure in Spring in Northwest Territories, $2,200. (See also *Ski Touring / Snowmobiling*.)

S. Barnett for Tag-A-Long Expeditions, Utah (page 282)

Ski Touring / Snowmobiling

Gliding on freshly fallen snow through silent glens or Douglas firs, past ice-shrouded waterfalls and along frozen creeks—cross-country skiers may not match the speed and glamour of downhill skiers, but they have a much more immediate and inexpensive means of enjoying the winter wilderness. They can cross-country ski just about anywhere. And they can learn the skills of winter campcraft— how to build an igloo, how to live and survive in a snow shelter, how to travel backcountry in winter.

More commonly referred to as Nordic or cross-country skiing, ski touring was born in the Scandinavian countries and often used as a form of winter transportation. It requires little more than a few inches of snow.

Your choice of trails varies with the region. In Yosemite 35 km of track and skating lanes weave through spectacular beauty. In Utah's La Sal Mountains follow the hut system over superb deep powder that blankets the mountain landscape from November to April. In Montana there are wood trails, open meadows, exhilarating downhills and flat track. In Minnesota experts guide through heavily forested wilderness, sometimes to hut shelters for noon stops. In New England expect well-manicured trail systems and old logging roads.

In some regions you spend overnights in cabins with wood-burning stoves or lodges with huge stone fireplaces. In others sleep in an igloo, snow cave, wood-heated tent or yurt. Meals range from hearty dishes and gourmet cuisine to Mongolian fire pot fondue and grilled trout.

Would you like to ride with a dog team or on a horse-drawn sleigh? How about ice fishing or fly fishing? Viewing the geysers and wildlife in Yellowstone? Skating over groomed tracks? Trying some winter camping with dog team support?

CALIFORNIA

**Yosemite
National Park**

**Stillness and
beauty in
Yosemite**—*Robert
Homes for Yosemite
Cross-Country Ski
School, CA.*

YOSEMITE CROSS-COUNTRY SKI SCHOOL

*Dept. ATNA, Yosemite National Park, CA 95389. Attn.: Bruce Brossman.
(209) 372-1335.*

"Watch the mist as it waltzes past El Capitan. Gaze at Yosemite Falls. Discover a wild coyote. Experience the stillness of a Yosemite snowfall." This and more you are urged to do by the Yosemite Cross-Country Ski School, headquartered at Badger Pass, with 35 km of track and skating lanes and a variety of lesson/tours amid spectacular beauty. On a beginner's lesson you gain stability and learn basic techniques (2 consecutive 2-hour group lessons, $40). To improve your track skiing, bring a lunch and take the trail and off-track lesson/tour ($35). For intermediates, a morning lesson improves your track skills, and after lunch you return for basic down skiing and turning skills ($35 for both sessions). Telemark skiing is taught in 2 sessions ($35), and cross-country skating is the focus of another 2-hour lesson ($18). A mid-week package combines personalized camaraderie of new friends (Mon.–Fri. $150, or Wed.–Fri. $90). On backcountry overnight expeditions your choice is snow camping or staying in the school's hut ($90). Rentals are available for all lessons/tours. (See also *Mountaineering / Rock Climbing*.)

MAINE

**White
Mountains**

TELEMARK INN

RFD #2, Box 800, Bethel, ME 04217. Attn.: Steve Crone. (207) 836-2703.

Steve Crone's Telemark Inn ski center has been called "the hidden cross-country gem" of the area. The turn-of-the-century inn is tucked away in Maine's White Mountain

Weekend sleigh rides for X-country skiers—*Steve Crone for Telemark Inn, ME.*

National Forest, about eight miles from West Bethel off Route 2, with 15 miles of broad, groomed trails for classic and skating-style skiing. Access to the national forest trail system provides unlimited backcountry exploration. "The varying terrain is perfect for intermediates and experts—an ideal spot for taking some time off and enjoying the wilderness," says Steve. Well-groomed trails follow ridges and streams and are just wide enough for skating as well as striding. The outdoor hot tub is a focal point of non-activity after skiing or at night under the stars. On weekends Steve stages horse-drawn sleigh rides, skating on the pond by kerosene lamplight and relaxing in the wood-fired sauna. With cozy rooms in the lodge, and meals rated "superb" by guests, it adds up to rusticity at its best. A weekend ski package is $159 per person, or $375 for five midweek days. For a family package in December the 5-day children's rate is $250. (See also *Hiking with Packstock.*)

MINNESOTA

Boundary Waters Canoe Area

BOUNDARY COUNTRY TREKKING

Gunflint Trail HC 64, Box 590, Grand Marais, MN 55604. Attn.: Ted Young. (218) 388-4487 or (800) 322-8327.

For a little northwoods solitude, join BCT on a yurt-to yurt ski trek on Banadad Trail, Boundary Waters' longest groomed and tracked ski trail. Yurts, Mongolian round structures traditionally used by Asiatic nomads, provide a cozy setting for swapping stories around the wood stove after a day of skiing. Several itineraries are offered, from two to four nights, in this remote area amidst the lakes and forests. "A great adventure requires great food," declares Ted Young—an

Enjoying fire pot fondue in a yurt—Boundary Country Trekking, MN.

observation he follows through with a gourmet menu including Mongolian fire pot fondue (a Young specialty) and typical Minnesota delights such as grilled trout. Groups 2-8, $220-$440/person. Custom and scheduled trips. Also, 3-to 7-day lodge-to-lodge adventure, from $330/3 nights, $700/7 nights. (See also *Dog Sledding*.)

MINNESOTA

Boundary Waters Canoe Area

GUNFLINT LODGE & OUTFITTERS

Gunflint Trail, Box 750, Grand Marais, MN 55604. Att: Bruce & Sue Kerfoot. (218) 388-2294 or (800) 328-3325. Fax (218) 388-9429.

In winter the Boundary Waters Canoe Area becomes a snowy wonderland for ski touring and snowshoeing from December through April. For independent ski tourers and for guided trips, trails lead from the Kerfoot's lodge through the heavily forested wilderness on loops from 2 to 20 miles, with huts and shelters strategically located for noon stops. "They have great access to some tremendous wilderness areas," writes a satisfied guest. Ski-through program for intermediates and experts operates among four resorts in the area which provide comfortable accomodations complete with fireplaces, saunas and meals. Also ski/snowshoe rentals, hour- and day-long dog sled rides, and escorted trips into winter moose yards and across the lake to area frequented by timber wolves. The winter lodge offers a big rock fireplace, cocktails and full-service dining room. (See also *Canoeing / Kayaking, Wilderness / Nature Expeditions*.)

MONTANA

**Spanish Peaks
Primitive Area**

LONE MOUNTAIN RANCH

*Box 160069, Big Sky, MT 59716. Attn.: Bob and Vivian Schaap.
(406) 995-4644. Fax (406) 995-4670.*

One of the finest Nordic ski centers in the U.S., Lone Mountain maintains 47 miles of professionally groomed trails from level to steep terrain and many wilderness trails. The ranch provides a guide for every seven skiers and optional instruction ($20/lesson). Woodd trails, open meadows, exhilarating downhills or flat track—all are here for beginner to advanced ability on a trail system radiating from the ranch. An outdoor hot tub is an apre-ski attraction, and skiers gather in the spectacular rock and log dining lodge and saloon for ranch gourmet cuisine. Lodging is in spacious log cabins with fireplaces, Franklin stoves and electric heat. Several times a week the ranch arranges trips into Yellowstone National Park to ski among the geyser basins and wildlife—an experience not to be missed. Skiers encounter spectacular thermal areas, ice-shrouded waterfalls and animals in their natural habitat. Other ranch specials: sleigh rides to North Fork cabin for dinner, winter fly-fishing and ski-to-lunch buffets—with blocks of snow as serving tables. Nordic holiday rate: $900/person/week double occupancy, with airport shuttle, meals, 7 nights lodging, trail fees, evening entertainment, horse-drawn sleigh ride dinner and wonderful memories. Also short- and long-stay rates. Arrival: Bozeman, MT. (See also *Fly Fishing*.)

Chow-time in the snow—*Lone Mountain Ranch, MT.*

NEW HAMPSHIRE

White Mountains

BALSAMS/WILDERNESS

Dixville Notch, NH 03576. Attn.: Jerry Owen. (603) 255-3400 or (800) 255-0600 in U.S. & Canada, (800) 255-0800 in NH. Fax (603) 255-4221.

The Balsams maintains more than 70 kilometers of groomed cross-country ski trails in the open terrain and scenic wilderness of its 15,000 acres in the White Mountains. Used primarily by Balsams' guests, the trails are uncrowded. You can cross-country ski to the Base Lodge after breakfast, in time for classes and orientation tours at 10:30 a.m. On the Wilderness Trail while you sharpen your cross-country techniques you'll also sharpen your eye for animal tracks—fisher, beaver, bobcat or moose. Special Sunday-to-Friday ski package includes a welcome party, 6 days of alpine and cross-country skiing, group lessons, nighttime horse-drawn hayride, night club shows, 5 dinners and breakfasts, 5 nights lodging—from $400; or a ski weekend package, Friday to Sunday—from $200. Activities also include alpine skiing, snowshoeing, nature ski tours, ice skating, dancing, movies and the game room, with recreational program professionally directed. (See also *Backpacking / Hiking / Walking*.)

NEW YORK

Adirondacks

COLD RIVER TRAIL RIDES, INC.

Coreys, Tupper Lake, NY 12986. Att: John and Marie Fontant. (518) 359-7559.

"Our secluded lodge in the Adirondacks offers excellent cross-country skiing for novice to expert, wonderful food, and a relaxing atmosphere," explain John and Marie Fontana. You ski on set track and miles of wilderness logging roads through sections of the Cold River-Raquette Falls Wilderness Area. Trails tie into small lakes and ponds. A modernized, turn-of-the-century lodge with fireplaces and a heated ski preparation room accommodates nine guests. Complimentary wine and beer are served with a "fancy, home-cooked" dinner. Rate: $60/person/day includes lodging with semi-private bath, all meals and trail use (three miles groomed trails, 17 miles maintained); B & B, $30. Guides, rentals, instruction, custom ski tours, snowshoeing and ice fishing. Dec.-Mar. Free pick-up at Tupper Lake, Saranac Lake, Adirondack Airport. (See also *Trail Rides*.)

UTAH

LaSal Mountains

TAG-A-LONG EXPEDITIONS/LASAL MOUNTAIN HUT SYSTEM

452 North Main St., Moab, UT 84532. Attn.: Bob Jones. (801) 259-8946 or (800) 453-3292. Fax (801) 259-8990.

With peaks at nearly 13,000 feet, the LaSal Mountains, located in the heart of Moab's canyon country, are the second highest mountain range in the state of Utah. Reaching into the sky above a wild twist of sandstone, the mountain's laccolithic peaks capture winter snow and convert it into superb deep powder that typically blankets the mountain landscape from November to April. Lighter, dryer snow and a more temperate winter climate combine to provide the ultimate in winter nordic skiing. "Our LaSal Mountain hut system offers guests the same adventure and challenge that one would expect from other nordic skiing systems, but there's the added attraction of a mighty river, red rock canyons, searing blue skies and the isolated beauty of the historic country of the LaSals," says Bob Jones. The milder climate of the adjacent canyon country also means combining your nordic hut-to-hut ski experience with mountain biking, golfing and backcountry hiking. Enjoy basic, easy trails or challenging expert runs. Packages range from unguided, unsupported hut rentals only, to full service guided hut-to-hut skiing. Custom tours are available for four or more guests. (Rates begin at $28 per person/night.) Also one-day guided ski adventure with shuttle service. (See also *Van / Jeep / Rail, River Running*.) See photo page 276.

Gliding across meadow trails— *Mountain Top Inn, VT.*

VERMONT

Green Mountains

MOUNTAIN TOP INN

Box 567, Mountain Top Road, Chittenden, VT 05737. Attn.: Bill Wolfe. (802) 483-2311 or (800) 445-2100. Fax (802) 483-6373.

Glide over 100 kilometers (67 miles) of trails through white, glistening meadows at 2,000 feet altitude in the Green Mountains of central Vermont. Designed for all ages and all levels of ability, trails wind through forest and field over Mountain Top's 1,300 acres. Snow grooming equipment sets 40 kilometers of dual tracks daily and maintains a well-manicured trail system, including old logging roads which are ideal for exploring. Machine-made snow ensures good skiing from November to April. Cheerful instructors improve your skiing skills. "Relax in the Ski Touring Center, a converted horse barn warmed by a wood burning stove, and savor our specialty, Vermont farm soup, or take a break at one of our three trailside huts," suggests co-owner BudMcLaughlin. Horsedrawn sleigh rides whisk you away over the meadow and through the woods with bells a-jingling. You also can skate day or night on a lighted outdoor rink, sled to your heart's content, try snowshoeing or horseback riding, then warm up by a crackling fireplace or in a sauna and whirlpool. Rates range from $89-$123 depending on dates, and include lodging, use of Inn facilities, skiing (including equipment), a horse drawn sleigh ride, ice skating (and skates) snowshoeing, sledding and horseback riding. (See also *Trail Rides*.)

WYOMING

Jackson

BAR-T-FIVE OUTFITTERS

P.O. Box 2140S, Jackson, WY 83001. Attn.: Bill Thomas. (307) 733-5386. Fax (307) 739-9183.

A snowy evening activity in Jackson is provided by the Bar-T-Five Outfitters. Their old fashioned horse-drawn sleigh takes you to a historic pioneer cabin for a roast beef or Bar-B-Q chicken dinner with all the trimmings—plus "some hand-clappin', boot-stompin' entertainment by the Bar-T-Five Singin' Cowboys." Wear warm clothing and hats, gloves and snowboots, and don't forget your longhandled underwear! The sleigh ride takes off each evening, Tuesday through Saturday, from 5 p.m. to 7 p.m. at the Snow King Resort or the Stage Stop on the Town Square. Reservations necessary. Rate: $39/ adult, $20/children, + tax. (See also *Covered Wagons*.)

BRITISH COLUMBIA

Clinton

BIG BAR GUEST RANCH

P.O. Box 27, Jesmond, Clinton, B.C., Canada V0K 1K0. Phone or fax (604) 459-2333.

Cross-country skiing in a hospitable country setting is the winter specialty at the Big Bar. With 25 km of double track set trails in timber and meadow, skiers get lots of action. They intersperse it with sleigh rides, ice fishing, ice skating, horseback riding (as long as ice is not built up on the trails) and traditional country cooking with relaxed hours in front of a roaring fire. The ranch provides 12 full-service guest rooms and two log cottages for guests, dining room and fireside lounge. By car it's six hours from Vancouver, two and a half hours from Kamloops, four hours from the Okanagan; or take BCR train or Greyhound bus to Clinton, with shuttle to ranch. Rates per person, dbl.: 3 days $140 Cdn., 8 days $441 Cdn., children to 14 years less. (See also *Pack Trips*.)

WYOMING

Yellowstone and Grand Teton national parks

OLD FAITHFUL SNOWMOBILE TOURS

P.O. Box 7182, Jackson, WY 83001. Attn.: Noel Meeks. (307) 733-9767 or (800) 253-7130. Fax (307) 733-7980.

Superheated geyser steam blasts into chilled air, a sapphire sky hugs the glistening white earth in a frozen embrace, and ice crystals twinkle in the air like daytime stars. You are in Yellowstone National Park in the magical season of winter. OFST sleds you through this winter wonderland on three- and four-day snowmobile trips. Tours start in Jackson at the OFST office at 7:00 a.m. where you don snowmobile suits and gear, travel by van to Flagg Ranch, then to the Park on a snowmobile. Lodging in West Yellowstone after viewing Old Faithful. The second day is a 50-mile ride to Mammoth Hot Springs. Your ride the third day skirts the Grand Canyon of the Yellowstone River to the spectacular lower falls, and on to the East Gate with accommodations at Pahaska Tepee. After breakfast the last day start a 70-mile ride back to Jackson past Yellowstone Lake, herds of buffalo and elk and via van through Grand Teton National Park. Dec. through Feb., 3 days $715, 4 days $945. (See also *Pack Trips*—Hidden Basin Outfitters.)

Watching buffalo at a geyser—*Old Faithful Snowmobile Tours, WY.*

INDEX FOR OUTFITTERS AND SERVICES

Western Wildcat Tours, 26, 206
White Tail Ranch Outfitters, Inc., 75
Whitewater World, Ltd., 186
Wild Horizons Expeditions, 16
Wilderness Adventure, 268
Wilderness Alaska, 18, 173
Wilderness Aware Rafting, 179
Wilderness Outfitters, Inc., 154
Wilderness Southeast, 250

Wilderness Tours, 162, 196, 226
Willards Adventure Club, 25
Williams Family Ranch, 52
Windjammer Barefoot Cruises, Ltd., 145, 211
WindSong Llama Treks, 32

Yamnuska, Inc., 25, 46
Yosemite Mountaineering School, 40, 278

INDEX FOR REGIONS, STATES, PROVINCES